D0442041

THE TRIUMPH OF THE MEEK

For Alexandra

THE TRIUMPH
OF THE MEEK

Why Early Christianity Succeeded

Michael Walsh

1817

HARPER & ROW, PUBLISHERS, SAN FRANCISCO

Cambridge, Hagerstown, New York, Philadelphia
London, Mexico City, São Paulo, Singapore, Sydney

Published by Harper & Row Publishers Inc

First US Edition

This book was created and produced by
Roxby Reference Books
A division of Roxby Press
98 Clapham Common Northside
London SW4 9SG

Editor: **Angela Dyer**
Design: **Elizabeth Palmer**
Typesetting: **Tradespools Limited**
Reproduction: **F.E. Burman Limited**

Library of Congress Cataloging-in-Publication Data

Walsh, Michael J.
  The triumph of the meek.

  Includes index.
  1. Church history – Primitive and early church,
ca. 30–600. I. Title.
BR166. W34   1986   270.1   86–45030
ISBN 0–06–069254–5

Printed and bound in Spain by
Tonsa, San Sebastian

CONTENTS

Chronological Table

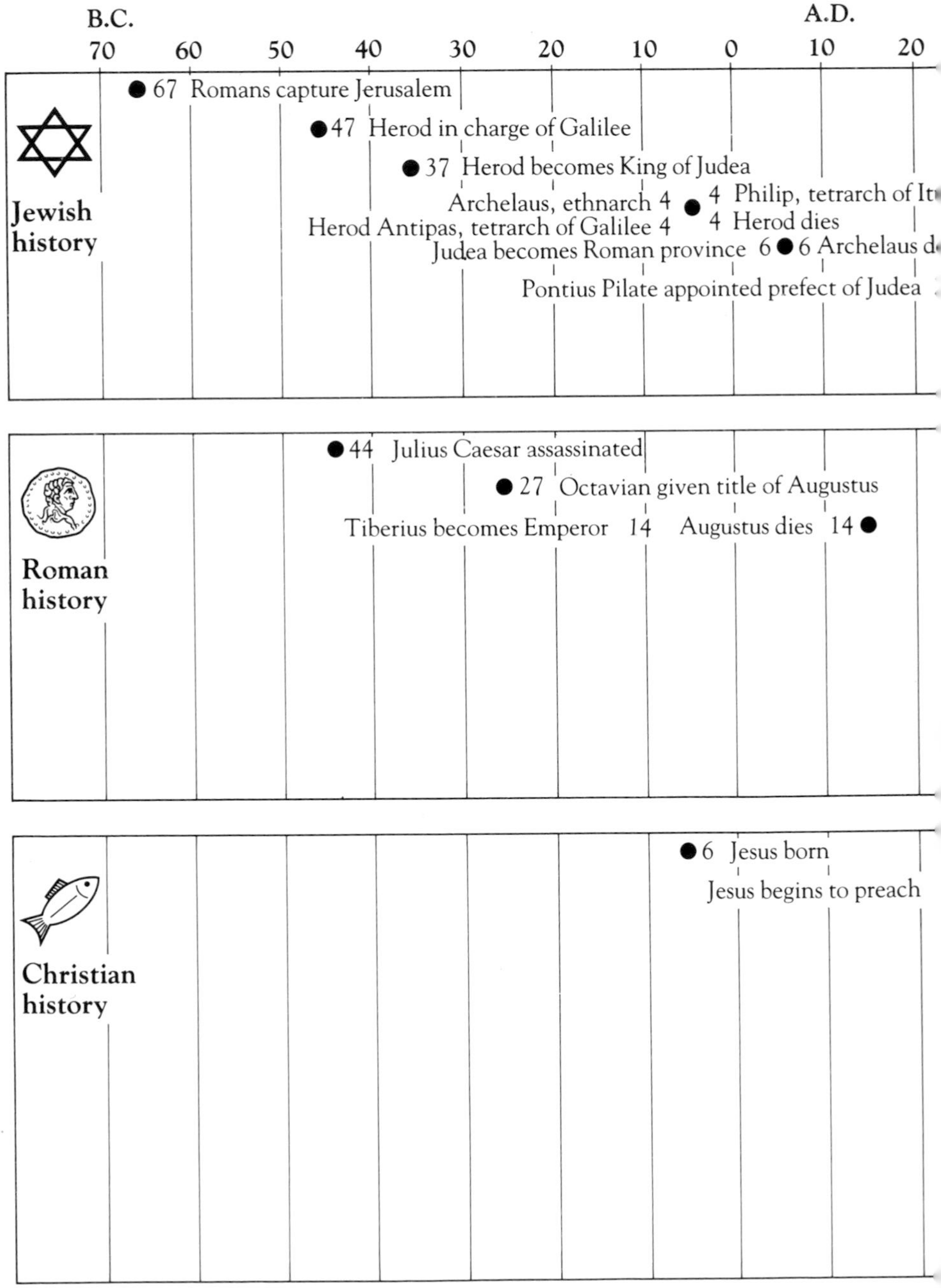

		B.C.							A.D.	
	70	60	50	40	30	20	10	0	10	20

Jewish history

- ● 67 Romans capture Jerusalem
- ● 47 Herod in charge of Galilee
- ● 37 Herod becomes King of Judea
- Archelaus, ethnarch 4 ● 4 Philip, tetrarch of It...
- Herod Antipas, tetrarch of Galilee 4 ● 4 Herod dies
- Judea becomes Roman province 6 ● 6 Archelaus d...
- Pontius Pilate appointed prefect of Judea

Roman history

- ● 44 Julius Caesar assassinated
- ● 27 Octavian given title of Augustus
- Tiberius becomes Emperor 14 Augustus dies 14 ●

Christian history

- ● 6 Jesus born
- Jesus begins to preach

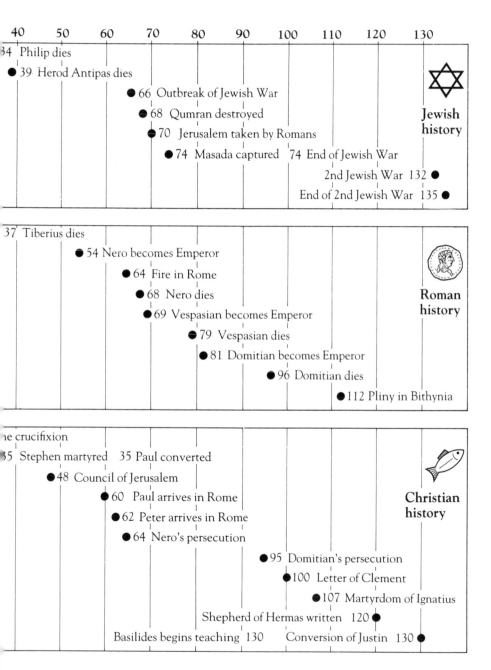

| 40 | 50 | 60 | 70 | 80 | 90 | 100 | 110 | 120 | 130 |

Jewish history

34 Philip dies
● 39 Herod Antipas dies
● 66 Outbreak of Jewish War
● 68 Qumran destroyed
● 70 Jerusalem taken by Romans
● 74 Masada captured   74 End of Jewish War
2nd Jewish War 132 ●
End of 2nd Jewish War 135 ●

Roman history

37 Tiberius dies
● 54 Nero becomes Emperor
● 64 Fire in Rome
● 68 Nero dies
● 69 Vespasian becomes Emperor
● 79 Vespasian dies
● 81 Domitian becomes Emperor
● 96 Domitian dies
● 112 Pliny in Bithynia

Christian history

he crucifixion
35 Stephen martyred   35 Paul converted
● 48 Council of Jerusalem
● 60 Paul arrives in Rome
● 62 Peter arrives in Rome
● 64 Nero's persecution
● 95 Domitian's persecution
● 100 Letter of Clement
● 107 Martyrdom of Ignatius
Shepherd of Hermas written 120 ●
Basilides begins teaching 130   Conversion of Justin 130 ●

Chronological Table

A.D.

140	150	160	170	180	190	200	210	220	230

Roman history

- ● 161 Marcus Aurelius becomes Emperor
- ● 180 Marcus Aurelius dies
- Alexander Severus becomes Emperor 222 ●
- Alexander Severus dies 23(

Christian history

- ● 140 Marcion begins teaching   140 Valentinus begins teaching
- ● 154 Polycarp in Rome
- 160 Marcion no longer teac
- ● 160 Valentinus no longer teaching   160 Melito of Sardis active
- ● 166 Polycarp martyred
- ● 172 Montanism begins
- ● 177 Martyrs of Lyons
- ● 178 Irenaeus becomes bishop of Lyons
- Pantaenus in charge of catechetical school at Alexandria
- 180 ● 180 Melito no longer active   180 Clement of Alexandria
- ● 185 Origen born
- Easter controversy at Rome 195 ●   195 Conversion of Tertullian
- ● 199 Zephyrinus becomes bisl of Rome
- Clement leaves Alexandria 202 ● 202 Martyrdoms in Cartha
- Origen becomes head of catechetical school at Alexandria ● 203
- Hippolytus active in Rome 210 ●
- Origen leaves Alexandria 215 ●
- Mani born 216 ●
- Zephyrinus dies 217 ●
- Callistus becomes bishop of Rome 218 ●
- Callistus dies 222 ●
- Fabian becomes bishop of Rome 23(

| 250 | 260 | 270 | 280 | 290 | 300 | 310 | 320 | 330 | 340 |

● 249 Decius becomes Emperor

● 251 Decius dies

● 253 Valerian becomes Emperor

● 256 Dura Europos falls

Roman history

● 260 Valerian captured   260 Gallienus becomes Emperor

● 268 Gallienus dies

● 284 Diocletian becomes Emperor

● 293 Tetrarchy established

Abdication of Diocletian and Maximian   305 ● 305 Constantius and Galerius become Emperors

Constantius dies | 306 ● 306 Constantine hailed as Emperor

● 312 Battle of the Milvian Bridge

● 313 Edict of Milan

● 248 Cyprian becomes bishop of Carthage

● 250 Persecution under Decius   250 Fabian dies

● 251 Cornelius becomes bishop of Rome

Christian history

● 253 Cornelius dies

● 254 Stephen becomes bishop of Rome   254 Origen dies

● 257 Persecution under Valerian

● 258 Cyprian dies

● 260 Persecution ceases

● 270 Anthony goes to the desert

● 277 Mani dies

● 298 Christians forced to resign from army

● 303 Persecution of Diocletian

● 305 Persecution ceases

● 306 Persecution in East only

● 309 Council of Elvira

Many of the above dates are only approximate.   ● 313 Edict of Milan

1

INTRODUCTION

The word 'gospel', whether in English, or Latin, or Greek, means 'good news'. But it does not demand much knowledge of history to realize that the Christian message, the 'gospel of Jesus Christ', has only too often brought disaster upon those to whom it has been preached, whether they accepted the gospel or rejected it.

Yet to those who first heard it, the gospel must indeed have been good news. In much less than three centuries from the death of Jesus, not only had the Roman emperor granted this new religion toleration, but he had endowed it with a number of privileges which in effect made it, by the end of the fourth century, the official religion of the Roman Empire. And that meant the official religion of most of the known world.

This all happened at a time when there were many different religions competing for the support of the peoples of the Empire. On the face of it, Christianity had little to commend it. It sprang from an insignificant corner of the Empire, far distant from the capital city, Rome. Its roots lay in the despised Judaism, and its founder had been executed by that most demeaning of deaths, crucifixion. It had, at least at first, attracted the least influential members of society, and it had been attacked in polemical tracts and held up to ridicule by some of the Empire's best writers. Christians seem to have been persecuted as much by the people among whom they lived as by the imperial authorities. Nonetheless, by the middle of the third century of what has since become known as the Christian Era, Church leaders were among the most powerful men in the Empire's major cities.

Christianity, then, presents the historian with something of a paradox. Within three hundred years or so of its unfavourable beginnings it had become a dominant force within the boundaries of the Roman world. And moreover, it had reached to every part of it. This book attempts to record, and to reflect upon, what happened to the early Christians, and what it was like to be a Christian, a member of a minority religion in a largely hostile society. History is reflection upon and interpretation of data preserved from the past. Most of what we know about the origins of Christianity comes to us in the form of written records, though there is also a small amount of

The gospel was proclaimed from a 'pulpit' such as this, found in a basilica in Leptis Magna, and constructed from fragments of pagan monuments. The basilica itself was originally built for civil purposes by the Emperor Septimius Severus.

11

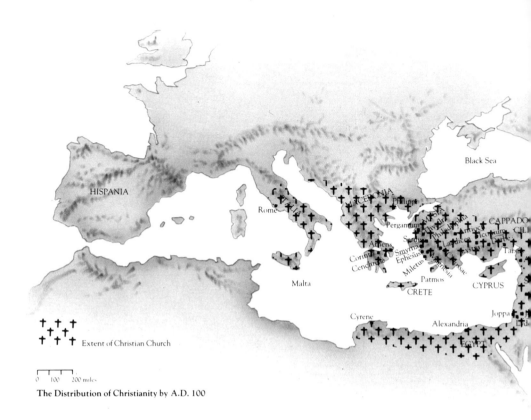

The Distribution of Christianity by A.D. 100

Above, by the end of the first century AD Christianity had spread out from Jerusalem –
north to Asia Minor, south to the Nile Delta and west across the Mediterranean to Rome.

Below, when determining the extent of Christianity by the year AD 200 (or by the year AD 300 in the map on the next page), it has to be remembered that our knowledge depends upon the chance survival of literary or archaeological evidence.

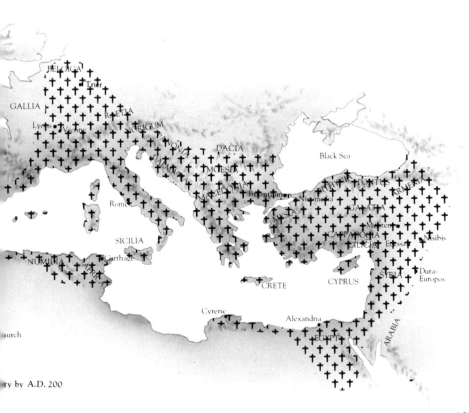

The Distribution of Christianity by A.D. 300

Extent of Roman Empire

Extent of Christian Church

York
Lincoln
Caerleon
BRITANNIA
London
St Albans

BELGICA

Paris
GALLIA
Autun

RAETIA

AQUITANIA

NARBONENSIS
Arles

HISPANIA

Tarragona

Rome
Ostia

Toledo

BAETICA
Illiberis
(Granada)

MAURETANIA

NUMIDIA

AFRICA

1:20 000 000

0   100   400 miles

14

archaeological evidence – surprisingly small, though this perhaps reflects the success of the Church, which in the course of time was able to overlay its old buildings with new ones. It is no accident that the most complete church building to have been discovered so far from the early years of Christianity is to be found in a town, Dura Europos (p. 140), which was suddenly abandoned soon after the Christian community had converted a house as a place for worship.

But it is not so much the lack of archaeological data that is the problem as the paucity of written records. This may seem odd. After all Christianity has, as its foundation documents, four accounts of Jesus' life, the Gospels; it has a series of letters written by one of its earliest converts, the apostle Paul, and a number of other letters written in Paul's style; in the Acts of the Apostles it has an account of the foundation of a number of local Christian communities; and in the Book of Revelation it has the account of a great vision vouchsafed, or so it is claimed, to one of Jesus' closest friends, the apostle John.

Historians have to approach these documents with considerable care, however. They are rarely what they seem. They were, as will be shown later, composed to serve the needs of particular communities, and reflect the outlook of those communities.

This does not mean that they cannot be trusted – only that they cannot be taken at face value. In order to understand these early documents the historian has to try to find a way back into the thought-world of those who wrote them, to see things more or less as they saw them, and to make allowances accordingly. Fortunately the four Gospel stories are quite different, so they can be examined in the light of each other, Fortunately, too, the Acts of the Apostles and the letters of Paul sometimes cover the same events from distinct perspectives, so that a more complex but possibly more accurate picture begins to emerge.

In the case of the writers who followed the New Testament authors the task becomes rather more difficult. Although they too composed their letters or treatises in specific contexts and in response to precise needs, they were not even claiming to recount the story of the origin and expansion of Christianity, as Luke had done in the Acts of the Apostles.

In any study of this period, therefore, a good deal of attention has to be paid to contemporary Jewish and Roman texts, to all the various kinds of information which might throw light upon detailed questions about Jesus, about his mission, and about the rise of the Church. It is important, for instance, to see Jesus against his background of first-century Judaism, to understand the make-up of the society in which he lived, and to follow the subsequent careers of his disciples within the history of first-century Palestine.

The results of this type of investigation can be disturbing. Many Christians, and even those who are not believers but who have been

16

brought up in a basically Christian society, cling firmly to traditional views which are based upon an uncritical reading of the text of the Bible. It may come as a shock to realize that the Pharisees were not as self-righteous and hypocritical as the Gospels present them, or that Jesus was not the only messiah-figure of his day, or that the early Christians were not always quite so full of charity as we would like to believe. And it may come as an equal surprise to many to discover that the Church to which they adhere today, with its complex structures and hierarchies, its fixed sacramental rituals and professional officials, is almost as far removed in spirit as it is in time from the Christian community of the first century.

One scholar has remarked, somewhat sourly, that Jesus preached the kingdom, but it was the Church which arrived. This book sets out to examine the truth of that statement. Was the Christian Church, by the time it was given official state approval in 313, the same Church that Jesus had founded three centuries earlier? But that begs a question that is rather more than strictly historical: did Jesus mean to found a Church at all?

This book seeks to avoid theological discussions of this nature. It aims instead to present evidence about the ways in which the early Christians thought of themselves. And it begins with the undeniable fact that, whatever Jesus may or may not have intended to do, the Christian Church is what happened. That does not settle the question, of course, since the Church changed. And it changed in response to the society in which it existed. But were those changes inevitable, were they implicit in the form of organization adopted by Christians after Jesus' death, or were they accidental? Did the Church compromise with the world around it, or did the Christians maintain the integrity of their belief? It is hard to accept that they retained their integrity when one compares the spirit-filled communities among which the apostles seem to have moved with the status-conscious community revealed in 302 at the Synod of Elvira (p. 185), determined to identify itself against the world around it – and to set the clergy apart from the laity.

Critical though one may be of the way the Church developed over the first three hundred years, it is important to remember that the Church was, ultimately, successful. Estimates vary, but at the Peace of the Church in 313 (p. 248) somewhere between one-tenth and a quarter of the population of the Empire confessed Christ. And even if it took another century for the Church to gain the majority of the population to its ranks, that is still a remarkable achievement.

It may simply be that the time of the Church had come. A world-wide political unity like the Roman Empire needed a universal religion. There was, of course, the cult of the emperors. But while that may have satisfied the political ends of religion as far as the imperial authorities were concerned, it scarcely provided for the spiritual and emotional needs of the majority of the Empire's citizens. These often took refuge in mystery

17

religions, in oriental cults that promised eternal life by way of the precise fulfilment of exotic rituals. But such cults were rarely universal, either geographically or socially. Traditional gods, too, were rooted to one spot. They were essentially local cults. In the third century growing centralization and an expanding imperial bureaucracy needed officials who could travel from one city to another in their service of government. And Catholicism, a name for Christianity from at least the beginning of the second century, filled the bill. An imperial emissary could take his faith with him wherever he went – almost literally so, for he carried his Christian credentials with him in the form of a letter from the bishop of his home community to the bishop at his destination.

Yet, curiously, almost the opposite, the private nature of Christianity seems to have attracted converts. Before the arrival of Constantine at the beginning of the fourth century, the Church enjoyed no special privileges. Its opposition to the imperial cult was well known, and this, quite apart from occasioning sporadic outbursts of persecution, had one very important

18

The frieze opposite and the sardonyx above both illustrate the deification of emperors, the first of Augustus, the second of Germanicus, who is being carried heavenward on a winged horse to be greeted by Augustus.

practical consequence: it forced Christians to avoid public office. Given the burden which such office placed upon those of high enough rank to hold it, there were no doubt many who welcomed any respectable excuse to refuse to serve. This would have been especially true of the third century, when inflation sent the costs of holding public office spiralling upwards. Some historians, indeed, see in the early monastic movement (p. 221) a way in which this tendency to shun social obligations because of their financial burden was almost institutionalized, and justified in the name of religion.

It would be wrong to ignore these somewhat negative reasons for the success of Christianity. But it would be equally wrong to ignore the positive attractions of the new faith. There was, among some pagans, considerable admiration for the moral stance adopted by Christians, and even respect for some of their stern injunctions about sexual behaviour and the practice of divorce. As will be seen later one Christian apologist went so far as to claim that, instead of persecuting Christians, the imperial authorities ought to support them, since both the Church and the State were concerned to promote the same values in society.

And then there was worship. It is no strange thing for people to seek reassurance on the subject of immortality and their personal redemption. Such assurance was offered by the mystery religions, and it was offered by Christianity. But despite some of the obscene practices of a couple of Christian sects, the form of religious worship that evolved within the Church was considerably less messy, and much more intellectually respectable, than that of the cults.

There was a constant danger that Christianity might become just one more cult. Different sects within the Church stressed this or that aspect of the faith in a way which made their version of the Church esoteric or exclusive. The great debate about who was, and who was not, in the Church reached its height at the beginning of the fifth century, a hundred years after this book closes, when widespread conversion to Christianity had meant that a good many people who were distinctly less than fervent had become part of any bishop's congregation on a Sunday morning. Yet somehow the main body of the Church seems to have rejected the path of elitism, whether the elite be one defined by holiness – authenticated by the

Contrasting attitudes to sexual morality: an idealized couple, Secundus and Projecta, depicted, opposite, on their silver marriage chest and, left, a prostitute's advertisement, cut into a marble paving stone at Ephesus.

21

ability to prophesy – or by knowledge.

Much of the early history of Christianity consists of the battles of one sect against another for a leading position within the faith. The battles are rarely edifying, but it is commonly assumed that the 'orthodox' tradition won through. That may be the wrong way of putting it. Was it the orthodox tradition which triumphed, or is it that we now denominate as orthodox that tradition which was ready to compromise with the weaknesses of humanity, and therefore survived? On the face of it, after all, the rejected faith of Montanus (p. 130) seems closer to the spirit of the earliest Christian communities than do the compromises of Pope Callistus (p. 215). And what we now tend to regard as the excesses of the early Syrian Church were closer to the literal teaching of the New Testament on poverty than were the practices of Bishop Cyprian (p. 160).

There were twelve tribes in ancient Israel: Jesus chose twelve men from among his disciples to spread his teaching and to build his new community. In this third-century catacomb painting from the tomb of the Aurelii in Rome Christ is shown seated among his twelve apostles.

When the followers of Jesus met together after his death to celebrate the Eucharist, there is no doubt that they constituted a community which was distinctly different from the world around them – even if, for a time, they continued to be thought of as a particular Jewish sect. But later on that distinctiveness became blurred. Some of the reasons why this happened are discussed at length in the pages which follow. Whether these changes were for the better, and if so, in what sense, it is for the reader to decide.

2

PALESTINE AT
THE TIME OF JESUS

I n order to form a realistic picture of the life of Jesus Christ, and to understand the achievement of his disciples in spreading his teaching throughout most of the known world by AD 313, it is necessary to know something of the background against which these events took place.

Jesus was born into a land with a turbulent political history, and into a culture in which religion and politics were inextricably intertwined. What follows is an attempt to pick out some of the more important aspects of both the political history and religious life of the land of Jesus' birth in the years before he began to preach and to teach, and to gather around himself a band of disciples.

THE LEGACY OF ALEXANDER

Alexander the Great died in 323 BC, at the age of thirty-two. In that short lifetime he established the greatest empire the world had yet known. His father, ruler of what to other Greeks was the almost barbarian kingdom of Macedonia, had united the city-states of the mainland by force. Alexander crossed the Hellespont to defeat the King of Persia and so inherit not only the kingdom of Persia itself, but all the territories which had been part of the Persian Empire. They included Mesopotamia and Egypt. They also included the lands of Samaria and Judea.

When Alexander died he had ruled from Macedonia down through Palestine and into Egypt, and to the east and to the south as far as India. This empire proved to be too large to survive as a single political entity. After the battles among his generals which followed Alexander's death, Ptolemy emerged as ruler in Egypt. His share of his master's conquests included not only Egypt itself but the land of Palestine as far as the northern borders of what had once been Canaan. Opposed to Ptolemy was Seleucus. He had won control of Mesopotamia, of modern Syria and Iran, and his lands stretched down to the northern border of Palestine. Thus Palestine, the country which the Jewish people had made their home, was a buffer state, a constant source of friction between the Ptolemaic dynasty and the Seleucids.

To the east the Bactrian Empire held sway in Afghanistan and over that part of India which Alexander's armies had reached. There were other states of varying size and significance – Macedonia being one of them. All had one thing in common: from their conqueror and his troops they inherited a shared culture.

This was a conscious policy. Wherever he went Alexander founded cities which were intended to be centres of Greek civilization. They were settled by Greeks, administered by Greeks, and defended by Greeks. The Egyptian city which bore the conqueror's own name, Alexandria, was perhaps the greatest of them, but other, lesser foundations were scattered across the length and breadth of the Empire. The culture they shared was 'Hellenism', 'Hellas' being the Greeks' own name for their homeland.

But so far from home Hellenism was inevitably influenced by the indigenous cultures it replaced, absorbing something of the exotic environment in which it found itself. In particular it gradually accommodated itself to the mystery religions of the East, and then transported them westwards.

A coin with the head of Alexander the Great from the late fourth century BC.

The word used to describe this assimilation of local culture into the culture of the Greeks – 'hellenization' – occurs first in the Greek version of the Bible. The Second Book of Maccabees was completed in about the year 124 BC. Its author complained about the hellenization introduced by a godless high priest. Across more than two millennia the author's indignation can still be sensed:

He went so far as to plant a gymnasium at the very foot of the citadel, and to fit out the noblest of his cadets in the petasos [i.e., as athletes]. Godless wretch that he was and no true high priest, Jason set no bounds to his impiety; indeed the hellenizing process reached such a pitch that the priests ceased to show any interest in the service of the altar; scorning the Temple and neglecting the sacrifices, they would

The conquests of the armies of Alexander over the barbarians are graphically depicted on the fourth-century BC Alexander Sarcophagus, originally in the royal cemetery at Sidon.

hurry to take part in the unlawful exercises on the training ground as soon as the signal was given for the discus. They disdained all their ancestors had esteemed, and set the highest value on hellenic honours. (2 Mac 4:11–16)

Elsewhere there are more precise complaints. The athletes taking part in the games went about naked, which deeply shocked the orthodox Jews, and some of them, apparently by an operation, attempted to disguise the fact that they had been circumcised (1 Mac 1:15).

By the time Jesus was born, Hellenism had been a force in Palestine for three centuries. Very likely this importation of Greek ideas, customs, methods of administration and so on only affected the lives of the wealthier inhabitants of Palestine, the aristocracy of Judea's capital city, Jerusalem, in particular. But few if any could have remained wholly untouched. Even if the personal lives and day-to-day activities of Palestinian peasants carried on much as they had done since their forefathers settled the land, many of them lived in the shadow of the Hellenistic cities.

In the first century before Christ there was a great expansion of buildings in the Hellenistic style. A theatre and amphitheatre were constructed in Jerusalem by King Herod the Great, the Herod of the opening of the gospel story. There was another amphitheatre and a hippodrome at Jericho. Games were held every four years in honour of Rome's ruler – the Romans had seized Palestine in 63 BC – and many would have attended them, despite official disapproval from religious purists. A handful of the wealthier Jews spoke Greek, and some Greek words seem to have entered the language. In Judea there were colonies of Greeks – or at least of people who spoke Greek – who had been converted to Judaism. It is quite likely that

The grave stone of a Greek athlete, depicted with his boy-slave. The athlete is holding a 'strigil', an implement with a curved blade with which dirt and sweat were scraped from the body after exercise, or in the baths.

there were even groups of Greeks living in Galilee at the time of Christ.

The period of Hellenistic influence in Palestine, which began with Alexander's annexation in 332 BC, survived several changes of overlord. The evidence suggests that, despite the stories told in the Books of the Maccabees, first contacts between Jews and Greeks were positive, and the religious sensibilities of the Jewish people were respected. And that was true even of Herod the Great.

GOVERNMENT AND CULTURE

Herod the Great was appointed King of the Jews by the Romans in 37 BC, and he ruled until his death in 4 BC. It is true that he was himself a Jew by religion, but his family came from Idumea, a region to the south of Judea which had only recently, and forcibly, been converted to Judaism. For the most part he took his faith lightly and surrounded himself with Greek officers of state. He was, however, generally careful to avoid giving offence to the religious susceptibilities of his subjects. In accordance with the Jewish Law, for example, his coins did not have upon them any human image, and no images symbolic of the Roman occupying power were permitted upon any public building in Jerusalem. He rebuilt the Temple – naturally enough in the Hellenistic style – but only priests were allowed to take part in the reconstruction work.

He permitted himself one small, but very public, act of defiance of the law. When the Temple was completed he raised over its gate the statue of an eagle. Such was the feeling of outrage that two rabbis incited a crowd to pull it down. But Herod's reputation was so powerful that they waited until he was dying before they did so. The king clung on to life just long enough to order the arrest and execution of the ring leaders.

Herod owed his position to his father Antipater's good judgement – or good luck – in backing the winning side in the civil war between Pompey and Julius Caesar for control of Rome. As a reward Antipater had been put in charge of Judea, granted Roman citizenship, and exempted from taxation. The Jews, enjoying reflected glory, were permitted to rebuild the walls of Jerusalem and were given other privileges to be exercised both inside and outside Palestine. Chief among them, and of some significance for the early history of Christianity, was the freedom to practise their religion, and in matters concerning their faith to be governed by Jewish Law administered by Jews.

Antipater appointed Herod Governor of Galilee in 47 BC; he was then twenty-five years old. He immediately made his presence felt. A band of thieves was terrorizing the Galilean countryside. Herod captured and executed its leader. Leading Jews in Jerusalem thought this to be a usurpation of their authority, and Herod was summoned before the Sanhedrin, the supreme legislative and executive body among the Jews. The 71 members under the leadership of the high priest were drawn from the main aristocratic families of Jerusalem, both priestly and lay, and appointments seem to have been by co-option: admission to its ranks was signified by the laying-on of hands. The Sanhedrin had its own police force, and could certainly hear, and judge, cases which did not carry the death penalty; whether it had the right to try capital offences is not clear.

On this occasion it seems likely that the Sanhedrin was about to condemn Herod when orders came to the high priest from Caesar himself that he was to be set free. The sitting of the Sanhedrin was suspended, and Herod was advised to leave the city. But so incensed was he that, had his father not prevented it, he would have used his own troops to attack Jerusalem.

Herod and his family were obliged to flee Palestine when the Parthians invaded the country in 40 BC. He went to Rome, where he was granted the title of King of Judea and lent troops to recapture his kingdom. After a bitter siege, Jerusalem was recaptured in 37 BC. The Roman armies were persuaded to withdraw, and Herod the Great was left in undisputed command, able to wreak belated vengeance on the people who had humiliated him. Some members of the Sanhedrin were put to death, and Herod chose his high priests from among the Jews of Alexandria rather than from within the Jerusalem aristocracy. The more religiously minded in Jerusalem regarded their king as a divine punishment upon the Jewish people for their failings.

At Herod's death the succession was disputed. Two of his sons, Archelaus and Antipas, hurried to Rome. In Judea there was a revolt which had to be suppressed by Roman troops: two thousand rebels were crucified. An embassy went to Rome to beg that, whoever be put over Palestine, it should not be a member of Herod's family. The request was refused. The Emperor Augustus put Archelaus in charge of Judea, Samaria and Idumea, though with the lesser title of ethnarch rather than that of king; Antipas was given Galilee and Peraea with the title of tetrarch; and, also with the title of tetrarch, a third son, Philip, was given charge of an area to the north and east of the Sea of Galilee.

Philip was by far the best ruler of the three. At the source of the river Jordan he built the town of Panias, which he later renamed Caesarea. As Caesarea Philippi it occurs in the Gospels, as does another city he rebuilt, Bethsaida, situated where the waters of the Jordan enter the Sea of Galilee.

It was in the territory of Antipas, whom the New Testament rather confusingly – though accurately enough – also calls Herod, that both John the Baptist and Jesus lived and worked for most of their lives. Like his father and his brother Philip, Antipas was a great builder, but unfortunately for him his new city, Tiberias, was constructed over ancient Jewish burial grounds. That made it impossible for orthodox Jews to live there without incurring ritual impurity, so the town had to be colonized forcibly by foreigners and by those who were less religiously observant. Urged on by his

An aerial view of the Herodian fortress near Jerusalem. It was built by Herod the Great sometime between 24 and 15 BC, and it was here that he was buried.

ambitious wife, Antipas went to Rome in AD 39 to petition the Emperor Caligula for a royal title. This was refused, and Antipas was banished to Lyons where he died the same year, possibly executed on the orders of the emperor.

The third son, Archelaus, who also called himself Herod, was a disastrous ruler. He began his brief reign with a massacre of Jews gathering for the Passover in Jerusalem, and in general acted with such brutality and cruelty that he succeeded in the almost impossible task of uniting both Jew and Samaritan against him. In AD 6 a deputation of Jewish and Samaritan aristocrats appealed to the Emperor Augustus, and Archelaus was deposed. A Roman governor was appointed, with the title of prefect – though he came to be referred to more frequently as the procurator. A legate, Quirinius, was despatched to undertake a census of the new territories of the Empire: a preliminary step towards their taxation.

The Roman procurator generally resided in the palace at Caesarea which Herod the Great had built for himself. At the times of major feasts, however, when trouble might be expected, he took up residence in Herod's palace in Jerusalem, and his troops were quartered with him. These troops do not seem to have been full-scale Roman legionaries but auxiliary soldiers, recruited in Judea itself from the country's non-Jewish inhabitants. The procurator's authority was considerable, but for the most part he left the administration of the country to the Sanhedrin. His only real concern was with political crimes. Civil and criminal law in Jerusalem remained with the Sanhedrin, and elsewhere it was in the hands of lower tribunals.

The writ of the Jerusalem Sanhedrin did not legally run outside Judea. The territories inherited by Antipas and Philip constituted quite separate administrative units, and to govern the Jewish populations of these areas there were probably local Sanhedrins, scaled-down versions of the one in Jerusalem. But the Jerusalem Sanhedrin appears to have exercised a certain moral authority even outside the range of its own mandate.

The same was true of the high priest. As president of the Jerusalem Sanhedrin he exercised considerable influence over the Jewish population even beyond the borders of Judea, though he no longer had any direct political power. The Roman procurators controlled appointments to the high priesthood, and that gave them practical authority. During the period of procuratorial government high priests came and went with great frequency: Caiaphas, the high priest of the Gospel stories, survived in office for an unusually long period. He was appointed by one procurator in AD 18 and deposed by another in AD 36.

In AD 41 the right of nominating the high priest passed to the Jewish kings. Neither they, nor the procurators before them, were entirely arbitrary in their choice of candidates. These were selected from among traditional high priestly families, in order to avoid offending unnecessarily the religious feelings of the Jews. And that was all too easy, given the many factions into which, at the time of Jesus, the Jews were divided.

PARTIES AND PIETY

To present the political situation of Judea as a conflict between the Herodian dynasty, intruders from the region of Idumea, and the Sanhedrin, representing traditional Judaism, is greatly to oversimplify matters. The

31

Palestine in New Testament times showing the kingdom of Herod and those of his sons

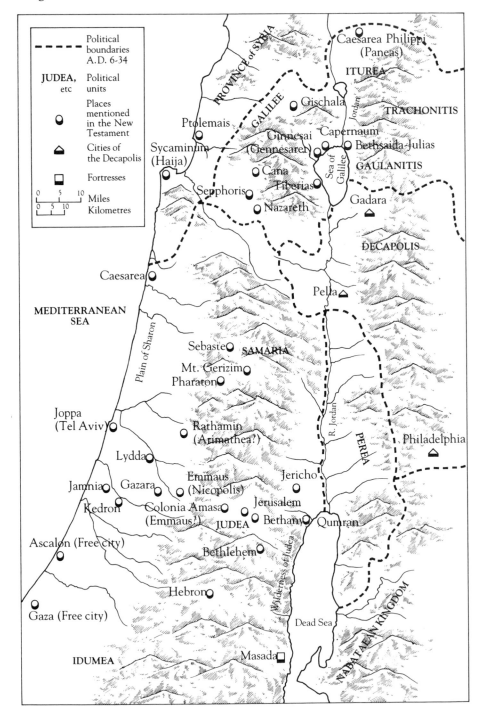

Legend:

Political boundaries A.D. 6-34

JUDEA, etc — Political units

Places mentioned in the New Testament

Cities of the Decapolis

Fortresses

0   5   10   Miles
0   5   10   Kilometres

Map labels:

PROVINCE of SYRIA

Caesarea Philippi (Paneas)

ITUREA

TRACHONITIS

GALILEE

Gischala

Ptolemais

Capernaum

Ginnesai (Gennesaret)

Bethsaida-Julias

Sycaminum (Haija)

Cana

Sea of Galilee

GAULANITIS

Sepphoris

Tiberias

Nazareth

Gadara

DECAPOLIS

Caesarea

Pella

MEDITERRANEAN SEA

Plain of Sharon

Sebaste

SAMARIA

Mt. Gerizim

Pharaton

Joppa (Tel Aviv)

Rathamin (Arimathea?)

R. Jordan

PEREA

Philadelphia

Lydda

Jamnia

Gazara

Emmaus (Nicopolis)

Jericho

Kedron

Colonia Amasa (Emmaus?)

JUDEA

Jerusalem

Bethany

Qumran

Ascalon (Free city)

Bethlehem

Wilderness of Judea

Hebron

Gaza (Free city)

Dead Sea

NABATAEAN KINGDOM

IDUMEA

Masada

reality was rather more complicated, and to understand it more fully it is necessary to go back about six hundred years.

In 587 BC King Nebuchadnezzar had captured Jerusalem and put its most influential inhabitants into exile in Babylon. The city was left in ruins. As the exiled families made their way back over the next century and a half, it was the priestly class which organized the rebuilding of the city and the establishment of a new community. The priests were the guardians of the Law, the Torah, which regulated the daily lives of the people. It was the priests who interpreted the Torah to meet new situations as they arose.

Priesthood was strictly hereditary. The great number of priests of Jesus' time all had to be able to prove their descent from one of the priestly families which had returned to Jerusalem after the exile. Before the exile the priests, as a class, had not been particularly wealthy. Afterwards they became so: the New Testament provides evidence of how severely the tithing laws were operated. According to these regulations, priests received a tenth of all produce of the land, in addition to the Temple dues, portions of sacrifices and other offerings. Collection and distribution of this income were centralized at Jerusalem. All priests received a share, even those who, because of some physical deformity, were judged unfit for service in the Temple.

In the course of time, and possibly because the priests were seduced by Hellenism and began to neglect their duties, lay people came to play an increasing part in the interpretation of the Torah. These experts were the scribes, the teachers of the Law who by New Testament times were being called 'my lord', or 'rabbi'. They dressed like the nobility or like priests, but generally earned their living by following some trade: their role as teachers and – sometimes – judges was usually unpaid. Everywhere they demanded the leading position: 'Everything they do is done to attract attention,' Jesus said of them, 'like wanting to take the place of honour at banquets and the front seats in the synagogues, being greeted obsequiously in the market squares and having people call them Rabbi' (Mt 23:5–7).

In that passage Jesus was speaking of both scribes and Pharisees. As strict observers of the Law, the majority of the scribes belonged, in all probability, to the party of the Pharisees. 'Pharisee' means 'the separated ones', and may originally have been used in a pejorative sense. Their own preferred name for themselves was 'haberim': the companions, or brothers, of the covenant. Their companions were not all other Jews, but only those who followed their particular interpretation of the Torah. Because of the severity of their understanding of the Torah, and especially of the regulations on ritual purity, the Pharisees constituted a fairly small group, few of them priests. But they appear to have been influential, especially in

The map opposite, clearly shows the divide between the coastal plain and the hill country of much of Judea and Samaria.

the cities and among women. Their ability to lead a six-year revolt against the warrior-king Alexander Jannaeus (103–76 BC) demonstrated that they could gain popular support.

The Pharisees were not, in theory, concerned with politics. Their chief concern was that the Jewish people should be allowed to pursue their religious duties without hindrance. They supported war in order to free the Jews of Hellenism, but when under Alexander the war appeared to become one of national aggrandisement against a weak Syria, they opposed it. Alexander gave in, and their victory in the struggle against the king left them with a degree of political control, so that even their arch rivals, the Sadducees, thought it wise to follow the Pharisees' interpretation of the Torah. The exact degree of their influence at the time of Jesus is disputed, but it is clear from the text of the New Testament that the Pharisees figured large in the life of the people.

While for the most part the Pharisees represented the lay interest, the Sadducees came mainly, though not exclusively, from the priestly families. Their name is thought to be derived from Zadok the Priest, whose descendants had served the Temple from the time of Solomon. They were drawn from among the Jerusalem aristocracy, from people of rank and wealth, and were much more concerned than were the Pharisees with political affairs. The Sadducees were attracted to Hellenism because it represented a form of government as well as a culture. They were prepared to come to terms with it, and with a Hellenistic overlord, if that was the price they had to pay to retain their status in society. The Maccabean revolt, which reasserted the traditional values of the people, considerably reduced their standing, and brought the Pharisees to prominence.

But the divide between the two was not a simple one. Where there is evidence – and it is not a great deal – of differences over the interpretation of the Torah, it is the Sadducean party which seems to have adopted the more conservative, and in that sense more traditional, stance. It is clear from the New Testament that the Pharisees believed in angels and spirits, to take one example, while the Sadducees did not. The latter view was the more traditional. Again, from the New Testament and other sources it is known that the Pharisees believed the righteous would rise from the dead to live in the glory of the messianic kingdom, while the unrighteous would be punished by eternal torment. Belief in survival after death came very late into Judaism. The Sadducean opinion, which rejected this conviction and with it the whole messianic hope of late Judaism, was the more traditional interpretation of the Scriptures.

Two magnificent examples of building carried out at the time of Herod the Great. Above is the palace at Masada, a word which probably simply means 'fortress', and below is the high level aqueduct, carrying drinking water five miles or so from Mount Carmel down to Caesarea.

The scrolls upon which the Torah, the Law, was written, were treated with great respect in the synagogues. The highly decorated niche above held the scrolls of the Torah at the Jewish catacomb in Rome.

It was on the issue of scriptural interpretation, or more precisely the interpretation of the Torah, that the most significant distinction between Pharisee and Sadducee was to be found. The Torah was constituted by the Pentateuch, the first five books of the Bible. The Jews had come to believe that the Pentateuch had been directly handed by God to Moses. Even the account of Moses' own death, which is to be found in the Pentateuch, had been included in the books when Moses received them. The Torah, therefore, was absolute. It was acceptance of the Torah as the rule of life, and the Temple worship laid down in it, that distinguished a Jew from everyone else.

Therefore both Pharisees and Sadducees had to accept the Torah. But that was the written Torah. Alongside it there was the 'oral' Torah: interpretations of the Law and its application to new situations as they arose. The Pharisees held these traditions to be as binding as the written Torah. In principle, the Sadducees refused to be bound by anything other than the written Torah although, in practice, they went along with the interpretations of the Pharisees. Nonetheless they continued to object to the oral Torah as being a limit to their authority both as priests and as the hereditary ruling class.

Though the two parties differed considerably, their diverse political outlook had the same result. Both supported Roman rule in Palestine. For the Sadducees it was a question of the survival of a national identity in a form which would allow them, as collaborators with the ruling power, a modicum of independence. The Pharisees on the other hand looked upon Roman rule as a punishment for the people's infidelity to God, and for the most part accepted alien government in that spirit.

But there were problems. As already noted, Rome and the local puppet rulers were generally careful to avoid offending Jewish sensibilities, but that was not always practicable. The only coins minted in Palestine, for example, were copper ones which carried no human image. But other coins, minted outside the country, were also in circulation, the gold aureus and the silver drachma. Both bore upon them the image of Caesar, and it was the silver drachma which was the coin paid in tribute to the emperor. The mere possession of such a coin was an implicit acknowledgement of the sovereignty of Rome, and a constant reproach to national pride.

For a century before the birth of Jesus and into his lifetime, the belief gained ground among the Jews that God had intended for the people of Israel a ruler from the house – the family – of David. Subjugation to a Gentile power, therefore, was contrary to Scripture. It was intolerable. This was the view generally held by the Pharisees, but opinion differed as to how best to respond. Some took the way of resignation: Roman rule had come, but in God's good time it would pass. Others, however, favoured a more active role: the coming of God's kingdom was to be hastened by the overthrow of the hated Gentile overlords.

For this latter group the crisis came in AD 6. Quirinius, Governor of Syria, imposed upon the Jews the census which is mentioned at the beginning of Luke's Gospel. In the eyes of the fanatical, or even of the merely zealous, the census was contrary to the Torah. It was forbidden to count God's people. Worse, it was illegal for them to be counted in order that a tax might be imposed which would help support Gentile rule over them. A Pharisee named Zadok joined forces with a certain Judas to create the revolutionary party known as the Zealots.

Judas was a remarkable man, and came from a remarkable family. His father was a rebel leader in Upper Galilee who had been executed in 47 BC by Herod the Great. Over forty years later, Judas broke into Herod's arsenal, just after his death, to steal weapons. In about AD 47 two of Judas' sons were crucified for anti-Roman activities. A third, Menahem, seized the fortress at Masada and then, dressed as a king, tried to enter the Temple in Jerusalem. He was killed in the fighting which followed, but his nephew led the last stand against the Romans at Masada in AD 73 (p. 109).

Judas' beliefs, sometimes called the Fourth Philosophy, profoundly affected another group within first-century Judaism, the Sicarii. Their name was taken from the *sica*, a curved dagger with which they committed political assassination. After the fighting which followed Menahem's attempt to seize power in Jerusalem, the Sicarii fled the city and took refuge in the citadel at Masada. Much of what we know about them comes from

37

Galilee in modern times – the citrus groves on the shore of the Sea of Galilee, not far from the site of Capernaum, demonstrate the countryside's fertility.

their activities in Judea's capital city, and the same is true for the Zealots. But Judas himself, like his father before him, was a Galilean, and that is significant.

A large area of Galilee had been annexed to Palestine as late as the end of the second century BC. Much of it was surrounded by Gentile territory, and it was cut off from orthodox Judea by highly unorthodox Samaria. It was populated for the most part by peasants. There were only two towns of any note, Sepphoris and Tiberias, both of which owed their existence to Herod Antipas and probably had not more than a handful of Jews among their inhabitants. When a revolt broke out in AD 66 Sepphoris remained loyal to Rome while Tiberias was only half-hearted in its support of the Jews. Galileans avoided the towns as far as possible. According to the Gospels, Jesus never went to either of them. The majority of Galileans lived in the countryside or beside the lake, where a good living was to be made from fishing or from the fertile soil.

The Galileans therefore were not poor, and they were highly independent. In addition to the owners or tenants of smallholdings, Galilean society produced labourers and itinerant craftsmen, people who had grown

The parallel rows of columns shown in this picture divided a nave from two aisles in this third-century synagogue at Capernaum, on the north-western shore of the Sea of Galilee.

up in a peasant society but who had both less stability than their kinsfolk and greater awareness of the social and economic disparities of first-century Palestine. Although they observed the demands of the Temple cult, their religious purity was not of the highest order and they were looked upon with suspicion by their Jerusalem-based masters.

From Galilee came brigands – or freedom fighters – such as Judas, his father and his sons. But there were also itinerant saints and healers, prophets and miracle-workers. Some of their names, and accounts of their careers, have been preserved. It was this society which produced John the Baptist – and Jesus, the village carpenter of Nazareth.

THE COMMUNITY OF THE DEAD SEA
While the Pharisees and Sadducees collaborated with the Roman regime and the Zealots and Sicarii opposed it, there was another group which did something entirely different. It set up an alternative society.

The name 'Essenes' possibly means 'the healers', although a more likely translation is 'the pious ones'. They were described by the two Jewish historians, the Pharisee Flavius Josephus (*c.* AD 37–100) and Philo (*c.* 20

BC–AD 50), who came from a wealthy priestly family living in Alexandria. The Roman writer Pliny the Elder (c. AD 23–79) also knew of them, and claimed that they were settled on the western shore of the Dead Sea. They have now been generally identified with the Jewish monastic community which has been revealed by the documents and the ruins found at Qumran. The link between the Essenes of history and the Dead Sea Scrolls so recently discovered has not been established beyond all shadow of doubt, but there are few scholars who now deny it.

The discovery of the scrolls began in the spring of 1947. A goatherd, looking for one of his flock, stumbled across a cave containing jars. Some of the jars were broken, others still intact. In them were scrolls of leather and papyrus which seem to have been deliberately placed in the caves – eleven caves were subsequently found to hold the jars – for safe keeping about the time when the armies of Vespasian came in to the Dead Sea region, in June AD 68. The buildings now lying in ruins near the caves show signs of having been occupied from the middle of the second century BC to AD 68, and the majority of the scrolls can be dated to within the same period. A number of them, however, appear to have been compiled as early as the beginning of the third century BC.

The manuscripts – there survive fragments of about 600 of them – are of various sorts. There are books of the Bible. There are other books which the Dead Sea community obviously considered may have been inspired by God as the Scriptures were, though more orthodox Jews and Christians have not chosen so to regard them. And then there were documents describing, and regulating, the community's internal life.

The isolation in which the Essenes lived, both physically and intellectually, constituted them a sect in the proper sense of the word. They were cut off. Unlike the Pharisees and the Sadducees, they were not a party within Israel, political or religious. They alone, they believed, were the true Israel, a faithful remnant, living on the fringes of Judaism. And in some ways the structures of the Dead Sea community reflected the structures of ancient Israel. Like the people of Israel they were divided into twelve tribes, or family groups. They were also categorized as priests, Levites (originally identical with the priestly tribe, but eventually allotted lesser ministerial duties in the Temple) and laity. The priests always took precedence, and were thought of as the sons of Zadok, who had been high priest at the time of King David.

From the scrolls a good deal is known of the internal organization of the community. It was governed by a council. Day-to-day management was entrusted to a guardian – presumably a priest – and there was a priest as president-general over all the groups. Membership was arranged in stages. No one might enter the community before the age of twenty as a full member, at which time, it was thought, a fully responsible, personal decision might be made. Before this came a year of spiritual preparation, or

A fragment of one of the scrolls found at
the Dead Sea site. It recounts Moses' clash
with Pharoah, from Exodus 5 – 8, and
dates from c. 200–175 BC.

noviceship, before the first of the ritual washings that were such a
prominent feature of Essene life. These were followed by two further years
of training, at the end of which an oath was taken to obey the Law of Moses
as it was very strictly interpreted by the community's priests. After the oath,
members were fully initiated. They were allowed to eat at the common
table. Anyone who seriously offended against the community's code might,

41

The Dead Sea Scrolls were first deposited in jars such as the one on the right, and the jars were then hidden from Vespasian's armies in caves like the one above. But not only scrolls were found. There were other artefacts such as baskets and beads (see opposite).

42

however, be brought before a tribunal and expelled from the community.

Both Philo and Josephus calculate that their numbers were about 4,000 or a little higher. The cemetery found at Qumran suggests that, at least in that particular community, the number of people dwelling in what can only be called a monastery was in the region of 150. It is necessary to speak of 'that particular community' because, although most attention has been focused on the area around the Dead sea with its ruins and its scrolls, it seems fairly clear that there were many different groups of Essenes living in the villages and towns of Palestine.

The village communities also attempted to live a common life of a quasi-monastic sort. They lived in a commuity under a superior. They, too, or at least the fully initiated among them, ate at a common table. Full members handed ownership of their property over to the community, and they then appear to have supported themselves by agriculture, though some are known to have followed other trades. Full members also probably shunned marriage and lived celibate lives.

Their style of life might be described as one of simplicity and moderation – but moderation only up to a point. They continued to pay their Temple dues, though they did not approve of Temple worship. They modelled their lives upon the lives of the Jewish priesthood and, like the priests serving in the Temple, took purificatory baths before eating. Baths, and washings of all kinds, played an important part in Essene life. The ruins at Qumran indicate a system of canals and cisterns too large to have just collected water for drinking; they must also have served as baths.

At the root of the Essenes' understanding of their service of God was the idea of 'covenant'. The covenant was an agreement between God and his people. The Essenes became members of the covenant by the oath they swore on membership, and it seems possible that a general assembly of the members of all the various communities in Palestine occurred each year on the Feast of the Renewal of the Covenant. The Essenes wished to live their lives in perfect fulfilment of the covenant. To do so it was necessary to study the Bible: study sessions with evening prayer were a feature of Essene life.

Their studies reinforced in them a strong sense that the Last Days, the end times, were fast approaching. Then there would appear not one but two messiahs. One of these would be a priest, the other a military leader. The age was to end in a great battle, to be fought both in heaven and upon earth. It is not surprising, then, that there should be just a hint that, when Qumran was abandoned, its former inhabitants threw in their lot with the Zealots: a fragment of their sectarian writings has been found at Masada, where the Zealots made their final stand against the Roman army.

So the Judaism into which Jesus was born was a complex mix of religious and political attitudes. It was made up of numerous sects and parties, of a range of views orthodox and unorthodox, of people who either hoped to retain their standing in society by collaborating with the imperial power or who set themselves apart in monkish solitude. Much of all this is reflected

An aerial view of Qumran, an Essene 'monastery'. The photograph pictures well the barren countryside in which the sectaries chose to live. In the background are the caves where the Dead Sea Scrolls were found.

in the New Testament which, when set against the background of the period, becomes more readily understandable.

And, as the New Testament relates, into this confusion of beliefs and practices, of messianic expectation and worldly ambition, 'a man came, sent by God. His name was John'.

THE COMING OF THE BAPTIST

The words just quoted occur at the very beginning of the Gospel of John. Both Luke and Mark open with the coming of John the Baptist, and John's story in Matthew starts immediately after the prologue which recounts the birth of Christ. In the Gospel of Matthew the description is most vivid:

> This man John wore a garment of camel-hair with a leather belt around his waist, and his food was locusts and wild honey. Then Jerusalem and all Judea and the whole Jordan district made their way to him, and as they were baptized by him in the river Jordan they confessed their sins.

John's curious diet may indicate that he was, or had been, a member of the Essene community, and felt himself still bound by the oath he had taken even though he was no longer living a community life. But it is not necessary to associate him with any known group in order to explain his appearance on the river bank, and his manner of life. It is quite likely that

45

The wilderness of Judea, out of which came John the Baptist preaching repentance. Contrast this part of Palestine with the view of Galilee shown on p. 39.

there were, in the Jordan valley, any number of competing groups practising baptism and proclaiming the coming of the end times. It may be that Jesus' sect was another such, preaching a similar doctrine, though clearly not having quite the same ascetic lifestyle as that adopted by the Baptist's community. Or alternatively Jesus may originally have been a member of John's sect but may have stood out, as John recognized by the Jordan (Mt 3:13–15), as one greater than he, finally setting out on his own.

John the Baptist's community survived his death at the hands of Herod Antipas. It may indeed have continued down to the present day. South of Bagdad there is a small sect called the Mandaeans; their origins undoubtedly go back to the Jordan valley, and at least to the second, if not to the first, century of the Christian era. For the most part, however, the followers of the Baptist were gradually incorporated into the Christian Church. The Acts of the Apostles tells how the apostle Paul travelled to Ephesus and there came across a number of people described as 'disciples'. They had become believers by the process of baptism, but had never heard of the Holy Spirit. '"Then how were you baptized?" Paul asked. "With John's baptism," they replied.' Paul insisted that John's baptism had only been one of repentance, and that the Baptist himself had wanted his disciples to believe 'in the one who was to come after him – in other words, Jesus'. Paul was a persuasive speaker. The book of Acts relates that they were then baptized in the name of the Lord Jesus, that the apostle laid his hands upon them, that the Holy Spirit came down, and that they began to speak with tongues (in foreign languages) and to prophesy.

46

Christian literature presents the community of the Baptist as in some sense a preparation for the coming of the community of the Church. John himself is similarly presented as a preparation for the coming of Jesus. He is the prophet who is to go before the messiah of David. He is made to say that Jesus 'must increase while I must decrease'. He plays a subordinate role, but not entirely subordinate. He is mentioned no less than ninety times in the New Testament – far more often than any of the apostles apart from Peter and Paul, far more, even, than his namesake John, the beloved disciple.

Why that should be so we can now only guess. The only sources about his community are Christian ones, and it may be that, at the time the Gospels were being written, the Baptist's community constituted an alternative, perhaps rival, form of life, with a similar message to that of the nascent Church. Or possibly Jesus saw in John's tragic fate his own ultimate end, bringing the realization of the role he was destined to play.

Such speculations trespass into the arena of theology. Whatever the motive of the Gospel writers in their accounts of the figure of John the Baptist, it is possible to glimpse behind the presentation something of the reality. John was one of the prophet-like figures of the period who called the Jews to repentance in the light of the end times which were, they believed, very near. He and they baptized as a sign of that repentance. John and his followers constituted a sect within Judaism, different in character perhaps from the sect of the Pharisees or of the Essenes, but a sect nonetheless. John was one of a number of religious leaders, revivalists they might be called today, or charismatics. His cousin Jesus was another.

3

THE MESSAGE OF JESUS

In examining the roots of Christianity we must look closely at the events of Jesus' life as told in the Gospels, and consider to what extent his teachings were reflected in the conduct of the early Christians.

All four Gospels tell the story of Jesus' preaching, of the wonders he worked, and of his resurrection. They all recount the events in a deceptively simple way. But the narratives are much more complicated than they appear to be at first sight. And perhaps of no part of the gospel story is this more true than the account of Jesus' birth.

THE FIRST CHRISTMAS

If one looks closely at the stories of the nativity in the Gospels, it soon proves very difficult to construct a coherent account of the event. Both Matthew and Luke, for example, claim to give detailed lists of Jesus' ancestors, tracing his family back to Abraham in the case of Matthew, and to Adam in the case of Luke. Yet the names in the two genealogies coincide only spasmodically. The lists are over-simplified. They are constructed of three times fourteen, or six times seven, groups of names. Matthew even draws attention to the fact: 'The sum of generations is therefore: fourteen from Abraham to David; fourteen from David to the Babylonian deportation; and fourteen from the Babylonian deportation to Christ.' (Mt 1:17)

There are also commonsense objections to the Gospel stories of the infancy of Jesus. Why, for instance, did Joseph and Mary have to go on the journey from Nazareth to Bethlehem, a distance of some ninety miles? Luke says that they had to be registered in the census of Quirinius. But people only had to go to a particular place to be registered if they owned property there, and it is highly unlikely that Joseph owned any property in Bethlehem. And even if he did, why did Mary have to travel with him? The Romans were reasonable. They usually allowed plenty of time for registration to take place, so there seems no reason for the couple to have made the journey when Mary was heavily pregnant.

It does not make sense. At least, it does not make sense if the accounts of the birth of Jesus in the Gospels of Matthew and Luke are taken to be precise records of what occurred.

Careful reading of the infancy narratives makes it obvious that they are an afterthought, even though they are placed early in the text. In all four Gospels the story they are intent to tell begins with the preaching of John

48

the Baptist. The accounts of the birth of Jesus and its immediate consequences are not there to provide a few colourful biographical details. They are there to set the theological scene.

Matthew and Luke are not primarily concerned to tell their readers how, when or where Jesus was born. Their chief concern is to tell them who he was. And they compiled their accounts from a patchwork of biblical quotation and allusion much more understandable to people in first-century Palestine than to us twenty centuries later.

Take, for example, the genealogies just referred to. Luke wishes to stress the universality of the salvation which Jesus has brought. So he goes back to Adam, the father of all humankind. Matthew, on the other hand, is much more interested in Jews who had been converted to Christianity, so he traces Jesus' family back to Abraham because Abraham was the father of the Jewish people. But both include David, the great Jewish king. The point of the lists of names is not their historical accuracy but their placing of Jesus in a historical context as saviour and messiah.

Further evidence of this bias is contained in the infancy narratives. Luke says that the news of Jesus' birth was revealed first to shepherds. They were the poor, for whom, according to the Bible, the messiah was to have special care. In Matthew the magi come from the East led by a star (magi were astrologers) to find the King of the Jews. They are told to seek him in Bethlehem, which was the town of David's birth: it was from Bethlehem that the Jews expected the messiah to come.

In the Gospels Jesus is presented not only as a king, like David, but also as a law-giver like Moses. In the infancy narratives, therefore, Herod massacres the innocents just as Pharaoh in the Bible massacred all the male children of the Hebrews in captivity in Egypt. But, like Moses, Jesus escapes death when Mary and Joseph flee with him into Egypt.

Matthew briefly mentions the flight into Egypt. But just as the writers of the Gospels built stories around Jesus' birth, later Christian writers embroidered the stories which the Gospels left too bare for their taste. The flight into Egypt was a popular incident for such embellishment. When the three refugees take a rest on their way, to give one example of later additions to the story, a palm tree bends down to offer its dates to Mary, while Jesus bids water spring up to quench the travellers' thirst.

These picturesque details have often been portrayed in art, though they have even less claim to historical accuracy than do the Gospel stories of the infancy. But they have a point. In this case they are emphasizing the power of Mary and of her son. The authors of these apocryphal stories were only doing what Matthew and Luke had done, though with rather less finesse. In the infancy narratives it is Jesus' future role in the Gospels rather than the nativity itself which is central to the writers' intentions.

This is even true of the actual date of Christmas. Nothing in the New Testament suggests a particular date for the birth of Jesus, and the first time

Scenes from the birth of Jesus, depicted on a very early Christian sarcophagus. The ox and the ass had already made their appearance, above, even though they are not mentioned in the canonical Gospels. The three 'kings', however, still remain 'magi', below.

50

that 25 December is mentioned is in a calendar representing liturgical practice at Rome in 336. From Rome, the custom of commemorating Jesus' nativity on that day spread to the rest of the Church in the West, though in the East the Epiphany, celebrating the visit of the magi, remained the more important feast. The choice of 25 December probably displays a Christian desire to replace the pagan celebration of the birthday of the Unconquered Sun, *Sol Invictus*, with an alternative celebration of their God as the new light, the new sun.

About the year, rather than the day, of Jesus' birth it is possible to be a little more precise. The system of numbering the years of the present era from the birth of Christ (*Anno Domini*, which means 'the year of the Lord') comes from a monk of Scythia, Dionysius Exiguus, or Denis the Little. It was wrong, wrote Dionysius in about the year 525 when he was living in Rome, that the years should still be counted from the reign of the Emperor Diocletian, for Diocletian had been a notorious persecutor of Christians. On some basis which is no longer clear, Dionysius calculated that Jesus had been born in 754 AUC (*Ab Urbe Condita*, or 'from the foundation of the city' – the city being Rome). So 754 AUC became AD 1.

Dionysius was Rome's resident expert on the calendar, but for all his supposed skill he got it wrong. The Gospels make it clear that Jesus was born while Herod the Great was still alive. By 754 AUC he had been dead for four years. Luke remarks that the census which brought Mary and Joseph to Bethlehem took place when Quirinius was governor of Syria. But that was in AD 6, long after Herod's death. On the other hand, a census was under way between 8 and 6 BC, before Herod's death. Based on this, the evidence suggests that Jesus was born about the year 6 BC. Some try to calculate the year from mention of the star, identifying it with Halley's comet (which passed close to earth in 11 BC) or with some particularly distinctive conjunction of planets. But that is to select one event from among the several which are alleged to have surrounded Jesus' birth and to treat it as if it actually occurred. It would be more in keeping with the style of Luke's narrative if all these details were regarded as part of a story built around the nativity to mark it out as an event of momentous importance.

PREACHING THE KINGDOM

The stories of the infancy of Jesus so far briefly described come from the Gospels of Matthew and of Luke. But it is generally believed that the first Gospel to be written, the one nearest Jesus' own lifetime and conveying his message most directly, was the Gospel of Mark. And Mark makes no mention at all of the events surrounding the birth of Jesus. The Gospel begins with the story of John the Baptist appearing in the wilderness, then making his way to the river Jordan where he offered 'all Judaea and all the people of Jerusalem' a 'baptism of repentance for the forgiveness of sins'. Jesus comes and offers himself for baptism, after which he goes out into the

desert for forty days, guarded by angels. Then he returns: 'After John had been arrested, Jesus went into Galilee. There he proclaimed the Good News from God. "The time has come," he said, "and the kingdom of God is close at hand. Repent and believe the Good News"' (Mk 1:14–15). Thus the first words attributed to Jesus, recorded in the earliest Gospel, are a proclamation of the coming of the kingdom of God.

Today, much of Jesus' teaching is known to people who would not consider themselves Christians. The parables of the Good Samaritan, of the Prodigal Son and others, the ethical teaching contained in the Sermon on the Mount, and so on, all contain powerful instruction about the way one human being should treat another. They reach through time and across religious divides. Such passages are taken to be the kernel of Jesus' teaching.

His first followers, however, saw it differently. For them, the all-important part of what Jesus had to say was the warning that the kingdom of heaven was at hand. This is his 'eschatological' teaching (from the Greek word *eschata*, meaning 'the last things'). Because the 'last things', the 'end times', have not arrived after two thousand years of Christianity, the eschatological element of Jesus' teaching has been overlooked. If and when

Illustrations of narrative scenes appear relatively late in Christian art. Portraits of Christ were much earlier. The beardless figure to the left, from the catacomb of Domitilla, is one of the earliest representations of a parable. It shows Christ the Good Shepherd.

it has been remembered, it has been seen in a symbolic, almost mythological, light. Christians have not been prepared to admit that Jesus was wrong in his expectation of the coming of the kingdom, so they have sought all kinds of reasons to account for the fact that his prophecies have not been fulfilled.

But the evidence of the Gospels suggests that Jesus preached the coming of the kingdom of God, if not in his own lifetime then shortly afterwards. Most of those who heard him took him at his word, but even those who disbelieved him knew what he was talking about. They had heard it before.

The beliefs and attitudes of some of the various branches, or sects, of Judaism have been sketched in the previous chapter. But these were the main ones, those which have left clear evidence of their existence, not least in the Gospels themselves. There were, however, many more groups, movements and sects of which little or nothing is known. Some of these are mentioned in later Jewish writings. Others have to be guessed at in order to explain some of the beliefs of which there is record.

The Qumran community provides an example. This sect produced abundant writings, although what is written is not consistent. It seems

The Jews expected the coming of the messiah, 'the anointed one'. Hopes centred on the return of King David, shown here being anointed as king by the prophet Samuel.

highly likely that even within the Qumran, or within the Essenes if indeed these two are identical, there were divergent groups. Indeed, some scholars argue that the many manuscripts which have been found in and around the area do not reflect the ideas of any one sect, but of very many different sects, and were simply hidden in the region when people fled from the Roman army.

Apart from Qumran, other groups can be guessed at from the writings which are often, though rather inaccurately, called 'intertestamental'. These books, those of Enoch, the Psalms of Solomon, the Book of Jubilees and others, contain much valuable information about Jewish beliefs in Palestine at or near the time of Jesus. And prominent among those beliefs is the conviction that a new era was about to dawn.

There is no single doctrine. Different religious groups had different opinions about the kingdom that was to come. The Qumran community, for example, believed that there would be three different messiahs. There was to be a priestly messiah, who would take precedence over the warrior messiah from the house of David, and there was also to be a prophetic messiah, perhaps a new Moses, who would have a new Elijah as his forerunner. Jesus himself is represented as believing this. 'It was towards John [the Baptist] that all the prophecies of the prophets and the Law were leading; and he, if you will believe me, is the Elijah who was to return', Matthew records him as saying (Mt 11:13–14).

A constant feature of the eschatology of the time, however, is the belief that there was about to dawn a new age of peace, righteousness and justice. In this new age those who had been faithful to God would be rewarded. But it was not to be born without conflict. Its coming would be preceded by disorder on a grand scale. In the Gospel of Matthew (24:6–8), Jesus says:

You will hear of wars and rumours of wars; do not be alarmed, for this
is something that must happen, but the end will not be yet. For nation
will fight against nation, and kingdom against kingdom. There will be
famines ánd earthquakes here and there. All this is only the beginning
of the birthpangs. . .

But this time of troubles was to be no more than a preparation for the coming of the kingdom. The kingdom would not be set in some other, future, world or life. It would be an event in this world, and Israel had a special role to play. According to some accounts, the righteous who had died before this millennium dawned would be brought back to life so that they might enjoy it.

The millennium was not going to be achieved without a struggle. A descendant of King David, a warrior anointed with the divine spirit, would prepare the way. He would wage war against, and defeat, Israel's enemies. He would cleanse the country, and the Temple, restoring peace on earth. This messiah – from the Hebrew word meaning 'anointed', as Israel's leaders had been anointed with oil to consecrate them to the service of the people – would be an ordinary mortal. In the Gospels Jesus is presented as such a messiah, one who would prepare the way for the new age. The title 'Christ', which is now used almost as if it were Jesus' surname, is a Greek word also meaning 'anointed'.

According to the Gospel narratives, Jesus believed the messianic era to be imminent. There are even sayings which suggest that he thought it had already arrived – 'The Kingdom of heaven is among you', he said on one occasion (Lk 17:21) – but they are the exception. In his own ministry, however, there were abundant signs that the messianic era was close at hand. Chief among these signs were Jesus' miracles. They were a recognized feature of the end times: without them Jesus' claims would have been regarded as empty, without them he would have posed no challenge to the Jewish establishment in Jerusalem.

This is not to suggest that Jesus saw himself as the messiah. On the other hand it is quite likely he saw himself playing some part in the coming of the kingdom. There was a dawning realization on Jesus' part that he would die at the hands of his enemies, as John the Baptist had done. His suffering and death would set the seal on the new covenant to be established between God and the people of Israel.

And there was his conviction that he would return again from the dead, most graphically expressed at the Last Supper. He prophesied that he would not drink wine again with his disciples until 'I drink new wine with you in the kingdom of my Father'. Resurrection from the dead was, like the occurrence of miracles, proof that the end times were at hand.

These eschatological elements in Jesus' teaching set the context for the Christian message. The more popular parables, the Sermon on the Mount, Jesus' lifestyle and that of his disciples: these provide the content. The parables describe the qualities required of people, and especially of his disciples, if they are to live the sort of lives acceptable in the kingdom. Jesus was not a social reformer. The ideals he set in the parables were not empty exhortations; they constituted a way of life which was followed by himself

Miracles were understood as signs that the messianic era was about to dawn. These two examples of early Christian art illustrate, left, the healing of the woman with an issue of blood and, right, the multiplication of the loaves and fishes.

The Gospel stories in which Jesus raised people from the dead were the most important signs of the coming of the messianic era. The medallion above depicts the raising of Lazarus.

and his disciples. And in some ways his attitude was at odds with the traditional view of the messiah. According to the stories which were circulating in Palestine, the Davidic messiah was a warrior. Jesus, on the other hand, expressed a clear opposition to violence. He refused to initiate violence, but himself suffered it patiently. As one of his disciples commented, the decision to go up to Jerusalem at the time of the Passover was tantamount to courting death.

And, as recorded in the Gospel of Mark, Jesus seems to have expected a similar fate for his disciples:

Take care that no one deceives you. Many will come using my name and saying 'I am he' and they will deceive many. When you hear of wars and rumours of wars, do not be alarmed, this is something that must happen, but the end will not be yet. For nation will fight against nation, and kingdom against kingdom . . . Be on your guard: they will hand you over to sanhedrins; you will be beaten in synagogues; and you will stand before governors and kings for my sake to bear witness before them, since the Good News must first be proclaimed to all the nations. (Mk 13:5–10)

It is obvious from this passage, however, that although Jesus may have expected the end times fairly soon, they were not to follow immediately upon his death. His disciples were to be witnesses of his message, and to spread the gospel. Like many another preacher of first-century Palestine, Jesus had built up a group of followers around himself, and he expected them to survive his death.

TRIAL AND DEATH

As has been seen, the Gospels present Jesus as going to his death, if not willingly, at least fully conscious that, as someone whose task it was to hurry on the coming of the kingdom, death was a destiny he could not escape. In the middle to late fifties of the first century AD the apostle Paul came to reflect upon the life and teaching of Jesus, and especially upon his death. To the Christian community in Corinth Paul wrote, 'Christ died for our sins, in accordance with the scriptures' (1 Cor 15:3).

From the way Paul writes, it sounds as if he is echoing an expression which is not his own. He tells the Corinthians that he is teaching them what he himself has been taught. But his words have resonances of a much older text, in the writings of the prophet Isaiah:

And yet ours were sufferings he bore, ours the sorrows he carried.
But we, we thought of him as someone punished, struck by God and brought low.
Yet he was pierced through for our faults, crushed for our sins.
On him lies a punishment that brings us peace, and through his wounds we are healed. (Isa 53:4–5)

This is the fourth of a mysterious set of poems or songs in the Book of Isaiah which tell of a 'servant' who suffered for the misdeeds of others. Paul understood it in terms of Jesus ushering in, by his death, the kingdom of God. He gives the song of the suffering servant a messianic intepretation. 'It is better for one man to die for the people,' the high priest says of Jesus in the Gospel of John, 'than for the whole nation to be destroyed' (Jn 11:50).

According to John, both priests and Pharisees were engaged in a plot to kill Jesus well before the events which led to his death. John's Gospel mentions a special meeting of the Sanhedrin to discuss the threat which Jesus posed to the stability of the regime. The three other accounts do not

This sarcophagus (c. AD 350) depicts scenes from the Passion of Christ, but with a difference. It is a victorious Jesus who is presented here; the crown of thorns, for example, has become a laurel wreath and the Chi-Ro symbol, in the centre, signals his triumph over death.

mention this, and place responsibility for Jesus' death squarely upon the priestly faction. This is curious, for in the countryside outside Jerusalem the Pharisees had appeared to be against Jesus at least as much as were the priestly Sadducees.

But it was the priestly aristocracy that had most to lose. They had good reason to be afraid. Mark records a story Jesus told in Jerusalem about the wicked tenants. They had been placed in charge of a vineyard. When the vineyard's owner sent servants to collect its produce the tenants abused them. The owner finally sent his son. He, too, was killed. And then the owner went himself, and slaughtered the tenants.

Priests, elders and scribes all took the point. They were, according to Jesus, all about to lose their privileged position because they had abused it. The same message was to be read in Jesus' action of driving buyers and sellers from the Temple precinct. Not only was this a grave insult to the priests whose responsibility the Temple was, it implied that Jesus was on the side of those eschatologically minded groups such as the Qumran sectaries who believed the Temple already to be defiled, and its priests unworthy.

Jesus entered Jerusalem in triumph, riding upon an ass and greeted by crowds waving palms, seen here on a sarcophagus.

TIBERIEVM . . .[PO]NTIVS PILATVS [PRAEF]ECTVS IVDAE[AE] The stone to the left records the dedication by Pontius Pilate of a building in honour of the Emperor Tiberius and shows that Pilate's title when he served in Judea (AD 26–36) was 'praefectus' rather than the more commonly accepted 'procurator'. It was found at Caesarea, the residence of the Roman governor and official capital of Judea. Pilate condemned Jesus to tread upon the stones of the Roman pavement, below, on his way to Calvary.

61

A crude piece of anti-Christian propaganda of the early third century, found incised into a wall on the Palatine hill. The crucified figure has an ass's head, and the inscription reads 'Alexamenos worships his god'.

Jesus' prophecy that 'the time will come when not a single stone [of the Temple] will be left on another: everything will be destroyed' (Lk 21:6) was an especially chilling threat. He was a clear target for the priests.

Jesus' presence in Jerusalem at the time of the Passover, when nationalistic expectations ran high, his triumphal entry into the city, with his supporters waving palm-branches and hailing him as messiah – all this was too much. He had to be done away with. But how?

And that remains a puzzle. Indeed the story of Jesus' arrest, trial and death upon the cross is full of puzzles. Was his appearance before the

Sanhedrin a formal trial? If so, what was the charge, and how was it proved? The Gospels present the Jews as responsible for Jesus' death. Jewish sources themselves agree. But if so, what was the role of Pontius Pilate?

Members of the Sanhedrin might have had good reason to wish Jesus out of the way, but who actually arrested him? Mark says 'a number of men armed with swords and clubs, sent by the chief priests and the scribes and the elders' (14:43) did the job. John insists it was a 'cohort' (18:3): that seems to imply a detachment of Roman troops. However, at this point in the story there was no reason for the imperial authorities to be involved. And even if they had been involved they would scarcely have sent a cohort, a thousand men or thereabouts, to arrest a single individual. Nor would they then have handed Jesus over to the Jews. The 'cohort' must have been a unit of the Temple guards.

The accounts of the trial, if such it was, before the Sanhedrin are full of anomalies. It appears to have taken place at night; to have been held on the eve of a festival; to have resulted in a death penalty on the very day it started. All these facts are contrary to the Jewish Law of the time, as far as it has come down to us: a strong argument against the historical accuracy of the Gospel accounts.

But the issue is more complex than this. Evidence about Sanhedrin trials comes from Jewish writings a century and a half after the death of Jesus. They come, moreover, from a Pharisaic tradition. It may be that the Sadducees, who were chiefly responsible for the events surrounding Jesus' death, did not follow the same rules.

The charge against Jesus was blasphemy. But, again according to second-century sources, blasphemy seems to have been limited to pronouncing the divine name, and there is no record in the New Testament that Jesus did this. It is clear that his accusers were having difficulty in proving the charge: witnesses contradicted one another. On the other hand Jesus' claim recorded in Mark's Gospel, 'You will see the Son of Man seated at the right hand of the Power and coming with the clouds of heaven' (Mk 14:62), may have been enough to incur the penalty if Jesus was thought to be saying that he himself would be sitting next to God on the heavenly throne.

The penalty, under Jewish Law, was death. Was that why Jesus was sent to Pilate? The gospel text appears to suggest that Jews did not have the right to carry out an execution on their own authority. But that, too, is debatable. One Jewish source indicates that the right to carry out the death penalty was withdrawn from the Jews at just about this time. On the other hand there is evidence of Jews executing people: they put to death Jesus' follower Stephen, for example, though that may have been a spontaneous act.

It was Roman practice to maintain local law, but in some instances sentences involving the death penalty were reviewed to avoid serious

A typical Jewish tomb,
showing the stone which was
rolled across the entrance to
block it, above. An ivory
diptych, right, which shows
the guards asleep in one
scene and women at the
empty tomb, talking to the
angel, in the other.

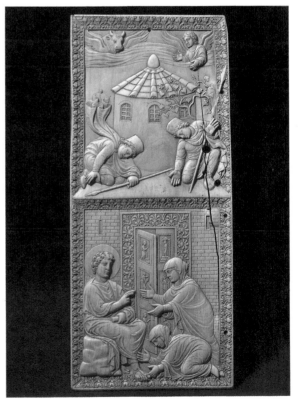

miscarriages of justice. That may have been Pilate's concern. Or he may have wished to ensure that the Sanhedrin's decision was politically acceptable. Perhaps he was not sure. In any case, Pilate bargained for Jesus' life against that of the robber Barabbas. It was hardly the act of a Roman but was not untypical of the Jews, and the procurator may have chosen to follow their example. Then he sent Jesus to be crucified.

It is often asserted that crucifixion was a Roman punishment. But we know that it was sometimes practised by the Jews, and the offering of myrrh to Jesus was a Jewish rather than a Roman custom: the Jews habitually dulled the senses of those about to die. At Jesus' crucifixion there were Roman soldiers around the cross, but other executions were taking place at the same time. Tradition has preserved the memory of two other deaths on Calvary, the thieves on either side of Jesus, but there is no reason to think that only three were put to death that day.

So although the accounts of the crucifixion are not free from difficulties, there is no real reason to doubt the main lines of the story as it is related in the New Testament. It has to be borne in mind, however, that at the time when the Gospels were written there was considerable tension between Christianity and Judaism. This is reflected in the hostility to the Jews, and especially to the Pharisees, as narrated in the pages of the New Testament. In contrast, many Christians wished to present the imperial authorities in as good a light as possible. The New Testament writers thus squarely shifted the whole burden of guilt for the death of Jesus upon the Jews.

Jesus was arrested by the Temple guards and taken to the Sanhedrin. It was night-time, so possibly the hearing was not a formal trial. The charge was blasphemy, but it proved difficult to demonstrate that Jesus was guilty. His claim that the Temple was to be destroyed and rebuilt (Mk 14:58) might have been sufficient to damn him, but the evidence was conflicting.

Jesus' real crime had been to proclaim the coming of the kingdom, and to associate himself with it. Had the national aspirations of the people been stirred to the point of revolt, it was the priestly aristocracy who would have had most to lose. They did not want a collapse of their *modus vivendi* with the Roman authorities. Thus the charge against Jesus was religious, but his real crime in the eyes of the Sanhedrin was political.

Pilate had no jurisdiction over crimes that were offences against the religious laws of the Jews, such as blasphemy. All he could do was to ratify the decision of the local court. This he did, though with some reluctance if the Gospel stories are to be believed. It is true that the accounts of Jesus' final hours make it seem as if the Romans had once again taken charge, but there are several possible explanations for that. As has already been pointed out, Jesus was not crucified alone. The two others mentioned, and possibly more whom we do not know about, were common criminals who would have come under Roman jurisdiction. Jesus' presence among them may simply have been a matter of administrative convenience.

THE RESURRECTION AND AFTER

It is quite likely that Pilate had to write a report about the events surrounding the trial and death of Jesus for his masters in the imperial capital. One Christian author, Justin, who lived in Rome and died about the middle of the second century, even writes as if he had seen the report. Had it survived it would no doubt have resolved the apparent inconsistencies in the story of Jesus' Passion.

But for Jesus' followers the significance of his death is as nothing compared to the account of the resurrection. The resurrection has so often been depicted that it is easy to forget that the Gospels do not describe what happened. They are concerned only with people's reactions to the news that Jesus had risen from the dead. Mary of Magdala, the two Marys, the two Marys and Salome, depending upon which account is consulted, came to the tomb where Jesus' body lay. They found it empty.

There have been more arguments about the resurrection than any other part of the gospel story, especially in recent years. The controversy arises because the event is so central to Christian belief. St Paul was the first Christian to comment upon it – or the first whose writings have survived. He told the Christian community at Corinth, 'if Christ has not been raised then our preaching is useless and your believing it is useless' (1 Cor 15:14).

What was at issue was the coming of the kingdom. It was not that Jesus' rising from the dead was the great miracle which endorsed all that he had said and done. But resurrection was one of the signs, perhaps the most important sign to the Jews of the time, that the messianic age had begun. Because it was so important, Paul listed all the evidence of eye-witnesses:

Well then, in the first place, I taught you what I had been taught myself, namely that Christ died for our sins, in accordance with the scriptures; that he was buried; and that he was raised to life on the third day, in accordance with the scriptures; that he appeared first to Cephas and secondly to the Twelve. Next he appeared to more than five hundred of the brothers at the same time, most of whom are still alive, though some have died; then he appeared to James, and then to all the apostles; and last of all he appeared to me too. (1 Cor 15:3–8)

Paul's inclusion of himself raises questions. He likens his own vision of Jesus on the road to Damascus to the appearance before the apostles. He makes them comparable. But visions of people who have died are not an uncommon psychic phenomenon. They are not to be identified with the experiences of the apostles or of Mary of Magdala as the Gospels recount them, who walked, talked and breakfasted with Jesus. The Gospels do not say that the apostles or Mary saw visions. Instead they emphasize the empty tomb.

The true face of Jesus? The 'negative' taken from the burial shroud preserved at Turin, which many believe to be the one in which Jesus was laid to rest.

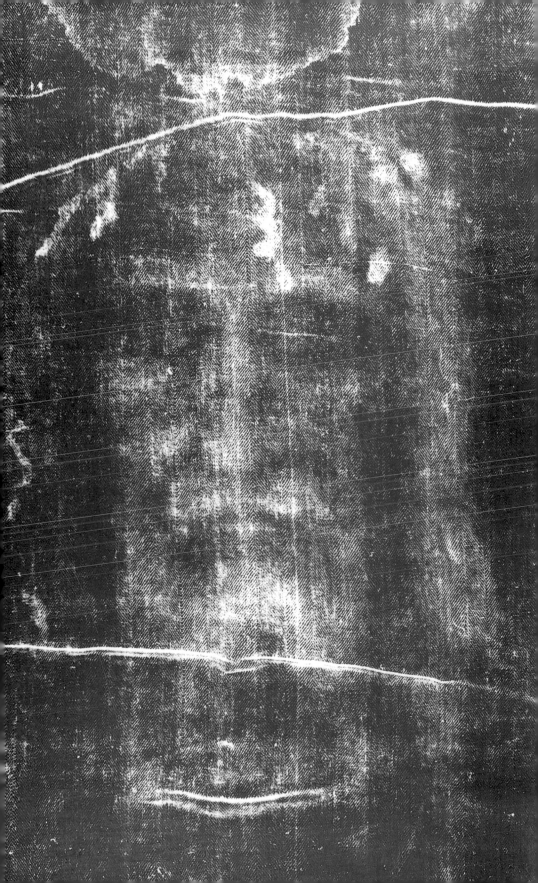

There are many possible interpretations of the empty tomb. St Matthew's Gospel itself provides an alternative to the resurrection. The guards who had been placed at the tomb:

> went off into the city to tell the chief priests all that had happened. These held a meeting with the elders and, after some discussion, handed a considerable sum of money to the soldiers with these instructions, 'This is what you must say, "His disciples came during the night and stole him away while we were asleep." And should the governor come to hear of this, we undertake to put things right with him ourselves and to see that you do not get into trouble.' The soldiers took the money and carried out their instructions, and to this day that is the story among the Jews. (Mt 28:11–15)

That particular story was self-evidently implausible, which may be why Matthew tells it. How could sleeping soldiers have known who took the body away? But there are other possibilities.

Jesus may have been in a coma. Or he may never have been put in the tomb at all. Or he might, as the Gospels claim, have risen from the dead. If so, then Jesus puts himself outside history. History has to do with finding similarities and contrasts in order to understand. But were the resurrection true, there is nothing with which to make a comparison.

Oddly, the Gospel stories seem to take account of precisely this point. After the resurrection, Jesus comes and goes at will. He passes through closed doors. He suddenly appears at a lakeside. He is not immediately recognizable, even though, along the road to Emmaus from Jerusalem, he talks at length with two of his disciples. The dimension of continuity in

The triumph over death: an allegorical frieze from a sarcophagus now in the Vatican which shows Jesus as sovereign of the universe.

space and time is wholly absent.

Jesus' message had been that the kingdom of heaven was at hand. Resurrection from the dead was a most potent sign of that kingdom. The disciples did not expect visions, but the reality of the risen Christ: the stress placed on the empty tomb in the Gospels is evidence of that. And next, they would have expected Jesus to eat with them. The notion of a meal, or banquet, played a large part in messianic thinking, and Jesus is constantly represented as eating with his disciples. In other words, the Gospel accounts stress the concrete aspects of evidence for the resurrection.

As will be seen in the next chapter, Paul's letters predate the Gospel accounts, but his description of the risen Christ is notably less realistic. Paul represents him in terms of a vision. His account is less practical, more theoretical: the Gospels seem to have retained a more primitive Christian tradition.

Two thousand years later the resurrection of Jesus is still a matter of debate. But in terms of the story of the Christian community, all that really matters is that those who followed Jesus believed the resurrection to have taken place. And they acted on that belief.

4

THE NEW SCRIPTURES

The story of Jesus' teaching, of his death and resurrection, is recounted in what has come to be called the New Testament. It is 'new' in contrast to the Old Testament, the books which tell the history and record the laws of the Jewish people. These were what Christians of the first century would have thought of as the Scriptures, a word which means 'writings', just as the word 'bible' simply means 'book'.

The authors of the books which constitute the New Testament were not conscious that they were adding to the body of the Scriptures. They were writing for communities of Christians which they knew, telling them about Jesus or commenting upon the way of life of the community in the light of Jesus' teaching.

So if the books of the New Testament are read with care, they not only tell us about Christ, but about the communities for which they were composed and which, in a sense, produced them. They reflect the precise interests and concerns of specific bodies of people. What is known about those people will be examined in the next chapter. But since it is the New Testament which provides most, if not quite all, of the evidence, it is at this we should look first.

FROM MEMORY TO RECORD

In any edition of the New Testament the order of the books which go to make it up is the same. First come the Gospels, then the Acts of the Apostles. The letters written by Jesus' first followers, Paul, James, Peter, John and Jude, are placed next, and the Book of Revelation, which is sometimes called The Apocalypse, comes at the end.

It seems a natural order. Obviously, the lives of Jesus, the Gospels, should precede the lives, or 'acts', of his chief disciples; and these disciples' reflections upon Jesus' life and teaching, as they wrote them down in their letters, should come before what looks like a description of the end of the world, as it is recounted in the Book of Revelation.

The order may indeed be natural, but it does not reflect the sequence in which the books were written. Without question, the earliest New Testament writings were the letters which are attributed to St Paul. Enough is known about Paul's life, or can be conjectured about the date of his death, to be certain that he had been executed before any of the Gospels – with the possible exception of the Gospel of St Mark – had been composed.

Paul's letters, therefore, constitute the earliest witness to the faith of first-century Christians about the life, death and resurrection of Jesus. And they are of particular interest because of what Paul has to say about the manner in which Christian teaching was communicated.

Some time between AD 54 and 57 Paul wrote to the Christian community at Corinth, which he had established a few years before. It is clear from the letter that there had been some distinctly unedifying behaviour during the celebration of the Lord's Supper. He recalled for the Corinthians what he had himself learnt:

> For this is what I received from the Lord, and in turn passed on to you: that on the same night that he was betrayed, the Lord Jesus took some bread, and thanked God for it and broke it, and he said, 'This is my body, which is for you; do this as a memorial of me.' In the same way he took the cup after supper and said, 'This cup is the new covenant in my blood. Whenever you drink it, do this as a memorial of me.' Until the Lord comes, therefore, every time you eat this bread and drink this cup, you are proclaiming his death. (1 Cor 11:23–26)

A few paragraphs further on Paul reminds the Corinthians of the gospel he

The Last Supper from the sixth-century Rossano Gospels, the oldest known copy of the Gospels to contain miniatures. Christ and the twelve apostles recline at table in late Roman style and dress. John's Gospel does not contain an account of the institution of the Eucharist. Instead he included the story of Christ washing his apostles' feet, above right.

THE ORIGIN OF THE GOSPELS

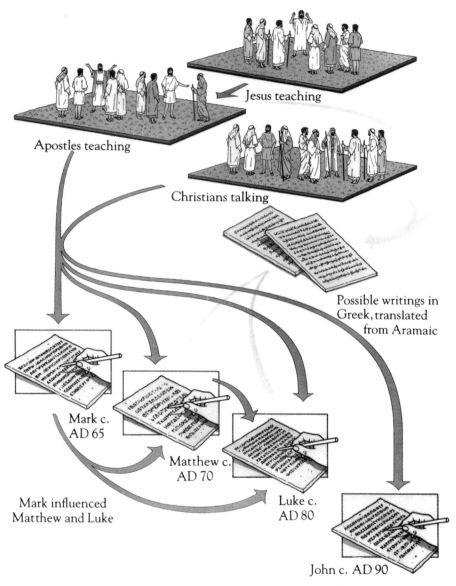

Jesus teaching

Apostles teaching

Christians talking

Possible writings in
Greek, translated
from Aramaic

Mark c.
AD 65

Matthew c.
AD 70

Mark influenced
Matthew and Luke

Luke c.
AD 80

John c. AD 90

*How the Gospels relate to each other is one of the major problems of New Testament
scholarship. The diagram above attempts to explain the way in which they might be
linked.*

had already taught them:

> Brothers, I want to remind you of the gospel I preached to you, the
> gospel that you received and in which you are firmly established;
> because the gospel will save you only if you keep believing exactly

what I preached to you – believing anything else will not lead to anything. Well then, in the first place, I taught you what I had been taught myself, namely that Christ died for our sins in accordance with the scriptures. (1 Cor 15:1–3)

He then goes on briefly to recount his teaching.

This second passage sounds like some sort of credal statement. That is to say, it may have been a very early formulation of the basics of the faith which Christians were expected to profess. The first passage quoted above appears to recount the central section of the ritual of the Lord's Supper, or Eucharist. Both quotations from the letter are precise formulae which, as Paul quite clearly says, had been handed on to him, and which he had handed on to those whom he had taught. In other words, both were traditions. And they had come into being by the middle of the first century, within two dozen years or so of the death of Jesus.

This method of passing on Jesus' teaching by word of mouth, oral tradition, reflects the conditions of the time. Books, or more correctly scrolls, were scarce in first-century Palestine. So teachers conveyed their instruction in such a way that their hearers might easily remember it. There were frequent repetitions. Poetical forms were used. Readily recalled stories, such as the parables, were employed to make a point in a narrative fashion.

The degree to which this formal type of oral teaching affected the construction of the Gospel narratives is much disputed, but it can scarcely have failed to make some impact. The four Gospels are very different from one another, each reflecting the context in which it was written. They were composed at different times and in different places. They would therefore have reflected different versions, perhaps even different stages, of the oral tradition.

They were, moreover, written for different kinds of audiences. Matthew was composed for a Jewish-Christian group, and is therefore full of links between the Old and the New Testaments. Luke's audience was a group of converts from paganism, and therefore stresses the universality of the offer of salvation. Mark's Gospel was also written for an audience drawn from a mainly pagan, rather than from a Jewish, background, and likewise emphasizes the widespread nature of the Christian message. Mark makes great play with the idea that Jesus' identity as messiah remained hidden until the crucifixion, at which point he was recognized as the son of God by the Roman centurion who was, of course, a pagan.

On the authorship of the Gospel attributed to Mark, the tradition is unanimous. It claims that the Gospel was written for a Roman audience by John Mark, a disciple of St Peter. It was composed after Peter's death, but probably before the destruction of the Temple in Jerusalem, which dates its final form to between AD 65 and 70. It may have been written to be read aloud at the Easter service.

73

Matthew's Gospel, on the other hand, was written in full knowledge of what had occurred in Jerusalem in AD 70, so must be dated after that. The author of Matthew was familiar with Palestinian traditions in general, and parts of the discourses of Jesus seem to reflect an Aramaic source – that is to say, a source in the language spoken in Palestine. There are even traces of an Aramaic style. But the Greek text as it has been preserved is very well written, in a much better style than might be expected from the tax collector named Levi whom Jesus renamed Matthew. The authorship of the Gospel, then, remains something of a mystery.

In the year 185, or thereabouts, St Irenaeus, who was the Bishop of Lyons in southern France, attributed the third Gospel to Luke, the 'beloved physician' mentioned in the letter to the Colossians (4:14), and a companion of Paul on many of the Apostle's journeys. Whoever composed the Gospel of Luke also wrote the Acts of the Apostles, a book explicitly intended by its author as a sequel to the Gospel, and there is a modest degree of evidence to suggest that he was a medical man. The text is in excellent Greek, and may have been written, as Irenaeus says it was, in southern Greece.

Most controversial is the authorship of the fourth Gospel. Irenaeus atributed it to John, the disciple of Jesus. His authority for that was his acquaintance with Bishop Polycarp of Smyrna who, he says, as a young man, had known John personally. He adds that the Gospel was written at Ephesus. A bishop of Ephesus, Polycrates, writing to Bishop Victor of Rome about the year 190, claims that John lived and died at Ephesus, although he does not mention the Gospel itself.

There is no real reason to doubt that the Gospel was written at Ephesus. The supposition fits the facts as far as they are known perfectly well. The identity of the author, however, is much more problematic. It seems likely that the book was composed in about the year 100. By that time the apostle John would have been a very old man indeed. He is, moreover, extremely unlikely ever to have achieved the high standard of Greek that the text of the Gospel displays. Nor could the same person – particularly one who had begun life as a Galilean fisherman – have compiled all the books attributed to him: the Gospel, the Book of Revelation and three Epistles. The differences between them are very considerable, as will become clear later.

Behind the fourth Gospel there is someone who remembered Palestine very well indeed. A possible, indeed likely, explanation is that the Gospel came out of a community of which the apostle John had been a member, and which preserved his tradition and his reflections, but which did not feel the need to recount once again the full story of Jesus because the Gospels of Matthew, Mark and Luke were already known to them.

These three texts are called the 'synoptic Gospels'. Taken together they present a complication of their own, which is known, not surprisingly, as 'the synoptic problem'. The word 'synopsis' in its original meaning signifies

74

Though the Gospel of John was the last to be committed to writing, it is the first of which there is manuscript evidence. The fragment of papyrus left was found in Egypt. It is a section of chapter 18 from St John's Gospel, and can be dated to the first half of the second century – to within fifty years of the Gospel's composition.

a table or chart. In this context it refers to the presentation of the three Gospels in parallel columns. If this is done, it rapidly becomes clear that they are very similar in content. About 90 per cent of what is in Mark can be found in Matthew, and more than half of what is in Mark is repeated in Luke. This could, and probably does, mean that Mark was the first Gospel – though it is not entirely undisputed – and that the material which he gathered from the oral tradition is repeated, in a slightly different fashion, in the two other synoptic Gospels.

The real problem centres on the material which is not found in Mark but is recorded in Matthew and Luke. It is possible that both drew heavily upon the same oral tradition. But it is fairly evident that Matthew and Luke came from very different backgrounds, and that their Gospels were written in quite different places. It is unlikely that a purely oral tradition could have produced such startling similarities.

To account for these similarities it has been suggested that, quite apart from Mark, there was another written source for Matthew and Luke. This source, if there was one, no longer exists – or has never been found; it remains a theoretical solution to a real problem. It is called 'Q' by the scholars, from the German word *Quelle* which means 'source'. It is thought

The 'four living creatures' from Revelation are thought to symbolize the evangelists.

to have consisted of the sayings of Jesus, though there are some who argue that it must have contained narrative material as well.

Because the similarities between Matthew and Luke are so great, it is said that 'Q' must have been in Greek. That is the language in which the Gospels have come down to us, and it is the language in which, in all probability, they were written.

There may have been other sources, no longer extant. It is possible, though unlikely, that a document might be unearthed which turns out to be a primitive form of one of the Gospels. Indeed there is already the Gospel of Thomas, as it is called, which was found at the beginning of this century, although the complete version only came to light as recently as 1945. This contains versions of some of the sayings and stories found in the synoptics – the parable of the sower, for example – in a form which indicates that Thomas was contemporaneous with the synoptics, if not somewhat earlier. Or there is the mysterious Gospel of the Hebrews which may, just possibly, have been composed about the middle of the first century, even before Mark. It now survives only in quotations from it by other, later writers.

Right at the start of his Gospel Luke seems to be hinting at the existence of these collections of Jesus' sayings. He begins:

seeing that many others have undertaken to draw up accounts of the events that have taken place among us, exactly as these were handed down to us by those who from the outset were witnesses and ministers of the word, I, in my turn, have decided to write an ordered account . . .

76

Whatever other writings there may have been, as time went by, and the events recorded by the Gospels became increasingly remote, the Gospels took on the status of being authentic accounts of Jesus' life. It has to be remembered, however, that none of the evangelists was chiefly concerned to recount the details of those events. They were not writing biographies. They were, it is true, especially interested in the events of the Passion, but beyond that their chief purpose was to record their Master's teaching, and to show how it applied to the particular situation in which those for whom they were writing were living out their Christian faith.

PAUL'S LETTERS

This heading begs two important questions. In the New Testament there are thirteen writings which are ascribed to the apostle Paul – fourteen if one includes the Letter to the Hebrews, though this is so different from the other letters that it has long been thought unlikely to be by him.

But are all the others by him? And what does 'by him' mean? At the end of the first letter to the Christians in Corinth there is a remark – 'This greeting is in my own hand' (1 Cor 16:21) – which suggests that Paul did not usually write his own letters, and the Letter to the Romans mentions Tertius 'who wrote out this letter' (Rom 16:22). Did Paul dictate the message, or did he simply indicate the main lines of his comments, and let a secretary get on with the business of filling out the framework? It may be at one time or another Paul used both these methods. That would at least help to account for the differences of style which have been perceived among them.

The second question is just as basic: are the letters really letters? Traditionally, Paul's writings have been called 'epistles', but that does not help very much because *epistola* is merely the Latin word for 'letter'. Some commentators, however, use the two words to indicate two quite distinct types of communication. In their sense of the words, an epistle is something fairly highly polished and intended for a wider audience than the apparent recipient. A letter, on the other hand, is just that: a communication on some particular topic or topics to a private individual, or a limited group of individuals.

Paul's missives fall almost entirely into the second of these categories. Only the Letter to the Romans, to a community which Paul did not know and apparently simply intended to visit on his way to Spain, reads more like a treatise. Some of the others are more or less difficult to understand simply because, quite obviously, they are discussing matters which had been put to Paul by members of the communities, either in letters or in the course of personal visits.

There must have been other letters by Paul which have not been preserved. It is hard to believe that he wrote only thirteen in the whole of his Christian ministry, and there is evidence in the surviving letters of others which have been lost. In his first letter to the community at Corinth, perhaps written in the early spring of AD 57, Paul refers to an earlier letter of his, while what is now known as 2 Corinthians, possibly composed that same autumn, suggests the existence of a further letter somewhere in the middle of the year.

These two letters, 1 and 2 Corinthians, are typical of Paul. He had founded the community of Christians during an eight-month stay at Corinth in AD 51–52. He now writes because he has heard, via messengers sent to him at Ephesus, of the various problems within the Church of Corinth, and in particular the major scandal, a case of incest. There are other difficulties too, concerning sex and marriage, and eating meat that had been offered to idols, and about how the gatherings for worship should be organized.

The next letter is quite different. Paul's integrity seems to have been called into question. He is upset, and springs to his own defence. It appears that the problem had arisen because a group of Christians who had come to Corinth were spreading strange notions about Jesus. Just who they were it is now impossible to determine. They may have belonged to a faction opposed to Paul. They certainly believed themselves possessed of superior wisdom, and they played down the importance of Jesus' humanity.

A somewhat similar group of people seems to have occasioned the letter to the Churches of Galatia, written c. AD 54–55. Paul's authority as an apostle has been called into question because he had not insisted on his converts observing every provision of the Law of Moses. Not only that, but whoever it was who had arrived in Galatia in Paul's wake wanted some special Jewish feasts to be celebrated. They also appear to have had a peculiar reverence for angels and other spirits. These traits suggest that the trouble-makers in Galatia may have been drawn from the Essenes, for the Essenes kept a range of feasts which were outside the usual Jewish calendar, and they believed in angels.

Angels were a problem at Colossae also. Here the Church had been founded by Epaphras, one of Paul's converts, perhaps at Ephesus. Epaphras reported to Paul that some members of his Church thought that angels controlled the world and that, in order to keep the angels happy, one had to know as much as possible about them. Paul's reply was to stress the unique role of Jesus.

But not all the letters were in response to problems. In about AD 50, for example, Paul wrote to the Philippians, thanking them for sending him money. The Church at Philippi had been Paul's first foundation in Europe, and it was probably predominantly Gentile. His letter, besides conveying his thanks, was one of general encouragement. The first letter to the community at Thessalonika was similarly encouraging: Paul had heard from his emissary Timothy that all was going well there. A few months later, however, he had to write in sterner fashion (2 Thessalonians). He had

Angels are mentioned in both the Old and the New Testaments, and they play a
particularly large part in non-biblical Jewish writings around the time of Jesus.

heard of disturbances in the Church brought about by some who believed that the new age for which Christians were waiting had already arrived.

These, then, are the letters generally acknowledged to be by Paul himself. In addition there is the letter to the Ephesians, which presents problems all of its own. Ephesus, later to be associated closely with John, had strong links with Paul. He went there on two of his missionary journeys, and in all spent some three years in the city. It is not unlikely, therefore, that he would have written to its Christian community. But from the letter it appears that the author does not know the community very well. Its style and its subject-matter are not typically Pauline. Above all, it seems quite likely that the address to the saints 'who are at Ephesus' was not part of the original text (it is omitted in some modern translations). Without that, the Letter to the Ephesians reads rather like a general treatise, as was the (undoubtedly Pauline) Letter to the Romans.

Finally, there is a group of letters which few consider to be by Paul, though they claim to be. These are the two letters to Timothy and one to Titus, known as the 'Pastorals' because they are addressed to individuals who have pastoral responsibility in the local Churches – Timothy had represented Paul in the region around Ephesus, and Titus had performed a similar function on the island of Cyprus.

The three letters clearly belong together. They share a similar style and vocabulary, and appear to oppose the same type of heretical teaching. Neither style nor vocabulary, on the other hand, has much in common with Paul's undeniably authentic letters. It is also difficult to place the Pastorals in the chronological framework of Paul's life unless, after his first imprisonment in Rome, he set off again on a missionary journey, and to the East, rather than to the West and Spain as had been his original intention. That is possible, and if so it is not too difficult to admit that the Pastorals may indeed have been written by Paul. The difference in vocabulary and style may be due to the fact that both were dictated by the subject-matter – the structure of the community, the importance of good works, and the need for orthodoxy, none of them common topics in Paul's writings. But whoever it was who wrote the Pastorals, they reflect a later stage in the development of the Christian community than that to be found in the less contentious letters.

NEW WRITINGS

There are twenty-seven 'books' in the New Testament, and of those all but six are called 'epistles'. Besides the epistles written (or possibly written) by Paul, and the Letter to the Hebrews, described below, there is a group which is generally known as 'the Catholic Epistles'. It is not clear why they should have been given that name: it may imply that early on they were accepted by all the Churches – the word 'catholic' means universal – as, in some way, the inspired word of God. These are the letter of James, the two

Paul's preaching caused a riot in Ephesus. Two of the apostle's companions were dragged into this massive theatre, and had to be rescued from the mob by the town clerk.

letters of Peter, the three letters of John, and the letter attributed to Jude.

But first, the Letter to the Hebrews. It is something of a misnomer to call this a letter at all, since it is more of a sermon or homily. We do not know who wrote it, or to whom it was addressed. From its style, and from the topics it treats, it would seem to have been by a Jewish Christian who had a Hellenistic background. That, of course, is a reasonable description of St Paul, and in mid-second-century Alexandria the letter was attributed to him. Some commentators have accepted the ascription, but many more have not.

There is no real reason to do so. It is generally agreed that the letter is a fairly late composition, written after the fall of Jerusalem to the Romans in AD 70, and therefore after Paul's death. On the other hand it was not a very late addition to the New Testament: it was quoted by a Christian writer called Clement of Rome, so must have been in existence by the end of the first century.

The two letters which bear the name of Peter are so different that they cannot both have come from the same hand. Quite possibly neither of them is by the apostle Peter, though both claim to be. The language and style of 1 Peter are certainly not what might be expected of a Galilean fisherman: the letter refers to the Greek version of the Old Testament, the Septuagint, which no Galilean would be likely to do.

If, however, it is acknowledged that 1 Peter was not written by the apostle personally but by someone else on his behalf, then most of the difficulties about accepting Petrine authorship disappear. Most, but not all. The author mentions persecution, but the first serious persecution from which Christians suffered was that under the Emperor Nero when Peter himself died – so he could hardly have written about it. It may be, though, that the 'persecution' of which the author writes meant no more than the problems encountered by Christians living among non-Christians under particularly harsh conditions.

If 1 Peter was composed during the lifetime of the apostle, then it must be dated between AD 60 and 64. Some scholars believe that the utterly different 2 Peter was not written until c. AD 140. So late a date does not have universal acceptance, but few dispute that it was the last of the New Testament books to be compiled.

Its purpose was to warn certain Christians – and the references are so precise that it must have been written to a particular group of communities and not to the Church at large – against false teachers. Specifically, these teachers are insisting that Jesus will not return. This denial of the 'parousia', as it is called, was no doubt occasioned by its delay in arriving – hence one of the arguments for the letter's late date.

A second argument for lateness of composition is that it seems to be dependent on the Letter of Jude, and this must itself be late because it talks of the apostles in the past tense as if they had all died. If that is the case, of course, the Letter of Jude could not have been written by the apostle Jude. So it appears that the Jude who claims authorship must be some other Jude. It has been suggested that he was the brother of James who, in the New Testament, is described as brother of the Lord. If that is so, then the letter cannot be very late – written perhaps in the last decade of the first century. It is similar to 2 Peter, being addressed to Christian communities and warning them against the false teachers who have appeared among them. In this instance, however, it is not only the teaching which is giving cause for concern, but the conduct of these teachers as well.

James, 'the brother of the Lord', has his name attached to one of the Catholic Epistles. It is a collection of brief recommendations and exhortations, urging that the faith be practical not abstract, and should lead to good works. The general tenor of the letter indicates that it is late, certainly later than the demise of James of Jerusalem, who died c. AD 62. It also lacks the strict ritualism one might have expected from James. But it displays an attitude to Jewish Christianity which, it is sometimes argued, is out of keeping with the situation after the fall of Jerusalem. Its date and authorship, therefore, remain a mystery.

Finally, and in a class by themselves, are the letters attributed to John. Almost everything about them is problematic. The second and third letters are very short indeed, consisting of, respectively, thirteen and fifteen verses. Their meaning is obscure, but that is partly because they are addressed to particular people or communities about specific issues. They are undoubtedly letters rather than epistles, in the distinction mentioned above (p. 77).

Despite their apparent differences, in terms of language, style and theology, the three letters seem to belong together. As a group, there might seem to be little connection between the Epistles and John's Gospel, yet between one of the letters, the first, and the Gospel there is a very close link. One possible explanation may be that 1 John was intended as a commentary, if not upon the Gospel itself, at least upon the traditions from which it sprang. Some passages of the fourth Gospel lend themselves to interpretations which are not exactly orthodox. Whoever wrote the letter was anxious that the Gospel should not be misunderstood.

MISSIONARY ZEAL

As we have seen, Christianity took a variety of forms in the first century of its existence. The Gospels sprang out of four different traditions, and Paul was constantly faced by problems which had arisen in the communities he founded when teachers arrived with a message unlike his own. These divisions are not something that hostile historians have read back into the story of the primitive Church. They were there from the beginning. They were recognized by Paul, and by the author of the Acts of the Apostles.

The book which is called the Acts of the Apostles is a sequel to the Gospel of Luke. Not only is it similar in style and in its particular interests; it is clearly presented as a continuation of the Gospel. The book begins: 'In my earlier work, Theophilus, I dealt with everything Jesus had done and taught from the beginning until the day he gave instructions to the apostles he had chosen through the Holy Spirit and was taken up to heaven.' 'My earlier work' is Luke's Gospel. That, too, is addressed to Theophilus – whoever he may have been.

There is little doubt that the author of Acts is 'my dear friend Luke, the doctor', as Paul describes him in the concluding verses of the letter to the

Above, four Old Testament prophets pointing to the event which their prophecies prefigured, the prophecies themselves being written out on scrolls beneath. They are pointing to the Last Supper scenes (p. 71). Right, St Stephen on trial for his life before the high priest, from the ninth-century crypt of the church of St Germain in Auxerre.

Colossians. In the accounts of Paul's travels, which take up the greater part of the second half of Acts, Luke falls into the first person plural, using 'we' as if to suggest that he was an eye-witness, or participant, in the events he records. This, at least, is the usual explanation of the 'we' passages. But it is not the only explanation, nor is it without its difficulties. Whoever the 'we' were, for example, they were clearly not Luke and Paul, for Paul is usually mentioned separately. So it may just be that these passages are no more than a stylistic ploy, intended to give a sense of immediacy to the narrative.

At first reading the Acts of the Apostles presents a very simple picture, spread over thirty years and related in chronological sequence, of the growth of Christianity. First it reaches out from Jerusalem to the Jewish world and then, when that mission falters, to the Gentile world, culminating with Paul's arrival in Rome. Closer examination of the narrative, however, reveals problems.

For example, Luke uses Greek, and the Greek text of the Bible. But behind it there are frequent signs of a Semitic source. Were there written sources for Acts as well as oral ones? And if so, in what language? Stephen was the first Christian we hear of being put to death for his faith, and Acts reports his final speech at some length. But what were the sources for this speech, and how were they preserved? It is particularly complicated because, as will be seen, Stephen's discourse seems to reflect Samaritan sources, and the Samaritans' branch of Judaism was distinctly unorthodox (p. 93).

The question of the origins of Luke's narrative may appear to be an academic issue, but it has practical consequences. For how far is Acts to be trusted as history? It seems clear that Luke thought of himself as writing history, the history of the expansion of Christianity. And about that he was very optimistic.

In this sixth-century portrait of Luke, scenes from his Gospel are arranged on either side of the figure to serve as a 'contents' to the book. Above, Luke is the winged ox (his symbol).

But he does not tell the whole story. Without Acts we would know nothing of Paul's origins, not even that he came from Tarsus. We would know little or nothing of the significance of the city of Antioch in the growth of the early Church (p. 101), nor of Barnabas' role at Antioch. Without Acts it would be impossible to work out the chronology of Paul's travels, and therefore to put his letters into some sort of sequence.

Yet there is much that we know which Luke does not mention, even though he, too, must surely have known it. Acts contains a vivid description of Paul's shipwreck upon the island of Malta. Paul claims to have been shipwrecked three times, but the other incidents pass by unremarked. Acts does not point out that Paul had been scourged three times. Or that, in Lystra, he had been stoned. Had Luke been a close personal companion of Paul he might have been expected to know these details. Why does he not recount them?

The answer may lie in Luke's purpose in writing Acts. As the next chapter will describe at some length, there was a tendency in the early Church for groups to emerge with their own particular brand of Christianity. Of these, the two most obvious were the Judaizers and the Hellenists, but nuances can be detected even among these, and other groups appear to have flourished – one descended from the Qumran sectaries has already been mentioned. Luke cannot disguise this, but he attempts to play it down. Just how sharp the battles must have been emerges only after an extremely detailed examination of Luke's text, in conjunction with a similar study of Paul's letters.

Luke has a neat plan for his book. First of all, Peter takes Jesus' message to Jews outside Jerusalem, and then turns his attention to non-Jews. From chapter 12, however, Peter disappears. Paul takes over completely. The Church is firmly founded upon the twelve apostles, regarded as a distinct group, and their authority is backed up by manifestations of the Spirit. In the later chapters that spiritual, or 'charismatic', authority does not play a significant part. This rather indicates that the account in Acts was intended to cut the ground from under those (whom Paul also had encountered) who were given to apocalyptic interpretations of the coming of Jesus.

As for Jesus, Luke stresses his earthly identity against a tendency to remove him from the real world, and emphasizes that he needed witnesses, and messengers, to make himself known.

Luke was reaching out. He was concerned to present Christianity as a respectable religion. The opening words to Theophilus suggest that the book was aimed at the upper classes, or at least at those who would look askance at any group which proved to be too revolutionary. Luke presents Jewish Christians as being, basically, faithful to the Law. It was the Jews, he argues, who had departed from the traditions of centuries.

He wanted to emphasize that Christians were not an amoral sect. Nor were they a hole-in-the-corner one. His attitude to the Roman state was positive; he displays sympathy for those in authority; his Roman officials are generally tolerant towards the Christians who are brought before them.

The Acts of the Apostles was probably written sometime in the decade AD 80–90. By that time, the Emperor in Rome had already persecuted Christians, a fact which must have been known to Luke. Yet despite that, he is optimistic that a united, rather than a splintered, Church would one day spread to all corners of the Roman Empire.

THE VISION OF JOHN

One of the constant themes of the story related so far has been that Jesus expected the end of the world to come either in his lifetime, or shortly after his death. Jesus' resurrection was to be a sign to his followers that they had indeed entered the end times.

Luke ends the Book of Acts with Paul's arrival in Rome. This painting depicts Peter and Paul either side of Christ. Later they were both taken as co-founders of the Church at Rome.

Paul had to contend with some who thought that the parousia would be indefinitely delayed, with others who were distressed because it had not already arrived, and with others again who believed that, because they lived in the end times, they could do as they pleased.

In the Acts of the Apostles Luke played down the coming of the Spirit, characteristic of the end times. In order to restrain the enthusiasm of some Christians, and to guide them into forms of behaviour which would not appear too bizarre to their fellow citizens, he proclaimed that the coming of the Spirit was confined to the age of the apostles.

Perhaps it was because to a respectable Church the Revelation, or Apocalypse, of John seemed so extraordinary that it was only reluctantly accepted into the group of books which go to make up the New Testament.

There is no doubt about the name of the person who wrote the book. 'John has written down everything he saw and swears it is the word of God guaranteed by Jesus Christ', it says at the very beginning. Probably because the author was early on identified with John the apostle, the Apocalypse was eventually regarded as the inspired word of God.

But, like so much else about the book, the identity of the writer is uncertain. There is enough similarity of themes and vocabulary to make it seem likely that it came from the same hand as the fourth Gospel – and just as many dissimilarities to make it unlikely. It may be that all the Johannine writings, the Gospel, the three letters and the Apocalypse, stem from a group of Christians who were disciples, possibly even close acquaintances, of the apostle while he lived, as tradition relates, at Ephesus. Detailed discussion of the Book of Revelation is out of place in a history of early Christianity. Its writing and its reception by the Church at large do, of course, need to be related to other events. But while the Gospels, the Acts of the Apostles, the letters of Paul and the other New Testament epistles can all provide useful information about both Jesus and the communities which put their faith in him, that is not quite so true of the writings of John the seer. A hint or two may be picked up, but little more.

Yet the Book of Revelation, or Apocalypse, became an accepted part of the New Testament. Excerpts have been read at church services down to the present day. And it does indeed have a theological message in emphasizing the triviality of worldly tribulations compared to the overall plan God has for the whole of humankind, a plan which cannot be thwarted. In the context of Christian history it has an important role to play as a reminder of the strongly apocalyptic nature, of the firm belief in the end times and their proximity, of the early Christians.

Spasms of apocalyptic fervour still occur among Christians. The outbreaks seem to take place at the end of centuries, and in particular towards the end of a millennium. Compared with these, the writings of John the seer seem relatively restrained. They are reminders that apocalypticism is a constant element of Christianity.

5

THE FIRST CHRISTIANS

Anyone who has held in his hand a copy of the New Testament has held most, if not quite all, of the evidence upon which is based modern knowledge of the history of Christianity in the first century. The collection of books which make up the New Testament has been subjected to closer examination than any other comparable set of texts. It has yielded a great deal of information, a surprising amount in view of the fact that none of the books, with the possible exception of the Acts of the Apostles, was composed as a work of history.

It has to be remembered, however, that the information we have about the communities for which these texts were compiled, rests upon very slender evidence. Some of that evidence comes from contrasting what the New Testament has to say with what is known from other sources – from the history of the Jewish war against the Romans in AD 66–70 by Flavius Josephus, himself a Jew despite his romanized name; or from the Mishnah, the collection of Jewish writings put together at the beginning of the third century; and so on.

The life of those earliest Christian communities in Palestine, and of the communities created outside the world which Jesus knew, is the subject of this chapter. It will also examine the effect of the war between Rome and the Jews upon Christianity, and its slow but inexorable development into a religion distinct from Judaism.

JEWISH CHRISTIANS IN PALESTINE

The Gospels relate that Jesus visited Jerusalem for the celebration of the great feasts. But his first preaching was in that area of Palestine called Galilee, and it was from there that his earliest converts were drawn. He travelled around its small towns and villages, avoiding the great Hellenistic cities such as Tiberias.

Perhaps because Jesus died there, Jerusalem appears to have been the first Christian centre. Yet in the accounts of the resurrection Galilee plays a much more prominent part than Jerusalem. The Gospels display a very positive attitude towards Galilee, and 'Galilean' seems to have been one of the earliest names for a Christian. (It survived as such at least until the middle of the fourth century.) But in the Acts of the Apostles there are no accounts of a mission to Galilee like the one sent, for example, to Samaria. The author of Acts clearly believes that Christianity was established in that

Three scenes from Paul's life illustrated on a fourth-century diptych. At the top he disputes with philosophers in Athens (Acts 17), in the middle he is bitten by a viper on Malta but is unharmed, to the obvious amazement of the onlookers who then, below, bring people to him to be healed (Acts 28).

Above, Galilee and its lake, the setting for Christ's earliest preaching. Right, a wall painting showing Christ in Samaria with the woman at the well. His disciples were taken aback when they found Jesus discussing theology with a woman.

region well before the time of Paul. Of the nature of that Christianity, however, there are only the vaguest of hints.

There is a clue in the large number of Jesus' sayings about leaving home and family, about living in poverty and having nowhere to lay one's head. This ascetic life is intended to lead to a share in the glory of the kingdom which is to come, and in the glory of the Son of Man who is its herald. This is the kind of life Jesus prescribes for his closest associates, the twelve apostles, and for the wider group of seventy-two disciples, mentioned in chapters 9 and 10 of the Gospel of Luke.

That these stories have been so carefully preserved is evidence that a number of Jesus' followers had been deeply affected by them. Jesus' own lifestyle, and that of the people around him, was of a wandering preacher. He was one of those who, in return for food and lodging, preached, prophesied and performed miracles.

It is clear from the stories about Paul and others that Christian preachers wandered about Palestine and beyond in the manner of Jesus, teaching and preaching in return for sustenance. Groups such as these were not uncommon in first-century Judea. They were to be found for the most part in rural areas, because the cities were associated with the persecution of prophets. So Galilee was a natural home for such a movement.

On the other hand this charismatic form of Christianity does not seem to have maintained its early momentum. John's Gospel, a late compilation,

shows respect for Galilee, but there is no suggestion of a notable influx of
Galileans into Christianity. At some time, perhaps about the year AD 40,
James, the brother of the Lord, went from Galilee to Jerusalem. The capital
with its Temple had always held a strong attraction for the pious Jews of the
Galilean countryside. But it may also be that James' decision to move to
Judea reflected a decline in the early momentum of Christianity in Galilee.
Jerusalem was now the place to be.

Between Galilee and Judea lay Samaria. Its inhabitants, like the
inhabitants of Galilee, were Jews, but the Samaritans were Jews of an
unusual kind. The Gospel of John displays a strong interest in, and
considerable knowledge of, the particular customs, beliefs and topography
of Samaria. It is this Gospel which recounts the meeting between Jesus and
a Samaritan woman at a well close to the town of Sychar. The woman
draws attention to the major differences between orthodox Jews and
Samaritans. The former believed that only in the Temple of Jerusalem
could true worship be offered. The latter had possessed a rival shrine on
Mount Gerizim, until John Hyrcanus had destroyed it in 129 BC.

There were other divergences. Samaritans venerated a different set of
biblical figures from those who played the largest part in Jewish life. That
was not surprising, for as their scriptures they accepted only the Pentateuch, and that in a form slightly different from the standard Jewish text.
Specifically Samaritan preoccupations occur not only in the Gospel of

John, mentioned above, but also in the account of the death of Stephen. Christianity in Samaria was strong enough, and had a distinctive enough identity, to be reflected in the New Testament.

But according to the New Testament, Christianity was founded from Jerusalem. Some four years or so after the crucifixion, some kind of persecution broke out against Christians in Jerusalem. Some fled the city, among them Philip, who went to Samaria to preach. He had such great success that Peter and John joined him in his mission. All this is reasonably straightforward: the puzzle is about the persecution in Jerusalem.

A first reading of Acts suggests that the whole of the Christian Church in Jerusalem was persecuted. A closer examination shows that only a part of the group suffered. The leaders, the apostles, are not touched: 'Everyone except the apostles fled', says Acts 8:1, though this can hardly be literally true.

This shekel, minted during the second great Jewish revolt that was led by Bar Kochba (AD 132–135), shows the Ark of the Covenant between two pillars of the Temple. The Temple had, of course, been destroyed during the first revolt: the coin is a symbol of the hoped-for rebirth of Judea.

It is not easy to reconstruct events, partly because the author of Acts, like the writers of the Gospels, strives to give an appearance of unity among Jesus' followers. But not all the divisions among them can be disguised, and one emerges quite clearly in Acts 6. There Luke recounts the disagreement between Hellenists and Hebrews over the distribution of food, a form of welfare service, to Christian widows.

Both Hellenists and Hebrews, naturally, were converts to Christianity, though both would have regarded it as more a conversion to a particular branch of Judaism than a rejection of their ancestral faith. The Hellenists were Greek-speaking. As Jews they had in Jerusalem their own synagogues where the Scriptures were read in Greek. Typically they were foreigners,

94

Jews by birth or converts to Judaism, who had chosen to live in their holy city. The Hebrews, on the other hand, were natives, if not of Jerusalem, then at least of Palestine. Their first language was Aramaic, but in their synagogues the Scripture readings were in Hebrew.

As far as the Jews, and some Jewish Christians, were concerned, the most controversial opinion espoused by the Hellenists was that the end time, the *eschaton*, had dawned with Jesus' death and resurrection. If that had happened, then the era of the Spirit had come, and the age of Temple worship was over. That appears to have been the tenor of Stephen's speech, and the belief for which he was executed.

More conservative Jewish Christians believed that the end time would arrive only with the return of Jesus as messiah – and that lay in the future. So although they met in private houses, as did the Essenes, unlike the Essenes they continued to visit the Temple to pray.

As Christians, both groups differed from traditional Judaism in their beliefs and their religious practices. But it was the Hellenists, the more radical group, who were persecuted. The apostles, as the more traditional Jews, were unharmed. Philip fled Jerusalem and engaged upon the first recorded missionary journey, to Samaria. Stephen was stoned to death. Both were deacons.

That, at least, is what they have traditionally been called. But in Acts they are not called deacons, though their service to the community is described, and *diakonia* means service. Luke presents them very much more as leaders, ones whose ministry is primarily to the Hellenists. They were appointed to ensure the fair distribution of food between the two factions. Seven are mentioned: Philip is named second, and Stephen is their leader.

So it is possible, very early on in the history of Christianity, to distinguish two Churches: the more traditional one led by the apostles, and the Hellenistic one led by Stephen, Philip and the other 'deacons'. When the persecution occurs, it is the leadership of the Hellenists which suffers.

Some indication of just how unorthodox the Hellenists were as far as Judaism is concerned can be gleaned from Stephen's last discourse, which is reported at length in chapter 7 of Acts. It emphasizes Israel's constant rebellion against God; it contains Samaritan interpretations of the Pentateuch; it is hostile to Temple worship. If Stephen was a typical Hellenist, their unpopularity among orthodox Jews is understandable.

Those who survived the persecution in Jerusalem seem to have preserved a form of authority over the Church at large. It appears that the approval of the Jerusalem Church had to be obtained to extend the reach of Christianity beyond Judaism. Both Peter and Paul had to justify their actions to the Jerusalem Church or, more specifically, to James the brother of the Lord.

After the crucifixion of Jesus, the leadership of the Christians in the capital city must have been drawn from those who had been closest to him.

Right, a portrait of Paul, believed to be the earliest representation of the saint and to be found in the third-century tomb of the Aurelii in Rome. Below, the south mole of the harbour at Cenchreae, the port for Corinth which Paul used. Phoebe (Rom 16:1) was deaconess of the Church here. A temple of Isis was built upon this mole, to be replaced later by a Christian basilica, the remains of which can still be seen.

In the early chapters of Acts Peter plays the leading role, and in one of his letters Paul describes Peter, James and John as the three 'pillars' of the Church. But then, sometime around AD 40 or perhaps a little earlier, James the brother of the Lord arrives.

In the Gospels this James is presented as being, at least at first, hostile to Jesus' teaching. But he emerged as a force to be reckoned with in the Jerusalem Church, governing it, apparently, through the typically Jewish system of a council of elders. How he came to such prominence is not recorded. But since it was not unusual for the leadership of Jewish sects to remain in one family, perhaps one need look no further than his relationship to Jesus. Whatever his background, he emerges as a powerful figure at Jerusalem, and a very conservative force in the development of first-century Christianity.

THE COMING OF PAUL

Everyone who has read the New Testament knows what a large role St Paul plays in the Acts of the Apostles, and how many of the letters included in the New Testament claim to be written by him. Clearly he was a religious genius. He was also a major figure in the early Church, and one who did not find relations easy with the leadership of the Church of Jerusalem.

Paul was a Jew, a strict observer of the Law, a Pharisee. He was born in Tarsus in about the year AD 10, the son of a freeman, from whom he inherited Roman citizenship. Around the year AD 30, presumably after Jesus' death for he never mentions having witnessed the crucifixion, he came to Jerusalem to study under the distinguished rabbi Gamaliel. He attended the stoning of Stephen, perhaps as an official observer. Then, armed with a personal commission from the High Priest to persecute Christians, he set off on the road to Damascus.

According to the Acts of the Apostles, just before he reached Damascus a bright light shone out. Paul was thrown from his horse. He heard Jesus' voice calling to him, and telling him to cease his persecution. He was struck blind.

When Paul (or Saul as he was known up to this point) reached his destination, the Christian Ananias, in somewhat reluctant obedience to a vision, visited the erstwhile persecutor, and cured his blindness. Paul was received into the Christian community and almost immediately, with the same zeal he had displayed in persecuting Christianity, he committed himself to propagating it. He went to the synagogue and preached that 'Jesus is the Son of God'.

The Jews now tried to kill Paul. A watch was kept on the gates of Damascus to prevent his escape, and he had to be lowered down the city walls in a basket. He fled into what, in the Letter to the Galatians, he calls 'Arabia'. In about AD 38 he made his way to Jerusalem to meet the leaders of the Church there, and then went home to Tarsus. But he must already

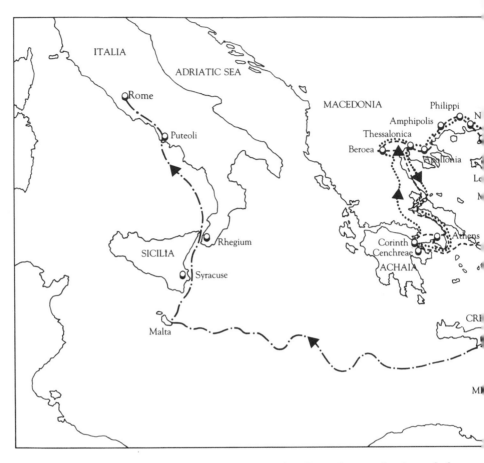

have gained fame as a Christian activist, for Barnabas, a leader of the Church in Antioch, travelled to Tarsus and persuaded Paul to return with him to Antioch. That appears to have been in about AD 43. Two years later Paul set off with Barnabas on his first missionary journey.

Up to this point Barnabas had been in charge, but in the course of that first journey Paul emerged as leader. The two attended the Council of Jerusalem in AD 45 (p. 104), but afterwards Paul set off again, this time alone. He had quarrelled with Barnabas over sharing meals with non-Jews. He went to Macedonia, to Athens – where he was rebuffed – and on to Corinth. He spent two years in Corinth before returning to Antioch by way of Miletus, Caesarea and Jerusalem. By this time it was c. AD 53.

Twelve months later he was off again. This time he spent two years in Ephesus. By AD 58 he was back in Jerusalem, where he was arrested. As a Roman citizen he exercised his right of appeal to Caesar. He was sent to the Emperor in Rome, where he arrived in the year AD 61 after being shipwrecked on the island of Malta. In the Empire's capital city he passed two years under a loose form of house arrest, but nothing at all is known of how he spent the remainder of his life. It is possible that he went east again.

A map of Paul's journeys — to Damascus as a persecutor of Christians, and to Rome as a Christian captive. In between occurred the three missionary journeys, the first of which has been calculated to have been nearly 1,400 miles, the other two some 2,800 miles each.

Key
—————— First missionary journey
– – – – – – Second missionary journey
•••••••••••• Third missionary journey
—·—·—·— Journey to Rome
····——····—···· Journey to Damascus

GALATIA
PHRYGIA
Antioch
Iconium
Tarsus
Derbe
Lystra   CILICIA
LYCIA   Attalia   Perge
Patara   Myra   PAMPHYLIA
CYPRUS   Salamis
Paphos
Antioch
Seleucia
SYRIA
Damascus
Sidon
Tyre
Ptolemais
Caesarea
Jerusalem

There is certainly a tradition that he visited Spain. Even his death is unrecorded, though it is believed to have occurred during the four-year-long persecution by the Emperor Nero. It is generally assumed that he died in Rome in about the year AD67.

These are the bare bones of the story. In his lifetime Paul walked some 10,000 miles, stepping out across the plains and over the mountains of Asia Minor in temperatures that must have reached 35 degrees centigrade. Only once did he reveal his feelings, and something of his suffering:

Five times I had the thirty-nine lashes from the Jews; three times I have been beaten with sticks; once I was stoned; three times I have been shipwrecked and once adrift in the open sea for a night and a day. Constantly travelling, I have been in danger from rivers and in danger from brigands, in danger from my own people and in danger from pagans; in danger in towns, in danger in the open country, danger at sea and danger from so-called brothers. (2 Cor 11:24–26)

This passage is interesting not only because it reveals details about Paul which are missing from the account in the Acts of the Apostles, but also because it reveals something of his view of the world.

When he is recounting the dangers he has lived through, Paul talks about towns, open country and the sea. What he does not mention is the cultivated countryside, the type of rural area in which Jesus began his mission. Paul was trained as a rabbi, and as a rabbi he was required to have a profession. He was a tent-maker, and was proud to be able to earn a living in this way and not to place a burden on other Christians.

As an itinerant tradesman, Paul worked mainly in towns, and it is quite clear that it was to towns he directed his mission. It is too much to claim that it was Paul who changed Christianity from being a religion of the countryside into an urban religion – that process had begun well before his time – but he certainly gave this movement added impetus.

Apart from when he was under Barnabas' leadership, Paul's strategy appears to have been to identify a leading city, especially a sea-port, where no significant Christian community existed already, and to spend up to two years working there. His first approach may have been to the local synagogue, but he seems to have thought of himself primarily as a missionary to the Gentiles. The apparent exception to this general strategy was his mission to Galatia. That was not an urban area, but a remote rural region. He supplies the explanation himself: 'Illness gave me the opportunity to preach the Good News to you'. Galatia lay on the road from Antioch to Bithynia and on to the Black Sea ports. Paul seems to have been passing through Galatia when he was taken ill, and to have stayed.

Rome also appears on the face of it to have been an exception. There was already a strong Christian community there before Paul expressed a wish to visit the city. But the visit was only to be a passing one. In his letter to the Romans, the only one of Paul's epistles addressed to a community he had not himself founded, he says that Rome is to be a staging post on the journey to Spain. It is only Luke in Acts who presents Rome as Paul's final goal.

Given the immense labour Paul undertook, and the fame which he has earned in the history of the Christian Church, it may seem strange to wonder whether he was a successful apostle. His letters survived, and that indicates fame of a sort. But even these epistles do not seem to have been widely circulated much before the end of the second century and the beginning of the third. And even Ephesus, a Church which he had founded, had by the end of the first century become more closely associated with the circle of the apostle John than with that of Paul.

This is a problem to which we shall return. But first let us look at the spread of Christianity outside Palestine, and examine Paul's role in that mission.

JEWISH CHRISTIANS IN THE DIASPORA

It is hardly surprising that when the message of Christianity was preached outside Palestine, the first people to whom it was addressed were the Jews of the diaspora. The turbulent history of the people of Israel had dispersed them (which is what 'diaspora' means) around the Middle East and further afield. They held on to their Judaism – but it was not always orthodox.

The Ebionites, who occupied a region to the east of the river Jordan, seem to have been one of the earliest Christian communities of the diaspora. Their name means 'the poor', and may reflect either a strict ascetic tradition or a general simplicity of lifestyle. The Ebionites seem to have believed that Jesus, having been dwelt in by the messiah from his baptism until shortly before his crucifixion, had purged the Law of Moses of all its distortions. It had now to be rigorously observed. Paul, who had a distinctly ambivalent attitude to the Law, they vehemently rejected. They refused him the title of apostle, and claimed he had been deluded by visions sent by the devil. They had one Gospel, that of Matthew, adapted to their own particular views, and fragments of it have been preserved in the writings of the fourth-century bishop, Epiphanius.

Occupying roughly the same geographical area were the Nazaraioi. They are less well documented than the Ebionites, but were apparently rather more orthodox. They, too, had a version of the Gospel of Matthew for their own use, written in Aramaic. They accepted Jesus as messiah, but observed the Jewish Law as far as circumcision, the sabbath and other rituals were concerned.

Towards the end of the second century Julius Africanus, who despite his name may have been a native of Jerusalem, reported that in the area east of the river Jordan there were Christians who believed themselves descended from 'the cousins of the Lord'. It had been suggested that this enigmatic phrase meant that this group had been evangelized not by the Christians of Jerusalem and Judea but by those of Galilee.

The argument is a tenuous one, but it does offer an explanation of why the Ebionites and the Nazaraioi developed a distinctive form of Christianity. They had their roots in a very early version of the faith, based upon the beliefs of those whom Jesus had gathered around himself in Galilee.

Between these Christians and the Jerusalem Church there was a considerable gulf. Other communities kept closer links. There was a very early community in Damascus which was obviously well known in Jerusalem, for why, otherwise, should Paul have chosen to go there on his momentous journey? But little is known about it. More important in the subsequent history of Christianity was the Church at Antioch.

Antioch, situated on the river Orontes, was the capital of the Roman province of Syria. It was the third or fourth largest city in the Empire, a hub of political and military activity, a commercial centre of importance, sitting astride the routes between Rome and the Persian frontier, and between Palestine and Asia Minor.

It was in Antioch, recounts the Acts of the Apostles, that the followers of Jesus were first called Christians. This was a significant development. It

A sarcophagus from the Jewish catacomb in Rome. Integration of Jewish and pagan symbolism shows how much the Jewish community had entered into the general culture there.

implies that Jesus' adherents had become sufficiently distinct from the Jews to merit a name of their own. The name is a Latin one, suggesting some sort of recognition by the Roman authorities.

Yet precisely when or how Christianity came to Antioch is unclear. In Acts we learn that the Jerusalem Church sent Barnabas as a missionary, but by that time the faith had already been preached there. Among the seven 'deacons' there is one, Nicolaus, who was a native of Antioch, and originally a convert to Judaism.

Likewise the leaders of the Antioch Church, when they are named in Acts, all appear to be Hellenists, and what is known of the Church there suggests that members of the Christian community rapidly discarded much of their Jewish past. Perhaps it was this that earned them their particular name of Christian. And from the list of the leaders of the Antioch Church we learn that one of them, Menaus, had been a childhood companion of Herod Antipas, an indication that the new sect was attracting high-ranking converts from very early times, for this was about AD 40.

It may have been as much as a decade later that Christianity reached Rome. That it did so by the middle of the first century should come as no surprise, for the city had one of the largest concentrations of Jews outside Palestine. The forty to fifty thousand Jews there enjoyed unique privileges. They were exempt from military service, had their own courts, were permitted to collect money for the Temple in Jerusalem (Vespasian diverted it to the temple of Jupiter Capitolinus), and had permission to assemble for meals, both ritual and social. They were served by over a dozen different synagogues.

102

The Roman historian Suetonius mentions disputes among the Jews occasioned by a certain Chrestus. As a name this is not uncommon, but circumstances suggest that it is a reference to Christ. He goes on to speak of an expulsion of Jews from Rome. Clearly not all went: such a mass exodus would have been remarked by other historians. So it may be that only Christians were expelled, and some certainly did leave. The activists Priscilla and her husband Aquila journeyed to Corinth, where they met Paul. These events occurred in about AD 49, so it seems that Christianity had made an impact in Rome, if an unfavourable one, by the middle of the century.

Ten years later Paul wrote to the Romans. His tone is cautious, even guarded. From what he wrote, it seems that the Church he was addressing was a moderately conservative one, and sympathetic to Jerusalem. The Jews themselves appear to have been rather more neutral. They avoided taking sides during the war waged by the Romans in Palestine from AD 66 to 70, giving no active support or finance to their warring co-religionists. They were apparently unmoved by the destruction of the Temple, though they would have watched its sacred vessels carried in triumph through the city's streets, and later have seen them engraved upon the Arch of Titus as a lasting memorial to the Roman conquest.

Paul's letter to the Christian community in Rome is a way of introducing himself, though when he eventually arrived, c. AD 61, it was as a prisoner. Peter's presence in the city has been a matter of acrimonious debate, though few would now deny it. Yet neither Peter nor Paul could claim to be founders of the Roman Church. Nor can Peter be called 'Bishop of Rome', though it is reasonable to imagine that two such eminent figures would have played a leading role in the city's Christian community.

That is, however, a supposition. It is also a supposition, though on firm foundation, that the two apostles both died a martyr's death in Rome, perhaps in AD 67. Tacitus records in his Annals that there was a fire, for which Nero made Christians the scapegoats.

The passage is an interesting one. Not only does it indicate that even by the year 67 Christians existed in the city in some numbers, but it is further evidence that they were recognized as distinct from Jews, even though Tacitus acknowledges their Jewish origins.

CHRISTIANITY'S WIDER REACH

The first converts to Christianity, then, were Jews. But it was one of the distinguishing features of the new sect that it appealed to Gentiles in a way which no other Jewish sect, such as the Pharisees or the Essenes, had ever done.

Not that Judaism itself was short of converts. Nicolaus of Antioch, the deacon mentioned above, was first a pagan and then a Jew before he embraced Christianity. And there were others who could not commit themselves fully to Judaism, but were devout followers of its teachings. They were the 'God fearers', some of whom are mentioned in the Gospels. In the Acts of the Apostles there is a long account of one such who was stationed at Caesarea, a Roman officer called Cornelius.

Cornelius was a centurion, in charge of what was probably a company of archers. He received a vision in which he was instructed to send for Peter. For his part, Peter had avoided Gentile areas on his missionary journeys, and was encouraged to go to Caesarea only because he, too, was vouchsafed a vision. In his vision Peter was instructed to eat animals that, according to Jewish Law, were unclean. A voice told him, 'What God has made clean, you have no right to call profane' (Acts 10:15). When he met Cornelius, Peter interpreted the vision for him: 'You know it is forbidden for Jews to mix with people of another race and visit them, but God has made it clear to me that I must not call anyone profane or unclean' (Acts 10:28). He then preached, and all the pagans who heard him were converted and baptized.

News of this event reached Jerusalem, and Peter was called to account for his actions. He retold the story of his vision and of the events which followed in vivid detail and, according to Acts, 'This account satisfied them, and they gave glory to God. "God," they said, "can evidently grant even the pagans the repentance that leads to life" (Acts 11:18). But no doubt the matter was not so simple, nor the story quite so straightforward.

As it is recounted in Acts, the conversion of Cornelius is surrounded by visions and outpourings of the Spirit. Such signs were accepted in Judaism as indications of the arrival of the messianic era, and, as has been pointed out, the Hellenists among the Christians believed just that. And in that case, argued the Hellenists, the old Jewish Law did not have to be observed in all its details. Peter was not by background a Hellenist, but in Jerusalem he had been tolerant of Hellenism. As has been seen, when they complained of discrimination he, as one of the twelve apostles, had appointed Stephen and six others to look after them. In AD 49 or thereabouts, however, Peter's tolerance was put to the test.

It seems that the Hellenists who had undertaken the mission to Antioch had not required that their converts be circumcised. This was one of the sections of the Jewish Law they believed to have been superseded. Then conservative Christians began to arrive from Jerusalem, teaching that circumcision was essential for salvation.

Paul was in Antioch at this time, and he, with Barnabas and a few others, set off to Jerusalem to defend the practice of non-circumcision. A meeting took place, sometimes called the Council of Jerusalem. Paul gives an account of it in his letter to the Galatians, and there is another account in the Acts of the Apostles. Both documents make clear that there was only one item of importance on the agenda: circumcision was required by Jewish Law, therefore could a convert from paganism neglect the prescription of

104

circumcision and still be saved simply by faith in Christ?

Peter said yes, and his voice prevailed. From then on circumcision was not to be demanded of pagan converts: a major tie between Judaism and Christianity had been broken. Paul and Barnabas promptly returned to Antioch.

Peter followed on shortly afterwards, and continued the practice he had adopted in the case of Cornelius. In clear contravention of the Jewish Law, he was prepared to eat with pagans. Messengers were sent from James in Jerusalem to rebuke him, and he gave way. Paul was distinctly put out. In his letter to the Galatians he says of himself with some pride that he 'opposed [Peter] to his face since he was manifestly in the wrong.' The

A plaque found at Antioch, and believed to represent the prophet Daniel. He is holding his arms upwards in the typically Christian attitude of prayer.

account of the whole affair in Galatians (2:1–14) presents Paul as having had the best of the argument, but that may be special pleading. On this occasion Paul lost the support of Barnabas, a leader of the Antioch Church and hitherto a keen supporter of his. Moreover, Paul fairly soon after left Antioch on his second missionary journey, and Barnabas did not go with him. The passage in Galatians which tells Paul's side of the story is the only time Antioch is mentioned in his writings. Something rankled.

For the Christians Paul left behind him in Antioch the dispute was not yet over. They sent emissaries to Jerusalem. They wanted James and his advisers to change their minds about the observance by Christians of Jewish dietary laws. They succeeded. A letter was sent from Jerusalem 'to the brothers of the pagan birth in Antioch, Syria and Cilicia':

> It has been decided by the Holy Spirit and by ourselves not to saddle you with any burden beyond these essentials: you are to abstain from food sacrificed to idols, from blood, and from the meat of strangled animals and from fornication. (Acts 15:28, 29)

The dispute was over. The Church in Jerusalem, whatever its own practice, had confirmed the discontinuity between the practices of Judaism and those of Christianity. The story highlights the part played by Jerusalem as a form of central authority. It also gives prominence to Peter in Caesarea, Jerusalem and Antioch.

But from then on Peter disappears from the story as it is told in Acts. And Jerusalem also disappears, except when it figures in the story of Paul. The form of Christianity which had emerged at Antioch was a radical departure from that taken for granted among 'Hebrew' Christians in Jerusalem. It followed the pattern established by the Hellenists. In the great cosmopolitan city of Antioch, Christianity looked outwards towards pagans, not towards the Jews.

THE EVENTS OF AD 70

In the year AD 70 the Temple in Jerusalem was destroyed, never to be

After Titus captured Jerusalem and destroyed the Temple he returned in triumph to Rome, bearing with him the spoils, including the Temple's seven-branch candlestick.

106

rebuilt. On 6 August of that year the perpetual sacrifice ceased. At the end of the month, perhaps on 28 August, the Romans burnt the Temple to the ground. For the history of the Jewish people it was a terrible, and momentous, event. For the links between Judaism and Christianity it had immeasurable consequences.

Conflict between Jews and Romans was perhaps ultimately inevitable, but the troubles of Palestine in the second half of the first century owed much to the incompetence of the Roman governors. For although during this period there was a puppet king, Agrippa II, it was Roman administration which dominated Judea.

The causes of the revolt which broke out are difficult to disentangle. Historians have to rely on Flavius Josephus for a great deal of their information about what happened. Josephus was a Jewish leader. When the fighting started in AD 66 he was put in charge of defending Galilee from the Romans. He drilled his soldiers along Roman lines and tried to suppress other Jewish groups. He attempted to construct a string of fortresses around Galilee.

These measures might have worked but, unhappily for Josephus, Nero sent Vespasian, his best general, to suppress the Jews. Against his legions the Jewish army melted away. Josephus was besieged for seven weeks before surrendering. When he did so, he went over to the Roman side. So Josephus is not the best person to record Roman insensitivity to Jewish practices, or the crushing burden of Roman taxation. But there is evidence of both those in what he wrote, and it is clear that the Roman procurators, who in the second half of the century seem to have been chosen largely from the eastern part of the Empire, were more sympathetic to the Greek element in Palestine than they were to the Jews.

The worst fears of the Jews were confirmed by the attitude of Cumanus, procurator from AD 48 to 52. A Roman soldier, on guard at the portico of the Temple, made an obscene gesture. The crowd demanded that he be punished for blasphemy. Stones were thrown. Instead of taking the Jews' feelings into account, Cumanus called out more troops. Although they did not attack, the crowd panicked and many were crushed to death in the rush to get away from the Temple.

Shortly afterwards a Roman caravan was set upon by brigands. Cumanus' soldiers raided villages near the place of the attack, apparently on the grounds that their inhabitants must have sheltered the attackers. In the course of one of these raids a soldier tore up and burned a copy of the Torah. Eventually the culprit was beheaded, but the delay in doing so further antagonized the population.

The final straw came when some Galileans travelling to Jerusalem were ambushed by Samaritans. The Galileans first appealed for support to Cumanus, but when he did nothing they enlisted the services of brigands to attack the Samaritans. Now that the Galileans had taken the law into their own hands, Cumanus supported the Samaritans. There was a battle in which some Jews were killed and others taken prisoner.

Yet Cumanus was not the worst of the procurators. Under his successors the situation deteriorated further. Outbreaks of sporadic violence were fuelled by the harsh exactions of the Roman authorities. When the rising began in earnest in AD 66, the first thing the Jerusalem rebels did was to burn the record of their debts.

It would be misleading to present the war against the Romans as a struggle of the poor and oppressed against their task-masters. There is some truth in that, but the immediate cause lay in Caesarea. There, six years before, the Romans had denied the Jews equal rights with the Syrians. Now they allowed Greeks to take over government of the city. It may have been a minor incident, but such was the intensity of feeling in Palestine that in no time most of the country had risen against the Romans.

At first the Jews were successful. Strongholds in Jerusalem were seized, and the Governor of Syria was repulsed in his attempts to retake the city; the 12th Legion was practically wiped out. But then three more legions arrived, under the command of Vespasian. First Galilee fell, then the coast road. Next he moved inland and reconquered territory, region by region, until Jerusalem was isolated. Nero died in AD 69, which brought fighting to a halt for a time. But Vespasian himself became Emperor, and sent his son Titus to take charge. Titus promptly laid siege to Jerusalem.

Within Jerusalem, the various Jewish factions had fallen out. In the fighting some of the food stores were destroyed. So when Titus built a wall around the city to starve out its defenders, the tactic quickly proved effective. Jerusalem was taken – though fighting continued for some time even in the city – and the Temple destroyed.

By that time some Zealots had already abandoned Jerusalem and taken refuge at Masada. This was a natural fortress atop a rock, and it was defended by some 960 persons. The Roman commander built a tower higher than the walls so that his troops could break through with a battering ram. A hasty repair was made, but the Romans set fire to it. They decided to delay the final assault for a day. That night, 2 May AD 73, every single person in Masada committed suicide.

The crucial event of the war, however, was the razing of the Temple. Inevitably, this changed the nature of Judaism. But did it also affect the tenuous relations between the Jews and the messianic sect which called itself Christian?

THE END OF THE TEMPLE

In the third book of his history of the Church, Eusebius reports the following:

> The members of the Jerusalem Church by means of an oracle given by
> revelation to acceptable persons there, were ordered to leave the City

[of Jerusalem] before the war began and settle in a town in Peraea called Pella. To Pella those who believed in Christ migrated from Jerusalem.

There they remained until the war between the Jews and the Romans was over. Then they returned to the city.

The Jews, after the destruction of the Temple, had to set about reorganizing their religion. The rabbis met at Jamnia (Yavneh). They determined the canon of Jewish scriptures, and formally excommunicated the Christian sect for their treason in time of war. From then on Christians were banned from the synagogue.

That is the traditional version. It may be true, but that is improbable. The Jewish canon of scripture, the formally recognized collection of books containing the Law and the prophets, had come into existence much earlier. And although it is true that a meeting of the Pharisee party took place at Jamnia, it is unlikely that there were any excommunications. The possibility of a complete expulsion from the synagogue probably did not exist before the year AD 200 or so.

In any case, the gathering at Jamnia faced problems more pressing than dealing with the Christians. It had to reconstruct the liturgy and the liturgical calendar. Letters were sent to diaspora communities announcing the dispositions agreed at Jamnia, and rabbis went too. It seems likely that the rabbis were critical of the new sect. The priestly party was at a disadvantage after the destruction of the Temple, and the Pharisees came to the fore. To the Pharisees the attitude of the Christians, and especially the Hellenists, to Jewish Law would have been wholly unacceptable.

In one of the reformulated prayers for the synagogue service there was added to the Eighteen Benedictions one, the twelfth, which appears to curse the Christians. But the reference to the *Notzrim*, the Christians, is awkward and looks as though it were added later to make more explicit the curse on all heretics.

That is not to say that the Christians did not understand the general curse being directed at themselves. Very likely they did. They would have felt distinctly uncomfortable in any synagogue service at which it was read out. And when Christian scriptures began to appear, just about the time of the meeting in Jamnia, they would have fallen under the general ban against the use of 'heretical' books in the liturgy. In practice, the Christians excommunicated themselves.

None of this proves, however, that the fall of Jerusalem and the destruction of the Temple were decisive in separating Christianity and Judaism, as the account in Eusebius suggests. The name 'Christian', which first came into use at Antioch as Acts relates, predates the fall of Jerusalem by many years. In Nero's persecution it was the Christian Church, not the Jewish synagogue, which was singled out as a scapegoat. The distinction between Judaism and Christianity was obvious to an outside observer long

The fortress at Masada where 960 Jews committed suicide rather than submit to Rome. The ramp which the Romans built to gain entrance to the fortress can still be seen on the right.

before the meeting at Jamnia.

Moreover, the destruction of the Temple does not figure large in early Christian literature, certainly not as large as one might have expected had it been a decisive moment in the history of the Church. For that matter it did not make a great impact on diaspora Judaism either. Until the second Jewish War (AD 132–135), and the establishment by the Emperor Hadrian of the cult of Jupiter upon the site of the Temple, it had always seemed possible that the building might have been re-erected.

The oldest reference to the story that the flight of Christians to Pella alienated the Jewish establishment from the new sect occurs in Eusebius. He was writing early in the fourth century, although he seems to have owed his information to Aristo of Pella writing about the middle of the second century. But how far should Eusebius have trusted his source?

It may be that a good many Jews fled Jerusalem before the war broke out in AD 66. It may also be true that a good many Jewish Christians went with them: a year later it would have been impossible to escape in any numbers. But was it likely that the Christians went to Pella?

It was not an obvious place of refuge. As a Gentile city it would scarcely

110

have been welcoming to Jewish Christian refugees. Secondly, and according to Josephus, it had already been sacked. In so far as the city was habitable at all, it would hardly have been hospitable to immigrants. Yet the story of the flight to Pella exists. If it were not true, then someone had an interest in inventing it.

Pella housed a Christian community quite early on. Of its foundation there is no record, the story of the flight there from Jerusalem apart. Apostolic origins were important to these early Christian communities. The suspicion must remain that the story told by Aristo was an attempt to supply Pella with apostolic ancestry, and that the events of AD 70 were not in themselves enormously significant in the separation of Christianity from Judaism.

THE END IS NOT YET

So far we have concentrated on what happened to Christians in the course of the first century. But during this time there also occurred a change in their perception of themselves as a messianic sect. This came about because Jesus did not promptly return in glory, as perhaps he himself and certainly many of the early Christians had confidently expected.

There is no doubt that this presented a problem. This is what 2 Peter had to say:

> We must remember that during the last days there are bound to be people who will be scornful, the kind who always please themselves what they do, and they will make fun of the promise and will ask, 'Well, where is this coming? Everything goes on as it has since the Fathers died, as it has since it began at creation.' (2 Pt 3:3–4)

The author did not deny that the last days had arrived, but he was faced with people who were saying that the return of Jesus had not happened soon enough. He had an answer:

> You must never forget: that with the Lord, 'a day' can mean a thousand years, and a thousand years is like a day. The Lord is not being slow to carry out his promises, as anybody else might be called slow; but he is being patient with you all, wanting nobody to be lost and everybody brought to change his ways. (2 Pt 3:8–9)

The prophecy has conveniently been reinterpreted. The end times which Jesus foresaw will last a long time, because the timescale of God and that of human beings do not coincide.

That was at the end of the New Testament period (c. AD 140). The same problem of a fading hope in the imminence of the parousia had presented itself much earlier. About the year AD 51, when he was in Corinth, Paul wrote to the Church at Thessalonika:

> We can tell you this, that any of us who are left alive until the Lord's coming will not have any advantage over those who have died. At the trumpet of God the voice of the archangel will call out the command

and the Lord himself will come down from heaven; those who have died in Christ will be the first to rise, then those of us who are still alive will be taken up in the clouds. (1 Thes 4:15–17)

From that it would appear that the preaching by which Paul won converts in Thessalonika had contained fairly explicit reference to the return of Jesus. So much so that the New Christians were puzzled, to say the very least, when they noticed some of their number dying before Jesus' return in glory.

In the passage just quoted, Paul appears to suggest that entrance into the new kingdom is something which lies in the not too distant future. A decade later he has changed his mind. In the letter to the Christians at Colossae, perhaps composed in Rome between AD 61 and 63, Paul expresses the belief that the kingdom has already arrived, already God 'has taken us out of the power of darkness and created a place for us in the kingdom' (Col 1:13). Similarly, in the earlier letter to the Church at Rome, resurrection, one of the signs of the arrival of the end times, lies in the future. In the letter to the Colossians it has already occurred. What had been seen as concrete events are now understood in a spiritual sense. The prophecy had been reinterpreted to fit the facts.

If Jesus did not foresee a long gap between his death and resurrection and the parousia, it is difficult to see why he should have invented an ecclesiastical hierarchy to run the Church in his absence from earth. If, that is, he laid the foundations even of a Church. That is a much disputed topic. There is less disagreement about the lateness of the date at which office-holders in the Church began to emerge. Luke has Paul appointing elders. In his own writings, Paul does not mention having done so.

Although disagreements occasionally show through, Luke wanted to present a picture in the Acts of the Apostles of a unified Church. It has a central authority residing in Jerusalem. Missions go out from Jerusalem to reach, eventually, Rome, the capital of the world. And authority resides in the apostles, in the Twelve.

It was not like that. Christianity did not spread out from Jerusalem according to some prearranged plan. And the term 'apostles' was, in the early Church, applied to a wider group than the Twelve – it included Paul, for example. This is not to say that Luke falsified his account. He was expressing what was increasingly becoming Christianity's understanding of its role. It had a long life ahead of it, therefore it needed a sense of unity and clear-cut lines of authority. These ideas may not have been well formulated at the time Luke was writing, but they were there.

The excitement of the early fervour died as the years passed. In his early Christian life Paul put the charismatic role of prophet above the much more staid role of teacher (1 Cor 12:28). By about AD 65, the likely date of 1 Timothy, prophecy is referred to in the past tense: it is over and done with. By the time of the Letter of Jude in the last decade of the first century, the faith has become normative. There is an orthodoxy which is handed down: 'Fight hard for the faith which has once and for all been entrusted to the saints' (Jude 3).

CHRISTIANITY BECOMES A CHURCH

Towards the end of the second century one of Christianity's most articulate opponents, the pagan Celsus, remarked that only the poorest classes were attracted to the new faith. It was meant as a jibe, and it has stuck. But it was not true.

Menaus has already been mentioned as a Church leader in Antioch who had been a childhood companion of Herod Antipas. Both in his first letter to the Christians at Corinth and in his letter to the Church at Rome, Paul refers to a certain Gaius, a Christian with a Roman name, and wealthy enough to own a house in Corinth in which, on occasion, all the Christians could gather.

On the other hand, no New Testament document hints that any member of any Christian congregation belonged to the senatorial class. And if there were any who were very poor, they, too, go unmentioned. It is true that the community of Jerusalem seems to have been reduced to poverty at some point (Acts 11:28–29), but that was probably because of an extensive famine. And Paul was able to gather money for it from other Churches he had founded:

> Now about the collection made for the saints: you are to do as I told the churches in Galatia to do. Every Sunday, each one of you must put aside what he can afford, so that collections need not be made after I have come. When I am with you, I will send your offering to Jerusalem by the hand of whatever men you give letters of reference to. (1 Cor 16:1–3)

The fact that such collections could be made indicates that if the congregations were not particularly wealthy, neither were their members destitute.

Paul himself was poor, but that was because he seems to have worked for one season of the year in order to finance his travels in another. The advice he offers in his letters sounds as though it is addressed to those in the same class as himself, moderately well-off tradesmen who lived in cities.

The first letter of Peter, however, was sent to an entirely different group. The letter calls them 'resident aliens', and they lived in Asia Minor in an area to the north and west of the Taurus Mountains. It has been calculated that, at the end of the first century, the population of Asia Minor was some four million. It is thought that possibly 80,000 of them were Christians, scattered thinly over a wide area. Racially, they were a very mixed population, and were predominantly village dwellers. 1 Peter urges them to cling together for support as members of the 'household of God'.

The word 'household' was an important one. In the Old Testament it had meant a community of believers, and was used in the New Testament in the same sense. It also had a secular meaning: the emperor was head of his family, or his household, the Empire; he was the *paterfamilias*, the source of authority.

The term was also used in the ordinary sense of a family under its head. In the New Testament letters there are several examples of what are known as 'household codes', or guides to social behaviour. Though, they are not peculiar to Christianity. In 1 Peter, for example, advice is offered to wives and husbands, and recommendations made on how slaves should treat their masters, and how Christians should relate to the State.

Whatever else these household codes may have done, they reinforced a fairly conventional manner of behaviour. That was probably their purpose. The letter-writer did not want the Christian way of life to appear too singular. If that was the intention, then the codes were not very successful. In the second century the complaint was made that the household was being undermined by Christianity. It was attracting to itself slaves, young people and women, to the detriment of the traditional authority of the *paterfamilias*.

From the time of Jesus onwards, it seems that the role of women in Christianity differed from their role in the world about them. It is true that there was a gap between legal theory on the position of women in society, and actual practice. There is plenty of evidence from inscriptions of New Testament times that women made a major contribution to their cities and their *collegia*, or clubs. It is also clear that women went to court, transacted business and owned property quite independently of the husbands to whom they were supposedly subjected.

Even granted that, it still seems that the place of women in the earliest Christian communities was especially powerful. The first hints that the Christian mission was to be extended outside Judaism come in two conversations between Jesus and women – the Samaritan woman and the Syrophoenician woman. Women are the first witnesses to the resurrection. The Gospel accounts are confused, but it seems likely that the apostles fled to Galilee after the resurrection, and returned to Jerusalem only after they had recovered their composure. The women stayed in Jerusalem all along.

The Hellenists in Jerusalem met in the house of Mary, the mother of John Mark. She seems to have been a woman of some means, for the house belonged to her not to her sons, and she had servants. Hellenistic Jews would have been accustomed to women in their synagogues. They would not commonly have been found, if at all, in the 'Hebrew' synagogues. Both groups would, however, have held festive meals which, in the Christian context, quite possibly became celebrations of the Eucharist. Was the involvement of women in the Eucharist one of the factors causing division between Hellenist and Hebrew Christians? It is impossible to know the answer for certain. Much of the history of women in the New Testament

114

A fourth-century portrait from the Roman catacomb of Trasona. Women continued to play a major role in the life of the Church throughout the fourth century.

appears to have been played down, if not actively suppressed. Enough remains, however, to construct some sort of picture.

Paul numbered women among his 'co-workers', and they worked with him on an equal basis. A disagreement between the two women Evodia and Syntyche, recorded in the letter to the Philippians, caused him particular pain because of the major role they had played in spreading the gospel (Phil 4:2–3). At Rome a large number of women are important enough to be mentioned by name in the last chapter of Paul's letter to the community there.

Among them is Phoebe, described as a 'deaconess of the church of Cenchreae'. Not only is she given a formal title, she is thanked because, says Paul, 'she has looked after a great many people, me included.' And after Phoebe come:

Prisca and Aquila, my fellow workers in Christ Jesus, who risked death to save my life; I am not the only one to owe them a debt of gratitude, all the churches among the pagans do as well. My greetings also to the church that meets at their house. (Rom 16:3–5)

Prisca and Aquila are a remarkable couple. They are a husband and wife team (another seems to be that of Andronicus and Junia, also mentioned in Romans, though it may be that Junia is a man, not Andronicus' wife), who were responsible for house-churches in Corinth, Ephesus and Rome. Prisca, also known in the diminutive form Priscilla, is always mentioned first. This may reflect her eminence as a missionary: at Ephesus she was the teacher of Apollo. But it is more likely to reflect the fact that, as a woman, she presided over the house, and it was in houses that Christians met for worship.

For many Jewish Christians at least, attendance at synagogue services continued until towards the end of the first century. But alongside these there were specifically Christian gatherings. The Christian meetings took place in private dwellings which, it would seem, were often owned by wealthy widows. Houses were locations where women, otherwise denied a leading role in society or politics, could exercise a considerable degree of power and influence.

Once baptism had replaced circumcision as initiation into the faith, there was established a new discipleship of equals. This is much emphasized by Paul. It would be strange if this level of equality had not attracted the hitherto underprivileged, women and slaves, to the new religion.

Equality was not without its own kind of tensions. It is very likely that the organizational model for early Christian communities within the structures of the Roman Empire was the *collegium,* or club. The Jewish community certainly seems to have followed this path. The *collegia* were private associations of people who pursued the same trade, or worshipped the same deity, or came from the same ethnic group. They were voluntary bodies which had special meeting places, and gave high priority to rituals and other cultic activities, particularly meals. They depended for survival upon wealthy patrons, whom they rewarded with statues and dedications. As well as providing a degree of social activity, these colleges or guilds also took care of the burial of their members, and commemorated the dead.

There were special problems for Christian associations of this sort. Commitment to Christianity excluded all other loyalties, and if Christians followed the Jewish practice and provided arbiters in disputes so that there was no need to approach the municipal authorities, the isolation of Christians from other social groups would have been all but complete.

There were as well particular tensions in the Christian associations. Paul records two very vividly in his first letter to the Church at Corinth. Both concern the class structure of early Christianity. Paul wanted to discourage the eating of meat which had been sacrificed to idols. It had been forbidden by the Jerusalem Church, probably because of its cultic connotations. But this prohibition was socially divisive. Sacrificial meat was cheap, and therefore available to the poorer members of society who might otherwise rarely have tasted meat. The wealthy, on the other hand, were acustomed to eating meat: it did not have for them any particular association with the cult. To deny sacrificial meat to Christians, albeit on perfectly valid religious grounds, may very well have been to deny any meat at all to the poorer members of the community.

The other issue tackled by Paul was the unwillingness of the wealthier members of the community to share the food set out in the house-church for the socially diverse group which met there. It was quite common in a *collegium* for a patron to provide a splendid meal at which he would entertain his friends, and thereby demonstrate the extent of his patronage. From the strength of Paul's insistence upon the common fellowship at the Eucharist in Corinth, it seems that someone was acting in a similar fashion within the Christian community.

A Christian patron may well have felt hard done by within a Christian *collegium*. He or she was not rewarded with visible recognition of benefactions made, nor automatically conceded authority in the community. Instead, in the early years of Christianity, leadership belonged to whoever, man or woman, had access to the Spirit.

The officers of the *collegia*, the bishop and the deacon – the first with administrative responsibility, the second in charge of communications with the association's members – were responsible to a committee of elders. They may have taken it in turns to hold the rank of bishop, or *episcopos*, a word which means 'overseer'.

Membership of this committee was determined by age and by gender. Although the existence of house-churches gave initial prominence to women, in most circumstances the head of the household was a man, and insofar as Christianity pursued the collegial model, the strongly hierarchical structure of the *collegia* promoted male dominance. Wealthy women elders, who might have expected to play a leading role in the community, were restricted on account of their sex to the subordinate task of instructing other women.

By the end of the first century the charismatic, itinerant group of preachers which had followed Jesus and learnt from him, had become an organization. It had its organizational model and code of rules, both geared to making the Church acceptable to the pagan environment in which it dwelt. One of the aspects of its early life which was sacrificed to convention was the leading role of women.

But it had also to come to terms with disappointment at the non-appearance of the end time. Because this was no longer expected in the foreseeable future, the Church had to structure itself for survival. Out of all the tensions and disputes and many varieties of Christianity, from all the books which recorded the teachings of Jesus and the history of his mission, the Church had to select a path down which it might securely go.

6

CHRISTIANS OF THE EAST

Asia Minor is of particular significance in the history of early Christianity. The Apocalypse mentions seven Churches there, and the problems each faced. An ancient kingdom within Asia Minor claimed to be the first to convert, with its entire population, to the new faith. Not too far away lies the earliest surviving church building. It was in Asia Minor that the bishop emerged as the dominant figure in the local Church.

But it was also in Asia Minor that, during the first three centuries of its existence, the greatest challenges arose to the unity of Christianity. Marcion cast doubts upon the value of the Bible as a book for Christian use; Montanus rejected the organizational structures which had developed; Mani proposed a wholly new, and seductive, vision of reality; while problems over the Church's calendar threatened to divide one community from another. The region seems to have been a breeding ground of extreme religious movements. The effects of these movements were felt right across the Church, and for centuries to come.

THE CHURCHES OF THE APOCALYPSE

As he begins his Book of Revelation, John the seer, on the island of Patmos, writes seven letters to seven Churches on the Mediterranean seaboard. They display an intimate knowledge of the geography of the cities, and of the factors which influenced the lives of their citizens. The towns mentioned by the seer were, in sequence, Ephesus, Smyrna, Pergamum, Thyatira, Sardis, Philadelphia and Laodicea. In two of them, Ephesus and Pergamum, the Nicolaitans had been at work, and had incurred the grave displeasure of the seer. Who they were remains a mystery. In Pergamum they were associated with the disciples of Balaam, known from elsewhere in the New Testament to be libertines.

It is possible that the Nicolaitans thought it permissible for Christians to eat meat that had been sacrificed to idols, and held that they did not have to restrain their lust. The charge that Christians were morally lax in matters of sex even to the point of perversion was common among pagans. Groups such as the Nicolaitans may have provided evidence.

Several of the cities mentioned, Ephesus and Laodicea in particular, were notable for their devotion to the cult of the Roman emperor. In that, they were typical of the whole of the province of Asia. The Pastoral Epistles

The Seven Churches of the Apocalypse

and 1 Peter, as well as other Christian writings, are fairly friendly towards Rome. Even the author of the fourth Gospel plays down the guilt of the Roman representative, Pilate, in Jesus' death. The Book of Revelation, on the other hand, is hostile to Rome. Why the change of heart?

What had happened was that Domitian had become emperor. Eusebius linked the persecution of the Church under Domitian (AD 81–96) with the fate of the – supposed – author of the Book of Revelation:

> [Domitian] showed himself the successor of Nero in enmity and hostility to God. He was, in fact, the second to organize persecution against us. There is ample evidence that at the time the apostle and evangelist was still alive, and because of his testimony to the word of God was sentenced to confinement on the island of Patmos. (*History of the Church*, 3:17–18)

As Eusebius was careful to point out, Domitian was not the first emperor to persecute Christians. But Nero's persecution had been confined to Rome, and in any case he was known to be a tyrant. Domitian was a different matter. He demanded that worship be given him as 'lord and god'. Those punished for failing to do so included Jews as well as Christians: 'Many were the victims of Domitian's appalling cruelty', Eusebius remarks.

The members of the Churches mentioned in the Book of Revelation suffered with their fellow citizens in the economic decline of Asia Minor. They had moreover troubles of their own: conflict among themselves over the Nicolaitans and the followers of Balaam, if the two groups were distinguishable. They also clashed with the Jews. That would seem to be the significance of the reference, in the letter to the Church at Smyrna, to 'the synagogue of Satan'. (Rev 2:9)

119

Along with that of many other cities, the Jewish population of Smyrna had expanded enormously after the fall of Jerusalem. As will be seen in the following account of Ignatius and Polycarp, there was, by the early second century, little love lost between Jews and Christians.

IGNATIUS AND POLYCARP

The evidence of the letters to the seven Churches, therefore, is of a piece with what can be gleaned from Paul's letters, and to some extent from the Acts of the Apostles. Christianity was divided into many different, maybe even competing, factions. The attempt of the Council of Jerusalem to arbitrate between Hebrews and Hellenists has already been described. That event stands out because it was the single one of its kind. Apart from that 'Council' there was no structure within Christianity to determine what was, and what was not, acceptable belief. With the arrival of Ignatius, however, things began to change.

Ignatius was bishop of Antioch in the last part of the first century and the beginning of the second. But compared to what is known about what had gone before, Ignatius was a bishop with a difference. From the Pastoral Epistles it is clear that there existed in the Church before the end of the first century the office of bishop and a number of other ministries. But these were not differentiated. The writings of Ignatius, however, very clearly distinguish between bishop, presbyter (or priest) and deacon. He was a vigorous proponent of the role of the bishop in the government of, and as the centre of unity in, the local Church.

Little is known about Ignatius. His literary style identifies him as a man of culture. He called himself Ignatius Theophorus, 'the God-bearer', which may have been a baptismal name. It is more than likely that he was born of pagan parents and received baptism, and the name Theophorus, as a grown man. Though most of his life story remains obscure, a good deal is known of his last months. After he had been head of the Church in Antioch for many years, perhaps as many as forty, he was condemned to death as a Christian. Instead of being executed on the spot he was sent to Rome, and legend has it that he was thrown to the lions on 19 December. The day is precise, but not the year. It was sometime in the reign of the Emperor Trajan, so between 98 and 117.

It is difficult to explain why Ignatius was sent to Rome. Had he been a Roman citizen who, like Paul, had appealed to the emperor, he would not have travelled in chains, nor would he have been thrown to wild animals in the amphitheatre. It may be that there was no one of sufficient rank in Antioch at the time to confirm a death sentence. Or it may just have been that Ignatius was too popular a figure to be executed in his own city.

There is little doubt of his popularity. Even his arch enemies admired him, and all along the route through Asia Minor on his journey to Rome crowds of Christians came to greet him. His journey in the company of ten soldiers took him from Antioch to Tarsus and then on to Laodicea. At Laodicea, where they might have turned towards the sea at Ephesus, the group went on to Philadelphia, Sardis and Smyrna.

Because they took this route, they bypassed several cities to the south which apparently had sizeable Christian communities: Tralles, Magnesia and Ephesus itself. So Ignatius wrote to the Christians of these towns, and also to the Church in Rome, for he was afraid the Christians there might try to save his life. His heart was set on martyrdom.

From Smyrna he went on to Troas. There he wrote letters to communities in the towns he had just visited, Philadelphia and Smyrna, and a personal letter to Polycarp, head of the Church in Smyrna. And then, legend apart, he disappears from history. His reputation hangs upon these seven letters.

His correspondence reveals a good deal about the Church in Antioch and the problems it faced. These problems did not come from the Roman authorities. Though Ignatius himself may have been condemned to death, there is no suggestion in his writings that Christians as a whole were being persecuted. The difficulties were not from without, but from within the Church.

There were two groups which were causing trouble, the Docetists and the Judaizers. It is not clear from the letters whether they were the same people. It is possible that they were, although Ignatius proposes different remedies against them. He insists to the Judaizers that they should follow distinctively Christian practices, rather than those reminiscent of Judaism. In his letter to the Philadelphians he very firmly makes the Old Testament subordinate to the New, and tells the Magnesians that the Saturday Sabbath is to be exchanged for a Sunday one.

The docetic problem was different. The Docetists believed that Jesus only *seemed* to suffer: their name derives from a Greek word meaning 'appearance'. Even his humanity was more apparent than real, they claimed. Ignatius answered them sharply:

Suffer he did, verily and indeed; just as he did verily and indeed raise himself again. His passion was no unreal illusion as some sceptics aver who are all unreality themselves. The fate of those wretches will match their belief, for one day they will similarly become phantoms without substance themselves. For my own part, I know and believe that he was in actual flesh, even after his resurrection. (*To the Christians of Smyrna*, 2–3)

Ignatius' fame, however, depends not so much upon his defence of the faith against these heretics (he is very sure who is, and who is not, a true believer), as upon the means he proposes to maintain the unity of the Church. He is a vigorous proponent of the office of bishop. No other defence of the episcopal role is to be found in surviving literature of the period. Of what is known as the 'monepiscopacy', or monarchical

A pavement mosaic from Antioch, where Ignatius was bishop. Antioch was the Empire's third largest city with half a million inhabitants, and was also one of the richest.

episcopacy, Ignatius is the leading apologist.

In a famous book, *Orthodoxy and Heresy in the Early Church*, Walter Bauer, the German New Testament scholar, argued that Ignatius was constant in his defence of monepiscopacy because his position was so insecure. Ignatius had to argue vigorously in defence of the episcopy, said Bauer, both because this understanding of the role was relatively new, and because the group over whom he ruled, and whom he recognized as true Christians, was small and insignificant in comparison with other groups in Antioch.

It is true that the number of Christians was probably fairly small in comparison with the pagans. There is no real evidence that those represented by Ignatius (and Polycarp for that matter) were not in a majority among those who called themselves Christians. And it is unlikely, though not altogether impossible, that Ignatius invented the monepiscopacy. If that form of Church government can be ascribed any single home, it is almost certainly Jerusalem, where James had established a dominant position and where, it seems, the office of bishop may have become hereditary.

Ignatius draws fine distinctions between the various offices in the

122

Church. He does not, however, feel required to prove that these offices should exist. He takes them for granted. If he did not create the tradition, he stood at or near its beginnings, and had to argue hard for his ideas to be accepted. There was something novel about them.

Syrian Christianity had been accustomed to itinerant, charismatic preachers, born leaders who were inspired by the Spirit (or thought they were). They were licensed to preach by the laying-on of hands. The community in Syria, whose outline can be glimpsed in the Gospel of Matthew and which flourished in the same region as that ruled by Ignatius, stressed brotherly service: it was made up of elders, rather than the hierarchical structure proposed by Ignatius – and proposed as being in accord with the wishes of Christ.

Prophecy, and prophetic leaders, were a characteristic of the Syrian Church. But were they sufficient? The communities here were stable and expanding. It was highly unsatisfactory that a group of Christians should go off on their own to celebrate the Eucharist apart from the bishop – something which, apparently, had been happening both in Ignatius' Antioch and Polycarp's Smyrna.

The answer was to exalt the authority of the bishop. He was to become the touchstone of true adherence to Christianity. He was both source and symbol of the unity of the Church, and people defined themselves by their closeness to or distance from him. The Docetists wanted to associate themselves with Ignatius, but because of their views he would not have them. He had become the arbiter of what one may begin to decribe as 'normative' Christianity. And in his attempt to win other Churches over to his side through his letters, one may see a vision of a wider unity of the faith. As far as one can judge, he was the first to speak of the 'Catholic', meaning the universal, Church.

Ignatius represents a turning-point for Christianity. He did not explicitly claim to be a prophet, but he wrote in typically prophetic language. So though he may have achieved eminence in the Christian community at Antioch because of his charismatic powers of leadership, once in office he came to see the necessity of what might be called bureaucracy in the Church, and above all, the need for a strong central authority: the local bishop.

Ignatius addressed one of his letters of advice to another local bishop, Polycarp of Smyrna. Rather more is known about Polycarp's life than about that of Ignatius. Polycarp had a pupil, Irenaeus, who became bishop of Lyons in the last quarter of the second century, and Irenaeus maintained that Polycarp had been taught by the apostles, which is not impossible. Tertullian, an African theologian who died c. 225, went so far as to claim that Polycarp had been appointed to Smyrna by St John himself, then dwelling nearby at Ephesus.

Polycarp was born c. AD 69, and was probably martyred in 155 after governing the Church at Smyrna for nearly half a century. His period in office was a difficult one. In his letter to the Smyrnaeans mentioned above, Ignatius lays down instructions as to behaviour which make it quite clear that dissident groups were holding meetings apart from the bishop:

> Avoid divisions as the beginning of evil. Follow, all of you, the bishop, as Jesus Christ followed the Father; and follow the presbytery as the Apostles. Moreover reverence the deacons as the commandment of God. Let no man do aught pertaining to the Church apart from the bishop. Let that eucharist be considered valid which is under the bishop or him to whom he commits it. Wheresoever the bishop appears, there let the people be, even as wheresoever Christ Jesus is, there is the Catholic Church. It is not lawful apart from the bishop either to baptize or to hold a love-feast. (Letter to the Smyrnaeans, VIII)

Two other documents tell us something of Polycarp. One is an account of his martyrdom, which throws a good deal of the blame for his death and the manner of it upon the Jews. (This suggests that relations between the two communities of Jews and Christians were extremely strained at the time). The second is a letter he wrote to the Church at Philippi. It was a letter of general exhortation, much concerned with the dangers inherent in money, for money had recently brought about the downfall of Valens, once one of the Philippian clergy. But the letter also contained detailed advice about the character and the duties of the various offices in the Church. They were the sort of remarks any conscientious bishop might utter – except that Polycarp did not mention the office of bishop. Possibly it had not yet emerged at Philippi in the form envisaged by Ignatius and, presumably, by Polycarp himself.

CHRISTIAN ORIGINS IN SYRIA

No attempt to tell the history of early Christianity can ignore the story of Abgar for, if the story be true, the first Christian country was Abgar's kingdom of Osroene, with its capital at Edessa.

Edessa, 'the water city', is the modern town of Urfa in Turkey. It was an elegant city built on a river, famous for its fishponds, and featured baths, porticoes, colonnades and statuary. Its citizens were renowned for their skill with mosaics, and were especially fond of music. They were huntsmen and outstanding bow-men: a company of Edessan archers formed a crack unit in the Roman army. When they could be relied upon, that is, for the Edessans were not the firmest of Rome's allies. The site of their town was of strategic as well as commercial importance, for it lay across the junction of two ancient highways. One of them led from Armenia south down to Harran, then across the Euphrates and on to the cities of Syria, while the other connected the ports of the Mediterranean with the town of Nisibis and, much further afield, with India and China.

The story about this kingdom which Eusebius relates is as follows. King Abgar (who ruled from AD 13 to 50) was dying. Hearing of Jesus' miracles he sent for him. Jesus wrote back – this correspondence, Eusebius claims, can be found in the Edessan archives – to say that he could not come because he had been sent to the people of Israel, but he would send a disciple later. But Abgar was already blessed for having believed in him.

After Jesus' ascension, the story goes on, Thaddaeus was sent. He stayed with Tobias, son of Tobias, and cured Abgar of his illness. In return the King ordered all Edessans to listen to Thaddaeus' teaching. 'By his actions he exerted such an influence on them that he led them to reverence the power of Christ, and made disciples of the saving doctrine. From that day to this the whole city of Edessa has been devoted to the name of Christ,' says Eusebius. (*History of the Church,* 2:1)

Eusebius admits that he has only recently heard this story. That is at the beginning of the fourth century. Half way through the century St Ephraem, who died in 373, still knew nothing of it, though he was writing in Syriac, and at Edessa. He has, however, heard of the arrival of the disciple Thaddaeus, though he calls him Addai. By the end of the fourth century, Addai had taken on a life of his own, for, so the *Doctrine of Addai* relates, he sent the royal painter to Palestine to produce a likeness of Jesus. This he achieved just before the crucifixion, and brought the painting back to Addai.

According to this story, Addai was bishop of Edessa, and was succeeded by Aggai. Addai ordained Palut as deacon, and after Aggai was martyred Palut went to Antioch to be consecrated in his stead.

We should not regard this as serious history, though there may be hints in the legends to indicate what really happened. Thaddaeus, it may be recalled, lived at Edessa with 'Tobias, the son of Tobias'. These names suggest a Jewish connection in the establishment of Christianity at Edessa, which is what might have been expected. As late as the middle of the fourth century the Christian writer Aphraat describes some of his Syriac co-religionists as living by practices which had strong affinities to Judaism.

There is another element in the story. In the first century of Christianity the royal family of the neighbouring kingdom of Adiabene had become Jews. By the middle of the second century there seems to have been a strong Christian presence there, and its chief missionary was known as Addai. It seems quite likely, therefore, that the story of Addai–Thaddaeus at Edessa was a legend concocted towards the end of the third century or beginning of the fourth in one form, and towards the end of the fourth century in another version, to account for the foundation of the Edessan Church.

Little survives of the legend except the name Palut. Christians in Edessa were still known as 'Palutians' in the time of Ephraem, much to his irritation. The suggestion must be that some other group had appropriated the name 'Christian', and that group may have been the followers of Marcion.

125

Above, Urfa, the modern Edessa, still 'the water city'. Right, a mosaic from the second or early third century depicting an Edessan funeral, with portraits of the dead man's relatives.

Marcion's role in the history of the Church will be described later in this chapter. Here it is enough to say that even as late as the sixth century his followers were calling themselves Christians, forcing more orthodox Christians to use the title 'messiah worshippers'. So if Marcion had appropriated the name of Christian, it seems not unlikely that it was he who brought the faith to Edessa – which would date its arrival to c. 150. It was well established by the beginning of the third century. In 210, says the Chronicle of Edessa, the river which ran through the city burst its banks, killing some two thousand inhabitants. It is recorded as having flooded the church of the Christians.

By that time there was a group gathered round the poet Bardesanes. His moderation was totally at odds with the fanaticism of the Marcionites. He composed his own liturgies, and used a special version of the Scriptures. He also wrote hymns, one hundred and fifty of them, perhaps in conscious imitation of the psalms. Only fragments of these now remain, embedded as quotations in the writings of others whom the Christian Church regarded as orthodox. Bardesanes' own views did not win approval.

So there were at least three Christian, or quasi-Christian, groups in Edessa competing for the religious allegiance of its citizens. In 313 Bishop

126

Qona, so the Edessan Chronicle records, put down the foundation of his cathedral. His name stands at the beginning of a thousand-year line of bishops. If this community of his was threatened by Marcionites on the one hand and Bardesanites on the other, it would not be surprising if he had been tempted to construct a history of his flock which reached back to the time of Jesus himself, thereby establishing unimpeachable apostolic credentials. It was this story which within a dozen years or so, filled out with a wealth of circumstantial detail, reached the ears of Eusebius.

The picture in Edessa is therefore anything but that of a straightforward expansion of orthodox Christianity. Once again there are several competing groups, of which the Marcionites were the most visibly prominent.

MARCION AND THE PROBLEM OF THE CANON

Marcion was born c. AD 70, and seems to have died c. 155. He came from the city of Sinope in the Roman province of Pontus. It is clear from the first letter of Peter that there was a Christian community in Pontus, and the younger Pliny who was proconsul, or governor, of the province c. 111–112 wrote to the Emperor Trajan concerning the life of the Christian community. He describes the men and women of every class and age who

127

assembled before sunrise to sing a hymn to Christ as God, and to bind themselves by oath to high standards of moral behaviour.

That Marcionism had spread far is evident enough. Opposition to his teaching was widespread. He was opposed by Polycarp, as has been seen, and there are good grounds for supposing that the Pastoral Epistles were directed against him. From Polycarp's letter to the Philippians, for instance, it emerges that there is a false teacher claiming to be teaching in the name of Paul. He has persuaded some that marriage is evil. He does not believe that the prophecies of the Old Testament refer to Jesus, nor that the God who raised Jesus from the dead is judge of the world.

According to Marcion there were two gods. The God who occurred in the Old Testament was a minor deity, though he was the creator. The God of Jesus, on the other hand, was a higher God than the Old Testament one. He wants those who believe in him to be saved, and to be released from the law of sin and death, but because he is not the creator and the world does not belong to him, he has no control over human beings. Marcion did not believe, however, that the lesser of the two gods was in any way an offshoot, or 'emanation', from the greater. His theories did not spring out of a philosophical system. The problem was Paul.

Marcion had read the letters of Paul, and had taken them very seriously indeed. He had read, for instance, that false preachers were subverting the gospel which Paul was proclaiming. In Marcion's view, that gospel was that Jesus had come to free people from slavery to the Law, and the Law was enshrined in the Old Testament. This had been entirely replaced by a new law, contained in the letters of Paul.

The Gospel texts, of course, made frequent links between Old Testament prophecies and the coming of Jesus. In Marcion's view they were in error in so far as they did so. He would accept only one of the four Gospels, that of Luke, and then only after considerable editorial emendation. Marcion's account of Jesus' teaching was derived from the letters of Paul, which Marcion ordered in his own particular way, giving priority to the Letter to the Galatians.

Marcion developed an alternative Church. Its services were so like the 'orthodox' ones that people might have been misled into attending the wrong one. His ecclesiastical structures, likewise, had many similarities, with bishops, presbyters, deacons and deaconesses. He did not permit women priests, but allowed women teachers and prophets to function – both these being offices in the Church of his day. It may be that he was simply reproducing the greater freedom which at this time was accorded to women by the Jewish communities of inner Anatolia, from which he came. The stricter, orthodox tradition would have none of it. In the Pastoral Epistles is a response which is direct and condemnatory: 'During instruction, a woman should be quiet and respectful. I am not giving permission for a woman to teach or to tell a man what to do. A woman ought not to speak, because Adam was formed first and Eve afterwards.' (1 Tim 2:11–13).

The same epistle recommended marriage for everyone, from bishops to widows, in opposition to a sect which forbade marriage. Sexual abstinence was another facet of Paul's teaching which Marcion took over and emphasized. But Marcion's reaction to sex was almost pathological. 'Language about sex', remarks Professor Henry Chadwick in his introduction to *Alexandrian Christianity*, 'and the process of reproduction shows him to have been a psychopathic case; the contemplation of sex overwhelmed him with a sense of nausea.' This attitude, together with their severe dietary laws, gave his followers a reputation for the strictest asceticism.

It is not wholly clear why Marcion chose to place so much stress on the writings of Paul to the exclusion of other works. He may have been aware of how little Paul's letters were in use in the Churches. The second letter of Peter describes Paul's teachings as 'hard to understand' (2 Pt 3:16), and the letter of James, which defends the value of good works, can be seen as a rejection of Paul's teaching on the supreme value of faith. Justin, a convert to Christianity, and a philosopher, was the first major defender, or

The Epistles of Paul appear here on a third-century papyrus fragment.

'apologist', of Christianity to the pagan world. He makes no use of Paul's correspondence. It may be that it was Marcion who, by his heretical use of the Pauline epistles, brought them to centre stage and thereby ensured their survival. And that raises the whole problem of the 'canon'.

'Canon' is a Greek word which originally meant 'reed', and came to mean 'measuring rod'. In Christian circles it was applied to the norm, or

129

rule, of faith. It was only in the fourth century, when a list of 'canonical books' was being drawn up, that the term 'canon' came to be applied to the books which contained the rule of faith, the Scriptures. In some special sense, the writings included in the canonical lists were regarded as the revelation of God to human beings. But it was not easy to determine which of the many early Christian writings were to be included in the lists.

Why, for example, were four Gospels included, and not just one? Why was the Apocalypse of John included, admittedly after some hesitation, and not the Apocalypse of Peter? The Petrine Apocalypse was certainly an early Christian book, and it was still being used in the liturgy of Good Friday in Palestine as late as the fifth century. So it was not simply a matter of chronology. The Church of Alexandria, for example, for a long time considered the letters known as 1 and 2 Clement to be canonical. They date from before the composition of 2 Peter, yet they were excluded from the canon.

The final form of the canon was achieved only after a long period of evolution, but by 170, when Melito of Sardis wrote of the 'old' Testament, thereby implying the existence of a new one, clearly the idea of a Christian set of Scriptures to set against the Jewish one had been reached. The expression 'the New Testament' was used for the first time some thirty years later, by the African theologian Tertullian.

The evolution of the canon cannot now be determined with certainty. In any case, its final form lies outside the period covered by this book. It seems very likely, however, that the radical views of Marcion, an unorthodox Christian evangelist from Sinope in the province of Pontus in Asia Minor, notably contributed to the high status which the letters of Paul have been accorded in the Church's canon of Scripture.

There is, however, a further question. Granted that Marcion's own understanding of what was, and what was not, part of the inspired word of God was unacceptable to the Church at large, why should it be presumed that inspiration had ceased? For the most part Christians were satisfied with the knowledge of Jesus and his teachings contained in the Gospels and the other writings included in the New Testament. That was the tradition they had received. But for some the tradition was not enough, and chief among those was Montanus.

MONTANUS AND THE PROPHETESSES

Montanus came from the village of Ardabau on the border between Phrygia and Mysia. He was baptized in about 170, and shortly afterwards began to prophesy. He was seized in ecstasy, began babbling in a strange language, and proclaimed that he was the spokesman for the Holy Spirit. Eusebius, who records the story from what he claimed as a contemporary source, attributed it all to the devil. And after his success with Montanus, the devil went on to take possession of two women, Priscilla and Maximilla.

130

Belief in the 'New Prophecy', as it quickly came to be known, spread rapidly through Asia and into Africa. In Africa it won its most distinguished convert in Tertullian, a Carthaginian who was one of Christianity's foremost defenders. Tertullian claimed that even the bishop of Rome, Zephyrinus, had been on the point of recognizing the prophecies of Montanus and his prophetesses as genuine expressions of the Holy Spirit, but had held back at the last minute.

The prominent role played by women in the New Prophecy was one of the major factors in turning ecclesiastical authority against it, as it had been in the case of the Marcionites. Reaction to the movement was so strong that it affected Christian attitudes to the Holy Spirit. Irenaeus in Lyons had to issue a stern rebuke against those who wanted to reject the whole of the Gospel of John because it spoke of the sending of the Spirit.

Official disapproval was slow to spread, however. In Carthage at the beginning of the third century it was still perfectly possible to adhere to Montanism without abandoning orthodox Christianity. The story of the martyrdom of Felicity and Perpetua (p. 157) makes that clear: Perpetua pleaded that the New Prophecies be read in church alongside the traditional scriptures.

Though Montanist practice may not have been entirely orthodox, at least at first it was orthodox in its beliefs. Yet the more traditional Christians did their best to denigrate it. Eusebius quotes Apollonius (who was writing, or so he said, only thirty-nine years after Montanus had started prophesying) as pouring scorn upon his claim to the title of prophet:

> Does a prophet dye his hair? Does a prophet paint his eyelids? Does a prophet love ornaments? Does a prophet visit the gaming tables and play dice? Does a prophet do business as a moneylender? Let [the Montanists] say plainly whether these things are permissible or not, and I will prove that they have been going on in their circles. (*History of the Church*, 5:18)

Montanism revived itinerant, charismatic preaching in the Church, which a century earlier would have been commonplace, especially in Asia Minor. It is not so easy to account for the revival of this form of Christianity in the second half of the second century of the Christian era. A clue may perhaps be found in local events at the time.

Disease seems to have been brought to the coastal area in particular by Roman troops returning to celebrate in Rome after a victory at Seleucia on the Tigris. Then the region was rocked by a series of earthquakes. It would have been easy to believe that these disasters, together with the renewed persecution, presaged the end of the world: there was a strong eschatological side to Montanism. Montanists believed that the New Jerusalem was shortly to arrive, and that it would be established at the village of Pepuza, some fifteen miles east of Philadelphia. Maximilla was bold enough to claim that 'After me no other prophet will come, but there will be a

Prophecy began to fade from Christianity by the end of the first century, but was revived by Montanus. The 'prophet' above is from the Jewish synagogue at Dura Europos.

consummation of all things.' Of the three prophets, she was the first to die. Yet the world did not end, which must have shaken the faith of some.

Most of the Montanists, however, went on with their practice of strict fasting and observance of celibacy as a preparation for the coming of the New Jerusalem. Their severe asceticism was an excellent preparation for martyrdom and, during the reign of the Emperor Marcus Aurelius (161–180), persecution broke out again in Asia Minor. Tertullian believed that only those who had undergone the strict discipline of Montanist asceticism could endure persecution.

Yet Tertullian, its greatest apologist, in some ways tamed Montanism. He denied women the prominent role they had hitherto held in the movement. They were to have no priestly function, they were not to teach nor to speak in divine service. Any utterances they might wish to make had to be made in private. And Tertullian played down talk of the coming of a New Jerusalem.

Montanism was a dangerous threat to an increasingly settled Church, and a threat all the more severe because it was not quite clear that the movement was unorthodox. As has been pointed out, the Montanist style of life and the role it gave to women when it began would not have been out of place a century or so earlier in Asia Minor. Yet it seems that the first gatherings of bishops in formal meetings, or synods, were to discuss what to do about this new movement.

Montanism arose in a remote community, one not wholly up to date with developments in the Church elsewhere. As the second century wore on, women seem to have been increasingly subordinated to men within the Church. Montanism restored them to something like the position they had held in the first-century Church. It also offered them virginity or celibacy as a way of life, which was another means of escape from male domination. Opponents of the New Prophecy were outraged because Priscilla promptly rejected her husband after the Spirit had descended upon her.

The rejection of marriage was a clear challenge to the traditional structure of society. A growing, and increasingly respectable, Church was unhappy that such a clash should develop; yet voluntary celibacy was an option offered to Christians in the teachings of Jesus. There was a tension in the Church between the ideals it proclaimed and the compromise it reached with the world in which it existed. As will be seen later, voluntary celibacy began to flourish in the Church only when society had a need for it.

MANI AND THE LURE OF GNOSTICISM

Gnosticism is one of the most complex subjects in the history of early Christianity. Like Marcionism and Montanism, it seems to have arisen in Asia Minor. There are some historians of this period who believe that Marcion was a Gnostic, though there is really no reason to suppose it.

Basilides, however, certainly was, and he was a Syrian. His writings included twenty-four books of commentary on the Gospels and a collection of prayers and hymns, but all were destroyed by the orthodox. What little of his work survives does so only because his adversaries quoted it.

Rather more is known about Basilides' younger contemporary, Valentinus. He was an Egyptian, and started teaching in Alexandria. About the year 135 he went to Rome to set up a school, where for some time he seems to have been a highly respected member of the Christian community. Thirty years or so later he returned to Alexandria. His teachings can be reconstructed from the writings of his disciples, and Irenaeus mentions that, among other books, he wrote a work entitled *The Gospel of Truth*. A book of that name, the contents of which coincide with Valentinus' views, was discovered with other texts at Nag Hammadi in Egypt in 1945.

In all, thirteen papyri were found, containing forty-nine Gnostic books. They were written in Coptic, the language of the native population of Egypt from the third century of the Christian era, and their discovery was as important as that of the Dead Sea Scrolls. Yet, as Professor Drijver has said in an article on 'The Origins of Gnosticism':

> It would seem that in a hundred and fifty years the problem of the origin of Gnosticism has not advanced one step towards a solution, in spite of an immense increase of sources and a correspondingly increased stream of publications, the result of a great deal of scholarly research. (*East of Antioch*, XV, p. 349)

Perhaps the only thing to be said about its origins is that, as an identifiable collection of ideas, it does not seem to have existed before the Christian era.

It is difficult to give Gnosticism a precise definition. It is used of a number of schools of thought, which differed from one another quite considerably. The common element, however, was that human beings might achieve redemption, leading ultimately to union with God, through possession of gnosis (*gnosis* is a Greek word meaning knowledge). This gnosis might come through secret knowledge given to the apostles and handed on to a chosen few, or it might come through a direct revelation by God to the founder of a particular sect.

There is, therefore, nothing specifically Christian in Gnosticism itself, though clearly there was in the form it took under Basilides, Valentinus and others. Their views were attacked by more orthodox churchmen, but it is difficult to gauge the degree of influence they had. The most influential Gnostic was not a Christian at all, though for a time his teachings won over St Augustine, one of Christianity's most profound thinkers. His name was Mani, and the sect he founded was known as the Manichees.

Although next to nothing is known of the lives of Basilides and Valentinus, a great deal is known about Mani. He was probably born on 14 April 216 near Seleucia-Ctesiphon, the Persian capital beside the Tigris, in southern Mesopotamia. His parents were said to have been of noble birth, and his father's name was Pattak.

Pattak joined a Gnostic baptist sect called the Elkesaites, who had emerged east of the river Jordan in about the year 100. Mani seems also to have been a member, for when he was about twelve years old he had a vision he later took to be a revelation of the Spirit or Paraclete, and as a sign that he had to reform the Elkesaites. But the Elkesaites resisted reform, so Mani formed a breakaway group which, after a second vision on 19 April 240, he led to the capital city, where he founded a community.

This community sent missionaries to the West, while Mani himself went to India. On his return he won the support of the Persian king, who possibly saw in the Manichees an alternative to the Zoroastrian religion, with its priests, the magi, which was a dominant force in the kingdom. Unhappily for Mani, the old religion proved too strong. He was thrown into prison, perhaps towards the end of 275, and died there in the spring of the following year.

Manicheism did not die with him. From Syria it spread into northern Arabia and North Africa. It reached Palestine and went on into Armenia, then to Rome, from where it spread to Gaul (the Roman province roughly equal to France) and Spain. In the West it survived until the sixth century, though it has regularly reappeared in one form or another, but in the East it lasted until the Mongolian invasions of the thirteenth century. In the Far East, in China and Tibet, it may have lingered on until the seventeenth century.

Manicheism seems to have been specially devised to take on the complexion of the religion amid which it found itself. In Persia it was closely linked to Zoroastrianism. In the West it was regarded as a deviation from Christianity, and Mani was thought a heretic by the Christians.

It was also a highly literary faith. Mani insisted that his teachings be put down in writing to prevent falsification, and was most particular about the style of calligraphy and of decoration employed in the texts. In the course of the past century a great many Manichaean tracts have been unearthed, some of them dating from no more than a century and a half after Mani's death.

Finally, it was a profoundly spiritual creed. In many places, though not so much in the West, its devotees lived in monasteries, the easier to maintain their strict form of diet. All of these elements added to Manicheism's popularity, but its success ultimately depended on being able to offer a convincing explanation of the universe and of people's role in the universe, and to hold out an assurance of salvation.

According to Mani, there were two equal and opposing gods, the 'king of the paradise of light', and the god of darkness and of matter. The two had engaged in a battle, during which some particles of the good god had become embedded in the being of the evil one. Human beings could liberate these particles from the material universe. Redemption consisted in the 'gnosis' of how to be actively involved in the process of liberating the being (light) of the good god from entanglement in matter. Manichees were to avoid tormenting light any longer. They were to help purify it, and lead it back to its source.

Mani believed that many Old Testament characters had been messengers of this gnosis, and so had Buddha, Zoroaster, Jesus and Paul. But of these messengers, Mani himself was the last. He was the messiah, the fulfilment of all religion.

The elect were the core of Mani's church. These were people who had removed themselves as far as practicable from temptation. They ate no meat and drank no wine. They fasted often. They had to avoid damaging nature – even to look at plants was to do them harm. They refrained from sexual intercourse, and ate only that vegetarian food which was judged to have a high quantity of light particles embedded in it, so as to free as much as possible of the good god's being.

It is hardly surprising that the number of the elect was fairly small. There were women among them, but they could not hold office in a church whose structures were to some extent modelled on those of Christianity. The strict asceticism of the elect made a considerable impression on their contemporaries. Many converts were gained through the assurance of salvation offered by Manicheism, and by its mystical explanation of the universe. Augustine was attracted to it for a time because it seemed to provide a solution to the problem of evil.

Though Manicheism was not strictly speaking a Christian sect, to many in the third century and early fourth it seemed so. It had something in common with those versions of Christianity, also stemming from Syria and Asia Minor, which put their trust in visions, prophecies and a severely ascetic discipline. It had little in common with the form of Christianity which was gradually establishing itself as the norm.

The Marcionites, the Montanists, the Manichees all provided a rather more lively, and more demanding, alternative to this safe, 'establishment' Christianity. Yet the first two, at least, were basically conservative sects, preserving something of the charismatic and prophetic experience of the first century into a second-century Church which had outgrown it. There was another form of conservatism, however, which arose in Asia Minor as a challenge to the practice of the West, though this time it was not so destructive of the unity of the Church.

PROBLEMS WITH THE CALENDAR
When Anicetus was bishop of Rome (c. 155–166), Polycarp of Smyrna visited the imperial capital. The story is recounted by Irenaeus, whom Eusebius quotes in his *History of the Church*.

Although Irenaeus does not exactly say so, Polycarp's visit appears to

A fragment of Manichaean text showing scribes – the Manichees were concerned with the quality of handwriting – and behind them fruit trees. As far as possible Manichees ate only those things which released imprisoned light particles so they could return to the god from whom they had come. Fruit was chief amongst such foods.

137

have been to settle a disagreement between the local Church, ruled by Anicetus, and immigrants into Rome from Asia Minor. The nub of the dispute was a divergence of opinion on the date upon which Easter should be celebrated.

The argument was this: should Easter, the feast of Jesus' resurrection, be marked by a service beginning on 14 Nisan (the first month of the Jewish year, roughly coinciding with April) and ending in the early morning of 15 Nisan with the celebration of the Eucharist? Or should it be celebrated on the Sunday following 14 Nisan, which was the Roman practice?

According to the Jewish calendar, 14 Nisan was the feast of the Passover. To celebrate Easter on that day was to link the Christian feast directly to the Jewish one, and this, one must presume, was the older practice. It was followed in Asia Minor and by those who had come to Rome from that part of the Empire. They looked to Polycarp for leadership. The later tradition, which moved the feast of Easter to the Sunday following 14 Nisan, separated it from the Passover but placed it on the day on which, week by week, Christians then celebrated Jesus' resurrection. According to the letter of Irenaeus just quoted, the newer practice had been followed in Rome ever since the time of Xystus, that is the second decade of the second century.

Polycarp and Anicetus could not agree, but the outcome was a happy one:

Anicetus could not persuade Polycarp not to keep the day, since he had always kept it with John the disciple of our Lord and the other apostles with whom he had been familiar; nor did Polycarp persuade Anicetus to keep it: Anicetus said he must stick to the practice of the presbyters before him. Though the position was such, they remained in communion with each other, and in church Anicetus made way for Polycarp to celebrate the eucharist – out of respect obviously. They parted company in peace, and the whole Church was at peace, both those who kept the day and those who did not. (History of the Church, 5:24)

The peace, unfortunately, did not last. Victor, who was bishop of Rome in the last decade of the second century, made another attempt to bring the Asians into line with Roman practice. This time it brought a letter of protest from Bishop Polycrates of Ephesus, which Eusebius has also preserved. It seems that Victor was trying to bring uniformity of practice not only in his own Church but throughout the Empire. He had synods called to discuss the issue. There was one in Pontus, another in Palestine, and a third in Osroene. The majority agreed with Victor until he tried to cut off those Asian Churches which insisted on maintaining their old tradition. Then he was met with a storm of protest.

Rome eventually had its way. The celebration of Easter on a Sunday was made obligatory by the synod of Arles in 314. The Quartodecimans (from

138

the Latin for fourteen) those who celebrated on the fourteenth day, were expelled from the Church at the Council of Nicea, thus achieving in 325 what Victor had tried to do in 195.

So strong were the feelings that one suspects there was rather more to the story than a disagreement over dates. Polycrates, in the letter mentioned above, cites Melito of Sardis as an authority on the Quartodeciman side. Melito 'lived entirely in the Holy Spirit', he wrote, 'and lies in Sardis waiting for the visitation from heaven when he shall rise from the dead' (5:24). Very little is known about Melito. From the letter there is a clear inference that he was a prophet, and there is a somewhat less clear inference – though Eusebius drew it – that he was bishop of Sardis. He probably died c. 190. Polycrates implies he had died fairly recently, and the letter was written to Victor c. 195.

Among the fragments of writing attributed to Melito are the words 'Under Servillius Paulus, proconsul of Asia, at a time when Sagris bore witness, there was a great dispute at Laodicea about the Pascha'. The passage implies that even within Asia Minor there was an argument about the 'Pascha', quite apart from the dispute between Asia Minor and Rome. But if so, what was the cause of the dispute?

Much turns on the meaning of the word 'Pascha'. It can, of course, mean Easter, but it can also mean the Jewish Passover. It has been suggested that the more conservative Quartodecimans were marking Easter with a traditional celebratory meal in the style of a Passover meal. If so, such behaviour was dangerous. It was likely to draw the unwelcome attention of the Roman authorities. Regular public meals were illegal, and the Church had already abandoned them.

So there may have been two quite distinct disputes involved in the Quartodeciman controversy: one about the precise date of the Easter celebration, the other about the manner of celebrating it. Both date and style, however, linked the Quartodecimans with the practices of the Jews. They had to rely upon the Jews for computation of the date of what had become a Christian festival.

The impression left by the arguments over the date of Easter as they are recorded by Eusebius is of the powerful hold which tradition and religious conservatism had, especially over the Quartodecimans. The Christians of Asia Minor could claim to have been the first people outside Palestine to have heard, and responded to, the gospel of Jesus. But, perhaps more important, is the fact that wrapped up within the controversy was a Christian search for identity: an identity which was distinct from that of Judaism, for Sunday rather than Saturday became the Sabbath; an identity tied to precise formulations of calendars and sacred times by those who opted for 14 Nisan.

The Churches of Asia Minor had retained something of their prophetic–charismatic origins, and charismatics tend to conservatism, perhaps as a

139

foil for the freedom of the Spirit which they claim to enjoy – or perhaps as a form of insurance. Whatever lay behind the quarrel, which for the first time pitted one part of the Church against another, one suspects it was not wholly rational.

DURA EUROPOS

A company of British soldiers patrolling the banks of the Euphrates in the aftermath of the First World War made camp in a ruined fortress near the village of Salihiyeh in the Syrian desert. A gust of wind blew sand from part of the ruins, exposing life-sized murals. As a Greek inscription was later to reveal, 'the troops had camped upon the abandoned settlement of Dura. A first-century reference to it names the city 'Dura, called Europos by the Greeks'.

Dura – the word means 'fortress' – was most probably founded by one of the generals of Alexander the Great. The Greek origins of the city are evident in its ground-plan, laid out in accordance with the Hellenistic grid

Below, the ruins of Dura Europos with, in the background, the Euphrates river and left, the splendidly rich interior of the Jewish synagogue which was found there. The decoration of the Torah niche is relatively restrained, but the surrounding walls mingle biblical scenes with pagan imagery. The hand of God appears in the upper right hand corner of the niche – the earliest known representation of what became a common iconographic device.

pattern. It was settled first by Macedonian and Greek veteran soldiers, then, in or about 113 BC, Parthians from across the Euphrates marched peacefully into Dura to ally themselves with its citizens against the aggrandisement of Rome. There followed a long period of prosperity, but in AD 164 the city fell to the Roman legions. They held it for less than a century. In 253 Dura was captured once again, this time by the Persian King Shapur I who, three years later and for reasons which now can only be guessed at, laid it waste.

There was nothing particularly spectacular about the rise and fall of Dura. Over the centuries its fate was no doubt mirrored by other cities which still lie hidden beneath the sands. What marked out this discovery on the distant banks of the Euphrates was the wealth of finds within the ancient walls. Not only was there great variety in the buildings revealed as season followed season of excavation – the Mithraic temple, the citadel, the splendid temple celebrating the gods of nearby Palmyra – but at least two of the finds were unique. The first was a magnificently decorated synagogue. It was as if, wrote one of the archaeologists long afterwards, 'Aladdin's lamp had been rubbed, and suddenly from the dry, brown, bare desert, had appeared paintings, not just one nor a panel nor a wall, but a whole building of scene after scene, all drawn from the Old Testament in a way never dreamed of before.' (Hopkins, *The Discovery of Dura Europos*).

So unusual were the pictorial representations on the synagogue's walls that some experts still believe the building to have been a Christian meeting-place. But the arguments against that are strong – and none more so than that a few doors away and still in the same part of town, a private house was uncovered which at some point in the history of Dura (probably AD 232) had been converted into a Christian church. It is the earliest ever to have been found.

Presumably the Christian community was destroyed, along with the city, twenty-four years later, so occupancy of the house-turned-church was short-lived. What little can be gathered about the community which worshipped there suggests that the majority of its members were natives of the city, though the evidence is very slight – just five inscriptions which contain names. Two of the names seem to have been those of Roman soldiers who came to Dura when the garrison was strengthened in a vain attempt to repel the Persian threat. At least one cohort which had been part of the garrison of Jerusalem after the war of AD 66–70 later came to Dura.

Among the graffiti on the walls of the church is the Syriac alphabet, the language which locals might have been expected to speak. But there are also Greek letters and Latin names. A fragment of a harmony of the Gospels composed by the Christian Syriac author Tatian was found at Dura – but in Greek rather than in the local dialect. It may be that the community at Dura, and other known concentrations of Christians in the region, came

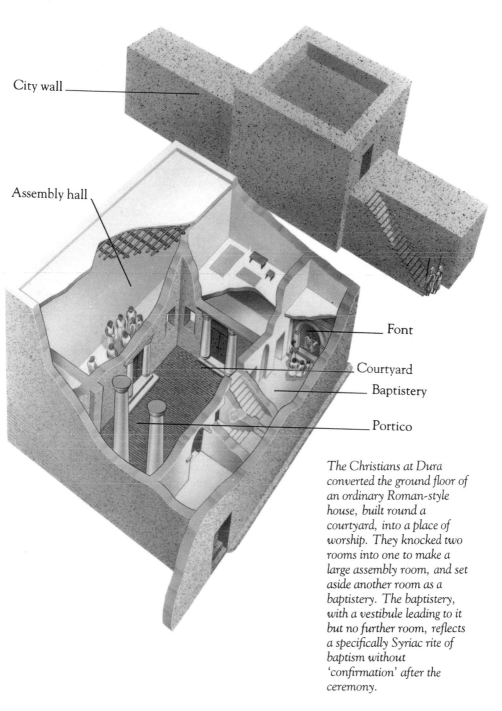

City wall

Assembly hall

Font

Courtyard

Baptistery

Portico

The Christians at Dura converted the ground floor of an ordinary Roman-style house, built round a courtyard, into a place of worship. They knocked two rooms into one to make a large assembly room, and set aside another room as a baptistery. The baptistery, with a vestibule leading to it but no further room, reflects a specifically Syriac rite of baptism without 'confirmation' after the ceremony.

into existence fairly independently of one another. If that is so, they were associated not with some major centre but with important highways along which passed both merchants and armies, some speaking Syriac, others Greek or Latin, and all bringing with them their own traditions.

Top, the baptistery in the Christian building at Dura. The font was located in the niche, and a convert would have had to step up into it. The decoration on the adjacent wall is much more modest than that of the synagogue. Bottom, a cameo of the brilliantly successful Shapur, self-styled king of kings of Iran and Non-Iran, who destroyed Dura Europos.

One caravan route passed through Antioch, crossed the Euphrates at Melitene (where the passage was guarded by Roman legionaries) and went on to Adiabene on the northern Tigris. A more southerly route out of Antioch crossed the Euphrates at Zeugma. From there it was possible to travel to the great crossroads at Edessa and so on to Singara. Yet another road linked Damascus and Emesa with Palmyra, home base for many of the troops in the Dura garrison, and ran on to Dura itself. From there the road turned south-east, following the Euphrates down to the Persian Gulf. Before the arrival of Rome this exposed route had been guarded by a Palmyran camel-corps, later to become Roman auxiliaries; from AD 165 the road was protected by legionaries. An up-turn in Dura's fortunes can be dated from that time.

The improvement in Dura's economy did not, however, greatly benefit the Christian community. It is true that, by the fourth decade of the third century, the Christians had acquired a fairly substantial house, and had adapted it for their use by knocking two of the rooms into one, thereby creating an assembly hall large enough to hold sixty or seventy people installing benches around the walls and erecting a baptistery. But the murals were modest both in conception and execution. The worshipping community, certainly in comparison with its Jewish neighbour, seems to have been neither large nor wealthy.

Nevertheless, a Christian community there was – and it had a building dedicated to, and adapted for, its own liturgy. The house could not have been a secret place. Ownership by the community, rather than by a single rich patron, required the approval of the city authorities. Perhaps by the end of the second century, and certainly in the early years of the third, a small Christian community in this remote city on the distant frontiers of the Empire had the confidence to make preparations for the future. It was not to know that, like Dura itself, it had no future.

Elsewhere in this Syriac-speaking area, however, in Adiabene and at Edessa, Christianity survived and flourished. In Adiabene Christianity's distinctive style probably owed much to a form of pre-rabbinic Judaism. Out of this a Christian sect slowly emerged, dragging with it many early Jewish traditions. Edessa, as has been said, was more of a crossroads. From a great variety of influences, and from a mish-mash of competing sects, 'normative' Christianity developed, as one scholar has described it, 'as a sort of precipitate in a cloudy situation'.

If there is a common factor in the growth of Christianity in these diverse locations throughout Syria, it is the network of roads. Along these, ideas travelled as readily as did soldiers or merchants. The similarities between the various types of Christianity were little more striking than the differences. Even in those parts of the world geographically close to Jesus' birthplace, Christian teaching had not yet settled down into Church dogma.

145

7

THE NORTH AFRICAN EXPERIENCE

In 332 BC Alexander the Great conquered Palestine, and immediately marched on Egypt, which he took from the Persians. At the mouth of the Nile he ordered the building of the greatest of several cities to bear his name – Alexandria.

After Alexander's death Egypt was taken over by one of his generals, Ptolemy Lagos, and under the Ptolemaic dynasty the city flourished not

The city of Alexandria portrayed in this mosaic as 'mistress of the seas'. The city was built as a major sea-port, to accommodate a large fleet.

146

A copy of a wall painting from Karanis in Egypt, showing local deities both standing and enthroned.

only as a commercial centre but as a centre of learning. Within it Alexandria housed three very different groups of people. The Jewish community, inhabiting the north-east of the city close to its great library and 'university', was larger than that in Jerusalem itself. The Jews, however, vied for second place in importance with the Egyptians, the original inhabitants, for under the Ptolemies it was the Greek community which was the most privileged.

When Alexandria came under the control of Rome in 30 BC positions were somewhat reversed for, much to the irritation of the Greek community, the Jews enjoyed a special relationship with the new rulers. An 'intermittent civil war', as one scholar has described it, developed between the Greeks and the Jews. There was a massacre of Jews in AD 38, when King Agrippa visited the city, and another in 41. In 66 the Jews of Alexandria rose in sympathy with the Jews of Palestine against Roman rule: Josephus says that 50,000 people lost their lives. Rebellion broke out again in AD 115 while the Emperor Trajan was occupied in Mesopotamia. A year later the rebellion had become outright war. It was put down, finally, by the Emperor Hadrian in 117, and this time the Jewish community in Alexandria was all but wiped out.

Christians in the city could not have escaped the consequences of these events, but what happened to them is a matter of much debate. Until the time of Clement, head of the Christian school in Alexandria, very little is known about the Christians, although we know that a community existed.

The earliest Christians mentioned, by Clement among others, were Basilides, who taught in Alexandria in the second quarter of the second century, and his younger contemporary Valentinus, who went off to Rome. Both of these, however, were Gnostics and this has encouraged the view, espoused by Walter Bauer, that the first Christianity in Alexandria was unorthodox. Orthodoxy, on this hypothesis, was a later development.

But Bauer's views have recently come under fire. From the evidence of the style of manuscripts which survive, the scholar Dr Colin Roberts has argued convincingly for an early, orthodox Christianity in Alexandria, dependent in its earliest years upon Jerusalem but increasingly coming under the influence of the Church in Rome. Nothing is heard of it, he has suggested, because it had little reason to distinguish itself from Judaism until, under Trajan and Hadrian, the Jews were thoroughly crushed. It is at that point that Christianity begins to appear, and the evidence of the manuscripts does not suggest that it was confined to Alexandria, or that it was particularly Gnostic in tendency. When a clearer picture does begin to appear, at the time of Clement, Christianity is 'orthodox' – after a fashion.

CLEMENT AND THE SCHOOLS

Clement emerges out of the mists of early Alexandrian Christianity, but he does not emerge very far. He must have been born, of pagan parents, c. 150. The place of his birth is unknown, though it may have been Athens. Like many of his contemporaries he travelled extensively in pursuit of learning. At the beginning of his book *Miscellanies* he describes his tutors:

> One was an Ionian who taught in Greece. Others were in southern Italy; one of them came from Coele-Syria, the other from Egypt. Others lived in the east; one of these was an Assyrian, one a Palestinian Hebrew. After I met the last (who was the first of them in importance) I abandoned further search, having discovered him hiding in Egypt. A truly Sicilian bee, he drew honey from the flowers in the meadows of the apostles and prophets, and implanted in the souls of his pupils pure knowledge. (Quoted by H. Chadwick, *Alexandrian Christianity*, p. 16)

Sicilian bees were proverbially famous for their honey: Clement was describing a paragon. The name of this paragon was Pantaenus. Pantaenus also earns great praise from Eusebius, who describes him as:

> one of the most eminent teachers of his day, being an ornament of the philosophic system known as stoicism. He is said to have shown such warm-hearted enthusiasm for the divine word that he was appointed to preach the gospel of Christ to the peoples of the East, and travelled as far as India...After doing great work he ended up as principal of the academy in Alexandria, where both orally and in writing he revealed the treasures of the divine doctrine. (*History of the Church*, 3:13)

It is not impossible that Pantaenus did indeed travel to India: his pupil Clement is the first Christian to mention Buddha.

The 'academy', or catechetical school, seems to have been in existence before the time of Pantaenus, though he is the first principal of it whose name has survived. He was in charge during the later part of the second century, though the dates are uncertain. Dr Roberts has suggested that, as a Stoic philosopher, his outlook on life would have been very much at odds with that of the Gnostics, and that he may therefore have been chosen to head the school to counteract the earlier influence of Basilides and Valentinus. What is known of the organization of the school, from a slightly later period, indicates that it reflected the curriculum of academies of pagan philosophy. Pupils began with grammar and proceeded, via rhetoric and geometry, to music and astronomy. From there they moved on to study the ancient philosophers – excluding atheistic ones – and only after this preparation were they allowed to tackle the Scriptures.

It was probably in about 180 that Clement became Pantaenus' pupil, and not long afterwards that he succeeded him as head of the school. He held the post for some twenty years until, in 202, persecution forced him to flee from Alexandria. He is thought to have died in about 215.

Eusebius claimed that Pantaenus wrote as well as taught in the school, but none of his writings remain. Of Clement's books, on the other hand, several have survived. His *Miscellanies*, already mentioned, are a collection of disparate reflections; there are also *The Exhortation to the Greeks*, *The Tutor* and a number of fragments quoted in the works of others. Of particular interest is *Which Rich Man Will Be Saved?*, which represents an attempt to reassure wealthy Christians – implying there must have been a good number of them – that what Jesus had to say about giving up everything in order to follow him required rich people merely to have a right attitude to their possessions, and not positively to abandon them.

Clement's writings throw light on other aspects of Christian life at Alexandria and, one may suppose, elsewhere as well. For example, he was in favour of marriage – in theory, at least. He believed that even St Paul was married and that 'the only reason why he did not take [his wife] about with him was that it would have been an inconvenience for his ministry.' The other apostles, meanwhile:

> took their wives with them not as women with whom they had marriage relations, but as sisters, that they might be their fellow-ministers in dealing with house-wives. It was through them that the Lord's teaching penetrated also the women's quarters without any scandal being aroused. (*Miscellanies*, 3:53)

Clement's approval of marriage is half-hearted: sexual abstinence within marriage clearly makes it more acceptable, in his opinion.

There were, on the other hand, the Carpocratians. When these gather for feasts, alleges Clement, they:

overturn the lamps and so extinguish the light that the shame of their adulterous 'righteousness' is hidden, and they have intercourse where they will and with whom they will. They think [he continues] that wives should be common property. Through them the worst calumny has become current against the Christian name. (*Miscellanies*, 3:10, 5)

The moral standards of mainline Christianity would have rejected the behaviour illustrated in this fresco from Pompeii, but some fringe groups indulged in orgiastic practices.

The charge of moral laxity was commonly made against Christians by pagan authors. That licentiousness arose as a problem early on is clear enough: it was attacked in the Letter of Jude and in 2 Peter. The belief that Christians, having been saved by Christ, were then free to do as they wished, remained a problem well into the fourth century. It was difficult for Christians to refute the charge that they were licentious when pagans could point to the example of the Carpocratians and others.

Another problem faced by Clement was the belief of many in the

Alexandrian Church that it was unnecessary to acquire learning. All that was needed was simple faith. For the Christians of Alexandria such an attitude was especially dangerous. The city had a long, and strong, philosophical tradition. If the Christian community showed itself anti-intellectual, not only would it lack credibility, it would fail to win the allegiance of learned men and women, who might be attracted instead to the more philosophically sounding Gnostic doctrines. Clement therefore made it his business to show that the Christian faith was rooted in learning.

Clement himself, of course, was not from Alexandria, but he seems to have absorbed its culture remarkably quickly. From Philo he learned that philosophy was a preparation for theology, and that both the Old Testament and Greek philosophy – which he understood well enough – were meant to bring men and women to Jesus. He was a layman, one of the first teachers of Christian philosophy, and the Alexandrian Church revered him for that. He was awarded the title 'saint' even if, by the severe standards of a later age, his writings were not always orthodox. Fourteen hundred years after his death Pope Clement VIII stripped him of his halo, and banished him from the calendar of the saints.

ORIGEN

Despite Clement's best endeavours, the charge against Christians of anti-intellectualism would not go away:

> . . . some Christians do not even want to give or receive a reason for what they believe, and use such expressions as 'Do not ask questions; just believe' and 'Your faith will save you'.

These are the words of Celsus, a pagan philosopher. He wrote his attack upon Christianity, the first of its kind, in about the year 178. It survives only in long quotations contained in a book entitled *Against Celsus* written in 253 or 254 by the Alexandrian Christian philosopher and theologian, Origen. Though the criticism had been written seventy years or so earlier, it still exercised a force potent enough to elicit a response from Clement's successor as head of the catechetical school.

Origen had a singularly chequered career. He was born in c. 185, and his mother may have been an Egyptian. His father, however, was Greek, and a particularly fervent convert to Christianity. He died in the persecution of 202–203, cheered on by his son who wanted to be martyred himself: his mother wisely hid his clothes so that he could not go out. After Clement's flight, Bishop Demetrius asked Origen to take over the school. He was about eighteen years old.

At first he was a great success, and people came flocking to hear him. But, says Eusebius, because 'he discussed religious problems before a mixed audience', he felt it necessary to castrate himself 'to rule out any suspicion of vile imputation on the part of unbelievers' (*History of the Church*, 6:8). Eventually Bishop Demetrius turned against Origen. There were specific

Remains of the Roman harbour at Caesarea, to which Origen came after leaving Alexandria.

accusations: while on an unauthorized journey to Palestine Origen had received ordination without his own bishop's approval, and he aroused Demetrius' ire by suggesting that even the devil might be saved.

Synods in Alexandria, with the backing of Rome, condemned this view, but synods elsewhere, including Palestine, came down on Origen's side. He thought it better to leave Alexandria, and in 231 settled at Caesarea. He was succeeded as head of the school by an old friend, Heraclas, who in 232 became bishop of Alexandria. Origen never returned home: his views were too suspect.

Yet they were not as unorthodox as those of Clement had been. When he was a young man and an orthodox Christian, Origen had lived in a household very much under the influence of a Gnostic priest. Orthodoxy and unorthodoxy had survived side by side, apparently harmoniously enough. But later on, significantly with the backing of Rome, there came a drive for stricter orthodoxy. Origen was one of the first casualties.

152

In Caesarea, however, he continued his work, and during his lifetime he is said to have produced some 6,000 tracts of one kind or another. Some display great scholarship. His 'Hexapla' lists the Old Testament in six different versions, including Hebrew and Greek. Origen died in Tyre, shortly after completing *Against Celsus*.

Some of the accusations voiced by Celsus have already been mentioned. All of them taken together provide a remarkable witness to the way pagans saw Christians. Needless to say, the picture was not flattering:

In private houses also we see wool-workers, cobblers, laundry-workers, and the illiterate and bucolic yokels, who would not dare say anything at all in front of their elders and more intelligent masters. But whenever they get hold of children in private and some stupid women with them, they let out some astounding statements...

says Celsus – or at least, he is quoted thus in Origen's response. Christians, in his view, were naive and unintelligent, their religion spread by way of children and 'stupid women'. Such naivety made them ready listeners to, and believers in, the magic with which Christianity was replete. Celsus had no wish to deny that Jesus worked miracles: magicians abounded, and Jesus was one like many another. He wanted to know, however, where Jesus had learned his tricks: he suggested that he might have learned them from Egyptian magicians.

A more serious charge than that of gullibility, because of its implications, was that Christians believed Jesus was God. Christians had not yet worked out quite what this meant, but they worshipped Jesus as God and that angered the pagan critics because it seemed to detract from the honour

In the early centuries of Christianity the possibility of miracles was not in doubt: the problem was the source of the power to perform them. This mid-fifth-century ivory from Palermo shows Jesus healing a leper.

153

due to the one high God. Moreover, it put Christians at odds with the Jews – not that Celsus had much time for the Jews, but there were a great many of them. There was scarcely a major city of the Empire that did not have a Jewish presence, and in the total population of the Empire, reckoned to be at this time about sixty million, Jews constituted a tenth. Their religion was officially approved, and even had it not been, they would have the respectability which a long tradition brought with it. Compared to the Jews, the Christians – and Celsus knew that they were a breakaway group from Judaism – were upstarts, with no long tradition to commend them.

But all that, it must be remembered, had been written long before Origen's response. In between times Christianity had gained in respectability. Even if he had thought it prudent to withdraw from Alexandria when the Emperor Caracalla paid it a visit in 215, Origen had already been invited to address the Roman governor of Arabia. Later on he was summoned to explain Christian teaching to the Empress Mammaea. No matter what Celsus may have said in the second century, by the middle of the third century a Christian philosopher was someone to be reckoned with.

Long after his departure, Origen's influence remained at Alexandria. Another pupil, Dionysius, became bishop in 247, but he, too, avoided inviting his old master back for the last years of his life. Like his former teacher, Dionysius' own views were suspect, and a correspondence ensued between Dionysius of Alexandria and his namesake of Rome. The bishop of Alexandria was a scholar. He demonstrated that the Book of Revelation could not have been written by the author of the fourth gospel, and he seems to have begun the practice of announcing the date of Easter each year to the dioceses of Egypt. His courage during persecution, and his zeal in the matters of his diocese, earned him the title of 'the Great'. He quite overshadowed his Roman contemporary, who is remembered chiefly for his clash with the bishop of Alexandria. In little more than a century the Church of Alexandria had emerged as one of the most powerful voices in the Church.

CARTHAGE

At the beginning of the Christian era Alexandria could reasonably claim to be the Roman Empire's second city. But Carthage, much further along the Mediterranean's southern shore, could challenge for pre-eminence. Its history was every bit as dramatic as that of Egypt's capital, perhaps more so. Carthaginian, or Punic, people had dominated commerce in the western Mediterranean until the rise of Rome. Three times in just over a century Rome and Carthage went to war. The first war, from 264 to 261 BC, was largely fought at sea, and Rome was compelled to become a sea-going power. It was in the course of the second Punic war (218–201 BC) that Hannibal made his famous journey across the Alps with his elephants. And, during the third war Cato declared in the Roman senate, '*Carthago delenda est*': Carthage must be razed to the ground. It was. It was captured and destroyed in 146 BC, and the ground upon which it had stood was solemnly cursed.

The curse proved almost too effective. The Roman practice was to retire troops, the *veterani*, to land in the provinces where they might establish farms. After a failed attempt to move landless Italians to the site of Carthage, Julius Caesar tried to settle some of his veterans there. This, too, failed. The region began to prosper once again only after Octavian settled some 3,000 veterans there. Like Alexandria, the new Carthage became an important supplier of grain for the Empire's capital city, but it was not until

The estate of the rich landowner, Dominus Julius, displayed upon a pavement mosaic from Carthage. The living quarters in the villa would have been behind the first-floor colonnade.

A Roman funerary mosaic found at Carthage portrays the deceased, a Christian, in an attitude of prayerful supplication.

the second century of the Christian era that it began to display great public buildings, a sign of the wealth of the city's inhabitants.

A large and prosperous Jewish community existed in Carthage in the second century, and possibly earlier. There was an extensive Jewish cemetery, the only one to be found in Africa at so early a date. A good number of the Jews in the city spoke Greek and may have been immigrants from the east rather than long-term residents. Was it among these that Christianity first developed? One piece of evidence in favour of a Jewish origin is the fact that Christians were called 'Nazarenes' at Carthage. But had there been connections, the Jewish cemetery should display some signs of Christian interments, which it does not. It is hardly surprising, for by the time the Jews were established at Carthage the two communities had completely drifted apart.

If not the Jews, were the Greeks the bearers of the new faith? Both in Rome and in Gaul Christianity had taken hold first among the Greek-speaking community; and Tertullian, the first distinguished Christian author from Carthage, sometimes wrote in Greek for a Greek audience. As for Tertullian himself, eager to demonstrate the apostolic origins of Carthaginian Christianity, he hints that the source may have been Rome. But he only hints; he does not say so unequivocally. Tertullian did not know.

The first definite reference to the presence of Christians in Carthage is sudden and dramatic. On 17 July 180 a number of Christians were brought before Vigellius Saturninus, the proconsul, charged with confessing Christ. 'You can earn the pardon of our lord the emperor if you return to your senses', offered Saturninus. They refused. After a number of other attempts to persuade them of their folly:

156

Saturninus the proconsul ordered the herald to proclaim: Speratus, Nartzalus, Cittinus, Veturius, Felix, Aquilinus, Laetantius, Ianuaria, Generosa, Vestia, Donata and Secunda I have ordered to be beheaded. All said: thanks be to God. And so they were all crowned with martyrdom together.

This story of trial and martyrdom is of particular interest because it demonstrates not only that Christianity existed in Carthage in 180 but that it was already well established and had penetrated the hinterland. It is known that the martyrs came from Scilli, or Scillium, but the location of that town remains a mystery, and it was certainly not a major centre of population. The list of names does not suggest that they came from any one social group – two of the names were native to that part of Africa. They were uncompromising in their attitude when faced with execution. That was typical of the African Church, and especially of Montanists.

Montanism is even more evident in the martyrdom of Perpetua and Felicity. Perpetua was a noblewoman, Felicity a slave. Both were married, and Perpetua for a time had her baby son with her in prison, while Felicity gave birth shortly before her death. The day of their martyrdom was 7 March, but the year is less certain – the most likely date is 203. Perpetua's Montanism is clear from her support for the reading of the Montanist prophecies, the 'New Writings', in church, and from her accounts of her visions. The story is revealing in other ways. It demonstrates, for example, that women still played an important part in the life of the Church in third-century North Africa, and the story that one of the martyrs, Saturus, had a vision in which he saw bishops and priests being barred from the presence of God suggests that there was dissension within the Church of Carthage.

THE PREJUDICES OF TERTULLIAN

Some of the tensions can be conjectured from the writings of Tertullian. Rather less is known about this Carthaginian theologian than about his slightly younger Alexandrian contemporary, Origen. Tertullian's dates are usually given as c. AD 160–225, but this is an informed guess. He was a layman who, after his conversion, occasionally preached at Christian services – some of his writings are in the form of homilies. At some point he became a Montanist, though in the first quarter of the third century, at least in Carthage, this was no great impropriety. Bishop Cyprian (p. 160) was particularly fond of Tertullian's works. He would not have been so had he judged them unorthodox.

From Tertullian's writings it is possible to learn something of the daily life of Christians in Carthage. His was a rather jaundiced view, however. He had a strongly sectarian inclination. He wanted Christians to cut themselves off from the world, whether in their social life or, in a definitive form, by martyrdom. He was, for instance, much opposed to Christians visiting the amphitheatre. The spectacles there, he argued, could arouse

emotions forbidden to Christians and it was impossible to watch them
without being drawn into the behaviour of the crowd.

In any case, the games were associated with pagan rituals. Just as
Christians had to avoid any compromise with sacrifices to idols, so
Christian magistrates could not preside at games. This injunction effective-
ly barred Christians from holding public office, though this may not have
bothered them too much. Games were expensive, and religious objections
to becoming involved with them may not have been unwelcome to the
minor aristocracy of a provincial town. Tertullian's moral rigorism,
however, touched the common Christian as much as the would-be
magistrate. Any slave or servant of a (pagan) magistrate might continue to
serve him, but had to avoid involvement with the sacrifice itself.

Perhaps Tertullian raised these issues himself, but a more likely
explanation is that Christians from all walks of life came to him seeking
advice. Builders asked if they might construct a shrine or temple; an artist
who had been commissioned to paint a picture of a pagan deity wondered if
he might accept the task. There is plenty of evidence that Tertullian drew
upon his own experiences. One of his books he addressed to his wife.
Should he die before her, he advises, it would be better that she should not
marry again. But if she chooses to remarry, then let her husband be a
Christian, for a pagan would not understand her need to be up before dawn
to attend divine worship, or to stay out all night for the vigil of Easter.

He had firm views about women. Even though his Montanism urged
celibacy upon him, he was susceptible to female beauty. Neither by dress
nor by demeanour, he warns women, should they encourage lust: they
should seek only to please their husbands. They should not plaster

158

Tertullian was opposed to Christians attending games such as those portrayed opposite, because they were associated with pagan rituals and because it was too easy to be caught up in the blood-lust of the crowds. Two centuries later in the same city St Augustine had to issue an identical warning. The detail on the left (from a mythological wall painting at Pompeii) illustrates the kind of elaborate hair-style against which Tertullian also inveighed.

themselves with cosmetics, dye their hair or, worst of all, go in for fancy hairstyles. Virgins as well as widows should wear veils in church.

Though these warnings might suggest otherwise, Tertullian had high expectations of the morality of Christians. Christians make good citizens, he argued. Whenever there was some sort of a calamity, man-made or otherwise, the cry was 'Christians to the lions', he ironically remarks. In this the people of the Empire are being singularly ungrateful. Without Christians, he claims, the world would be a much more evil place. By their prayers Christians protect the world from evil spirits. On a rather more practical note, he pointed out that while Christians might be accused of withdrawing money from temples, this was more than counterbalanced by their charity to the needy – and by their unusual honesty in paying their taxes.

What if Christians could not live up to these high standards? There was need for absolution, and Tertullian had firm views about that. He was scornful of those who went to seek absolution from Christians imprisoned for their faith, as was the practice of the time. They went along, he alleged, to seek forgiveness laden with great quantities of food and drink. One man in prison for his faith had wined and dined so well that, when he wanted to recant his faith, he was too drunk to do so. He died a martyr's death.

159

It was Tertullian's view that within Christianity there was room for one repentance after baptism but not a further one. Later he was to change his mind. There was to be no second chance for anyone who had committed the gravest sins.

The question of the availability of penance for sin may seem a small one, but it had important consequences. For one thing, Tertullian's views reflected the sort of Church which he, and many other African churchmen after him, believed in. Their Church existed for the perfect, for a group which, because of its rigorist views, had all but withdrawn from society. Such a Church was no more than a sect. That was an opinion which affected Bishop Cyprian, and which for a time was to sour relations between Carthage and Rome.

THE TIMIDITY OF CYPRIAN

Despite the large number of bishops in North Africa, surprisingly little is known about them. In Carthage there was a Bishop Donatus who engaged in correspondence with the bishop of Rome over a heretic who had been condemned by a synod of no less than 90 bishops. And then, in 248, Thascius Caecilius Cyprianus was elected to succeed Donatus.

Before becoming a Christian Cyprian had been a wealthy lawyer. He signalled his conversion to the rest of Carthage by ridding himself of his property. He also simplified his literary style, avoiding pagan imagery, but it was his abandonment of riches that attracted attention. There was no tradition that converts should do so, but it marked dramatically his break with the past. Not that this gesture left him penniless. It was detachment from wealth that he sought, not penury, and he may have handed over his money to the Church to be used on behalf of the poor.

And then, only two years later, Cyprian was elected by the Christians of Carthage to be bishop of Numidia and Mauretania, the most important see in the provinces of Africa and almost equal to the great and apostolic see of Alexandria. It was an astonishing rise. It is clear that by then there existed a definite ladder of promotion. Cyprian had jumped all the rungs. The people's choice was approved by bishops of the surrounding sees, but there were at least five presbyters of the Carthaginian Church who resented the appointment.

Cyprian's election took place sometime between May 248 and May 249. In December 249 the Emperor Decius decreed that all were to offer sacrifice to the pagan gods. The decree was not directed specifically against Christians, but it included them. In Rome the bishop was martyred before the end of January 250. The bishop of Antioch died shortly afterwards. By mid-June there were executions in Alexandria, and soon after that altars were set up in Carthage for the sacrifices to be carried out. Cyprian fled.

Not surprisingly he was accused of cowardice. Long afterwards Pontius, his friend and biographer, was still trying to justify Cyprian's flight by

A wall painting showing a Roman household sacrifice. It is presided over by the leading household god, in the centre by the altar, and a slave brings in a pig for the sacrifice.

claiming it was to the benefit of the Church and its unity that the bishop survived persecution to care for his flock. The clergy of Rome, whose bishop had been one of the first Christians to die, mocked Cyprian, ironically excusing him on the grounds of his importance.

When he made a belated return, sometime after Easter 251, he found his Church in a state of collapse. Thousands had offered sacrifice. Many more had acquired certificates, *libelli*, to say they had sacrificed when they had not. Cyprian blamed the disaster on a lack of discipline. Christians, he said, had grown weak in the years of peace. Men – and that included the bishops too – had devoted themselves to looking for profit and to satisfying their greed. There was envy among members of the Church, and immodesty too: cosmetics had been much in use, by men as well as women. Christians were even marrying pagans. Wealth had undermined devotion, and the persecution was a divine punishment upon avarice.

The Church was certainly financially poorer for the persecution. Cyprian's remaining funds had been confiscated, and money had been needed to support the families of the martyrs and those who had been imprisoned. Requests for assistance came from outside Carthage. More money had to be raised somehow, so Cyprian commended to those who had offered sacrifice or purchased a *libellus* the value of almsgiving.

What more should those who had lapsed from Christianity do by way of penance? There was a difference of opinion in the Church, and the group of presbyters who had opposed Cyprian's election now resurfaced. Novatus may have been a rival candidate in the election. He was now the presbyter

161

in charge of the richer district of Carthage, and was all for readmitting those who had lapsed without prolonged penance. Cyprian was totally opposed to this. His policy was to readmit only those who were in danger of death, and who possessed a *libellus* signed by someone who had suffered in the persecution, petitioning their pardon.

Novatus, whose attitude to the lapsed was attracting wealthy Christians, fled to Rome to win support against Cyprian. The city was still without a bishop but was apparently under the charge of the presbyter Novatian who had already indicated that he personally shared the opinion of Cyprian. Novatian was not elected to the bishopric: Cornelius was chosen instead, and Novatian set up in opposition. Cyprian's hesitancy over whom to support for a time caused a good deal of tension between the two Churches.

In the course of this Cyprian wrote his book *On the Unity of the Church*. Unity he understood as the unity of all the bishops of the Church who together, as a 'college', had oversight of the whole body of Christians and who, as a group, stood in succession to the apostles. And especially in succession to Peter. In the first version of the book occur the words 'the primacy given to Peter', and they are applied to the Church of Rome. What precisely they mean is a matter of debate. Cyprian certainly did not have in mind the type of leadership, or primacy, which the papacy came to claim as its right. Nevertheless, he conceded Rome at least some special honorary role in the Church. Eventually he felt he had gone too far: he removed the words from a later edition. By that time he had fallen out with Bishop Stephen, the new bishop of Rome. The problem was rebaptism. In c. 220 AD Agrippinus, a former bishop of Carthage, had summoned a Synod in which it was decided that baptism performed by a heretic was inadequate. Anyone joining the Church who had been so baptized had to go through the ritual again. That had become the tradition of the Carthaginian Church. Bishop Stephen incensed Cyprian by implying that the Roman tradition of accepting heretically performed baptisms was older, and ought to be preferred. The bishop of Carthage called a synod which met on 1 September 256, bringing together 87 bishops from Africa, Numidia and Mauretania, as well as sundry presbyters, deacons and laypeople. The bishops spoke in order of seniority. All supported Cyprian.

Cyprian's argument turned on the phrase in Ephesians, 'there is only one baptism' (4:5). These words were taken to mean that baptism exists in the united Catholic Church and nowhere else. Stephen turned the argument the other way round: because there is only one baptism, it does not matter who performs it. Ultimately it was this view which prevailed, but Cyprian would have none of it. He pointed out in a letter (which even an ardent admirer of the bishop of Carthage has described as containing 'unmeasured abuse of Stephen') that the bishop of Rome did not believe heretics possessed the Holy Spirit, yet in granting them the power to baptize he was granting them the power to forgive sin, which was a power granted to the apostles and their successors by the Holy Spirit. It was a neat theological point, but argument was fast becoming a luxury. In 257, possibly in August, persecution broke out anew.

The persecution of Valerian was aimed specifically against Christians, and particularly against bishops and presbyters. The structures of the Church were under attack.

Cyprian again went into exile, sent, this time, by the proconsul. Eleven months later he was allowed back, to face trial for his Christianity. He was arrested on 13 September 258 and arraigned the following day before the Proconsul Galerius Maximus. The trial was short. First Cyprian's identity and office were established, then Galerius Maximus said, 'The most sacred emperors order you to perform the requisite ceremonies.' 'I will not do it,' replied the bishop. 'Consult your best interests,' said the proconsul, but to that Cyprian answered, 'Do what you are ordered to do.' He was condemned to death by beheading – a comparatively lenient, not to say honorable, way of death. The sentence was carried out the same day.

From his election onwards, Cyprian's tenure of the see of Carthage had been fraught: his rapid promotion, his flight, the problem of the lapsed, the rebaptism controversy. There is no doubt that to the faithful Cyprian was a generous man. His Church marshalled its resources to look after the imprisoned and the families of those who persevered in the faith until death. But in the matter of the lapsed, the future lay with a much more compassionate attitude than that displayed by Cyprian. Nonetheless, he was not so rigorist in his views that the Church was reduced to a tiny remnant. To that extent his moderation in countenancing the return of the lapsed on certain conditions preserved the unity of the African Church. He prevented it losing itself in sectarianism, as a Church of Tertullian's might have done, and as African Christians were always in danger of doing.

Although Cyprian undoubtedly had his squabbles with Rome, the degree to which Rome played a part in the life of the African Church seems now quite extraordinary. The Mediterranean was a link, rather than a divide, between the two Churches. There were regular comings and goings, though they were not always welcome to Cyprian. In the midst of the controversies he formulated a doctrine of episcopal responsibility for the whole Church which, in his annual synods at Carthage, he attempted to put into practice. The size of the gathering fluctuated as plague or persecution took their toll, but it is a measure of the respect in which he was held that the number of bishops attending was so high. It is a tribute both to his administrative genius and to the force of his personality.

Though he may at first have been timid in face of persecution, he was always a man of integrity. Rome, for all its pretensions, and for all the respect which Cyprian paid it, could not boast a leader of the stature of the martyred bishop of Carthage.

8

ROME AND THE WEST

'And so we came to Rome.' Luke's words at the end of the Acts of the Apostles (28:14) seem to imply a degree of inevitability. And so it was. In the sixties of the first century Rome was the centre of the world. Unless Christianity made its mark there it would wither and die.

THE CENTRE OF THE WORLD

When Julius Caesar was assassinated on the Ides of March 44 BC, the nineteen-year-old Octavius, grandson of Caesar's sister, hurried from Greece to Rome to claim his inheritance as head of the Roman Empire. In an uneasy alliance with Mark Antony he defeated at Philippi the armies of the chief conspirators against Caesar, Brutus and Cassius.

Then Mark Antony took his troops on a foreign campaign. Unsuccessful in Parthia, in 34 BC he overran Armenia. But by then he was already

A massive bronze head of Octavius, to whom, in 27 BC, the Roman Senate gave the title 'Augustus'. His supreme authority was intended to last ten years: but this authority was passed on to subsequent Roman emperors and continued for four and a half centuries.

164

High-rise living, Roman style. Perhaps the majority of Rome's ordinary citizens lived in buildings such as this insula.

enamoured of Cleopatra, Queen of Egypt, and so he retired to Alexandria. Octavius made considerable political capital out of his erstwhile ally's affair with a despised Eastern ruler. The war which followed ended with the total defeat of Antony and Cleopatra at the battle of Actium in 31. Their suicide in Alexandria left Octavius in undisputed charge of the Roman dominions which he ruled, in relative peace, for the next forty-five years. Augustus, the honorific title that became the name by which he was known, died at Nola on 19 August AD 14, at the age of seventy-seven.

This period, during which Jesus was born and grew to manhood in one of the Roman provinces, was something of a golden age. Augustus gave back to the Roman Senate some of the dignity stripped from it by Julius Caesar. He attempted, too, to restore the old Roman religion, rebuilding ancient temples and reviving ancient rituals. He made efforts to improve moral standards in family life, and encouraged the birth-rate by discriminatory taxation. Literature and the arts flourished. Ovid's *Ars Amoris*, The Art of Love, earned him banishment, but Livy, Virgil and Horace all wrote in praise of the virtues which Augustus fostered. There were new and splendid buildings – a new forum, the first of the imperial baths, the Pantheon. Some of these are still to be seen, such as the Theatre of Marcellus or the Ara Pacis, the Altar of Peace, dedicated by the Senate in 9 BC. Three new aqueducts were constructed to bring water to the million or so people who, it is estimated, lived within the city boundaries at that time.

For the most part, they lived in squalor. They inhabited high-rise tenements called *insulae*, a revealing term, for it means 'islands'. These stinking, jerry-built, badly lit apartment blocks were lodging houses from which tenants might readily be evicted. They were at constant risk from fire and, though sewers ran beneath the streets of Rome, only the houses of the rich were served by them. Epidemics were a way of life. There were no hospitals. At night the streets were hazardous.

This dismal state of affairs was vigorously attacked by Augustus. As part of his inner-city reform he decreed that no *insula* was to be more than 21 metres high. He recruited a force of watchmen-cum-firefighters. He divided the city into fourteen regions and, it seems, into 265 districts, each with its own officials elected by the people. There was a 'Tiber conservancy board' whose task it was to prevent the regular, and disastrous, flooding of the low-lying parts of the city. Those on the register of male citizens, just two hundred thousand at the turn of the era, were eligible for a ration of corn. The army was reduced in size, and veterans were settled. It was a period of calm which would not soon return.

Augustus was succeeded in AD 14 by his adopted son, Tiberius. The new emperor had lived in Capri before his accession, and to Capri he

A room in the Domus Aurea *built by Nero after the great fire of AD 64.*

returned for the last ten years of his life. His death in AD 37 was greeted with jubilation by the Romans, who had scarcely seen him. Gaius (known as Caligula), apparently mentally disturbed, was assassinated in 41; Claudius, in many ways efficient but nonetheless unpopular, died in 54, probably also assassinated. And then came Nero.

He began well. He enjoyed lavish spectacles, and because the people enjoyed them as well he managed to retain their support, even after the disastrous fire which left only four regions of the city untouched and utterly destroyed three others. Upon the ruins he built the *Domus Aurea*, the Golden House, a vast complex of buildings covering some 125 acres. Nero committed suicide in June 68 after an army revolt, but it was into his Rome that there came the apostles Peter and Paul.

THE BONES OF ST PETER

There is no argument about Paul's presence in Rome, but it is a different matter where Peter is concerned. Disagreement has been along denominational lines. For doctrinal reasons associated with the role of the papacy, Roman Catholics have asserted that Peter came to Rome and was martyred and buried there. Others have pointed out that there is no direct evidence of this.

According to Roman Catholic teaching, Jesus bestowed leadership of the twelve apostles upon Peter, and this leadership, or primacy, Peter passed on to his successors as bishops of Rome. Around the cupola of the basilica in the Vatican which bears the saint's name, Jesus' words are inscribed in Latin, 'You are Peter and on this rock I will build my Church'. Directly beneath the cupola there stands the magnificent papal altar.

That Jesus meant something special by this is impossible to deny. Not only did he change Peter's name (the saint had hitherto been called Simon), he also used a significant play on words. In Greek *petros* means stone: Peter himself, it would seem, was the stone upon which the Church was to be built. Nor is there any doubt that the New Testament, and in particular the Gospels, give Peter especial prominence. For example, lists of the apostles occur four times in the New Testament. The names are not always the same, and the order differs. But in every case the name of Peter is put at the head of the list.

Yet Peter fades out of the Acts of the Apostles halfway through. His name was attached to two letters which have found their way into the canon of the New Testament, but there is nothing to tell, except very indirectly, what may have happened to him in the closing years of his life. The literary evidence for a visit to Rome is extremely slim. Fortunately, however, other types of evidence exist.

What implications Peter's presence in Rome may have for the papacy is a separate issue, but there is no longer much doubt that he visited the city, and also that he died there. What appears to be his tomb has been found,

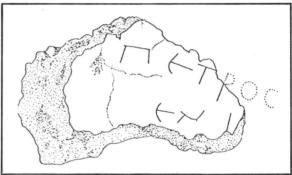

This graffito was incised in the red wall near Peter's tomb in the second, or early third, century. It undoubtedly mentions the saint's name, but the rest is not so easy to decipher. Its most likely meaning is 'Peter is within'.

and it seems very likely that some of his remains have been identified. They lay directly beneath the cupola bearing its legend. In his history, under the reign of Nero, Eusebius remarks that Paul:

> was beheaded in Rome itself, and that Peter likewise was crucified, and the record is confirmed by the fact that the cemeteries there are still called by the names of Peter and Paul, and equally so by a churchman named Gaius, who was living while Zephyrinus was bishop of Rome [199–217]. In his published *Dialogue* with Proclus, the leader of the Phrygian heretics [i.e., the Montanists], Gaius has this to say about the places where the mortal remains of the two apostles have been reverently laid: 'I can point out the monuments of the victorious apostles. If you will go as far as the Vatican or the Ostian Way, you will find the monuments of those who founded this church.' (*History of the Church* 2:25)

The monument to Peter, the *tropaion* or triumphal tomb, has been found where Gaius said it was, on the Vatican hillside. The slope had subsequently been levelled by the Emperor Constantine to make way for the basilica of St Peter.

Excavations under the high altar of St Peter's began in 1940. A long row of mausoleums appeared, in line with the nave of the church above. The latest of them dated from about AD 330, just before the work on the first St Peter's was begun. Then there was revealed a marble pillar (evidently there had once been two) holding up a stone slab, which in turn was set into a red wall with niches in it. The archaeologists first thought they had discovered an altar, but the column went down below the level of the Constantinian church: the height of the slab would have been too great for it to have served as an altar. It became clear that what they had found were the remains of the *tropaion* described by Gaius.

The red wall went down to a simple earth grave. Beneath the wall bones were found. The assumption was that these were the bones of Peter. The clinching argument was that no skull was found: Peter's head had long been venerated in another Roman church. The bones were said to be those of a powerfully built man in his late sixties, a description which suited perfectly what little was known of Peter. Later examination showed that they were the bones of a woman.

Unbeknown to the archaeologists, however, a Vatican official who had made it his business to care for scraps of bone unearthed in the excavations had taken some remains from an opening in a wall, covered with graffiti, at right angles to the red wall. When the opening was subjected to detailed study, the researchers wondered if it had ever served as a repository for the relics of Peter, but by the time they came to do this the remains had already been removed. It was not until 1953 that they were examined. These were indeed the remains of a powerfully built man in his late sixties. They had once been wrapped in purple cloth with a golden thread. The skull, or portions of it, was present, but the feet were missing. Still adhering to the bones was soil of a type identical with that to be found in what was thought to be Peter's grave.

Although on balance the evidence does seem to suggest that the bones of St Peter have been found, there are many unresolved problems. Why were they put in the graffiti wall? Why are there no bones remaining below the ankle? (though had Peter been crucified upside down, as tradition has it, the feet might well have been severed.) And what of the skull in the other Roman church, the ancient Lateran Basilica? Could not the bones just as easily be of someone other than Peter?

THE CHRISTIAN MONUMENTS

What happened to the Christian community in Rome after the death of Peter? The answer lies hidden in the catacombs. Over three dozen of these burial chambers have been identified, most of them dotted along the main highways leading out of Rome. The name 'catacomb' comes from one particular cemetery, Ad Catacumbas, meaning 'sunken valley'. According to Christian mythology it was here that people hid to escape persecution; but the one thing that is certain about the Christian catacombs is that the authorities in Rome knew where they were located. In order to excavate a

catacomb a title had to be acquired to the property. This was not difficult for individuals, and the earliest Christian burial chambers bear the names of individual Christians: Priscilla, Domitilla, Callistus.

Domitilla was in use from c. AD to 150 to 400. It was named after the grandmother of the Emperor Vespasian. She was married to Titus Flavius Clemens, who was himself a nephew of Vespasian, and in AD 95 held the eminent office of consul under the Emperor Domitian (who, to make it even more confusing, was Titus' cousin and Domitilla's uncle).

Shortly afterwards Titus was put to death for 'atheism against the Roman gods', a charge which looks suspiciously like that of being a Christian; his wife was exiled. After that both disappear from history, except that Domitilla gave her name to a catacomb excavated beneath land which, it is thought, had belonged to her, while Titus may have given his name to a church.

The present church of San Clemente in Rome dates from the twelfth century, but just over a century ago it was discovered that it had been constructed on top of a fourth-century church, which in turn had been constructed over a first-century building, erected on the site of houses destroyed in Nero's fire. One side of these houses is a typical Roman tenement block (where there was a small temple of the god Mithras, still to be seen), but on the other side there is a mansion which belonged to someone called Clemens, perhaps Titus Flavius Clemens. It is also probable that in that mansion, from the second century at least, there was a room set

170

Opposite, the wall of a first-century house has been found beneath the Roman church of San Clemente, which Christian tradition has associated with Titus Flavius Clemens, believed to have been martyred in AD 97. In the third century one room was converted into a temple to Mithras. Clemens' wife Domitilla owned property under which a Christian catacomb was excavated. The picture on the left, shows the cubiculum, *or little room, of the Good Shepherd, dating from the late second or early third century (p. 52–3).*

aside for Christian worship.

Ownership of a house was indicated in Rome by setting up a plaque, a *titulus* or 'title', on the building's façade. As the Christian community grew and it became necessary to take over whole houses to serve as meeting-places for worship, the houses seem to have continued to be known by the name of their original owner. In that way the *titulus Clementis*, 'the title of Clement', became the church of Clement. Christian piety of a later generation canonized the former proprietor, and transformed the building into the church of San (Saint) Clemente. By the middle of the third century the community had grown so large that it owned a considerable amount of property. That must be the implication of the edict issued by the Emperor Valerian in AD 257 to deprive the Christians of the ownership of their cemeteries; it was a provision which was intended to hurt even though three years later, under the Emperor Gallienus, they were restored.

So the existence of the churches, and still more of the cemeteries, reflects the status of the Christian community in Rome. But the cemeteries tell very little of the Christians who were buried within them. The catacomb of Domitilla was the final resting-place – at least until the advent of grave-robbers and relic-seekers – of between a half to three-quarters of a million people. There was one group which was shown special reverence in the catacombs: the bishops who ruled the see of Rome. Zephyrinus is the first bishop whose date of death and place of burial are reliably recorded. He was martyred in 217 and was interred not in, but above, the catacomb of

171

Callistus. Callistus himself, however, was hurriedly laid to rest in the catacomb of Calepodius, while Urbanus, Callistus' successor, has no known tomb. From then on a long line of bishops was buried in the catacomb of Callistus, in what is now called the Crypt of the Popes.

The presence of some of these tombs has been confirmed by the inscriptions which a rather later bishop of Rome, Pope Damasus, had erected to their memory. For others it is necessary to rely upon a generally trustworthy document from the middle of the fourth century. Clearly the men whose names and deeds were recorded in stone and on parchment, and who were buried side by side in the catacomb of Callistus, were eminent leaders of Rome's Christian community. But how far back did the succession of bishops reach?

THE OFFICE OF BISHOP

Although, as we have seen, it does appear that Peter was in Rome, it does not answer the question of whether he was the city's first bishop and, in Roman Catholic parlance, the first pope. The word 'pope' needs some explanation. In the first centuries of Christianity it was used of bishops in

The Crypt of the Popes is in the catacomb of Callistus, named after the man who looked after it, a former slave who himself became bishop of Rome.

172

general: it is an affectionate, but respectful, Greek term for father. The first bishop of Rome of whom the title seems to have been used was Callistus (217–222), but from the fifth century it appears to have been applied almost exclusively to the bishop of that city. Almost exclusively, but not quite. The word is still in use today for Greek parish priests, and it is also used of the Coptic Patriarch of Alexandria.

But the term 'pope' has come to imply a claim to leadership over the whole Christian Church and, in Roman Catholic thinking, the claim is as old as Peter's leadership over the apostles. This leaves two questions to be settled: was the Christian Church in the early centuries sufficiently conscious of its own unity and coherence to have had a leader at all; and, if the answer to that question is positive, did the bishop of Rome exercise this function?

The answer to the first question must be yes. The Christian community, despite its many disagreements about doctrine, nevertheless had quite a strong sense of its unity. An expression of this can be found as early as the letter to the Ephesians:

Do all you can to preserve the unity of the spirit by the peace that binds you together. There is one body, one Spirit, just as you were all called into one and the same hope when you were called. There is one Lord, one faith, one baptism, and one God who is Father of all, over all, through all and within all. (4:3–6)

It is true that the writer was speaking specifically to one community, but the passage is open to a worldwide interpretation, and such an understanding was not long delayed.

Ignatius of Antioch picked it up. In what is the first known use of the word 'Catholic' in the sense it now has, he told the Smyrnaeans in the passage quoted earlier, 'Wheresoever the bishop appears, there let the people be, even as wheresoever Christ Jesus is, there is the Catholic Church.' Though this is the only use of the term 'Catholic' in the writings of Ignatius, it occurs at least three times in the rather later *Martyrdom of Polycarp:* 'And when he [Polycarp] had finished praying, having remembered all whom he had ever met, both small and great, high and low, and all the Catholic Church throughout the world...' (8:1) This is just one example, but it is perhaps the most striking for it implies a prayerful concern for Christians in whatever part of the world they might be.

It is not difficult to show, therefore, that among even the earliest Christians there was a sense of unity in the faith which was universal – which is what the word 'Catholic' means. This universality or Catholicity, tied neither to the local gods of town or village nor to the élitist cults that came from the East, may well have been one of Christianity's most attractive features as far as the people of the Empire were concerned. Those whom the ancient gods no longer inspired were welcomed into an Empire-wide community, membership of which demanded neither money nor status. But there is nothing to suggest that this universal community needed a single over-all leader, from Rome or anywhere else. One Christian tradition, however, has understood that the undeniable role played by Peter as leader among the apostles was handed on by him from one bishop of Rome (Peter himself being the first) to the next. Whatever may be said of this notion of the 'apostolic succession', it does not quite fit the historical facts.

When Peter made his way to Rome he came to a Christian community that was already well established: in no way can he be regarded as the founder of the Church there. It is very likely that this first Christian group was composed of Jews. Rome was the first European city which is known to have had a Jewish presence. By the first century AD there were some forty to fifty thousand Jews living there, a very substantial number, though still rather fewer than those living in Alexandria. The Jews in Rome lived across the Tiber from the main centre of the city, in the region now known as Trastevere, and kept close links with Jerusalem. Palestinian rabbis regularly made the journey to Rome to act as teachers to the community, and as spiritual guides to the dozen or so synagogues which flourished in the city.

The various synagogues were not all of one mind, however. It is quite possible that, in the mid-forties of the first century AD, they were at odds among themselves over the recognition of Jesus as messiah. It was about the year 49 when Prisca and Aquila had to leave Rome for Corinth, a date which coincides with Claudius' edict, recorded by Luke, that 'all' Jews should leave the city. Clearly, not all obeyed. Were those expelled Jewish converts to Christianity who were causing trouble within the local community?

If the arrival of Christianity in Rome can be dated to the mid-forties, the faith could have been brought only from Antioch or from Jerusalem. There is no evidence of the involvement of Antioch, and plenty of evidence for Jewish links with Jerusalem, so the Jewish capital seems the more likely founding Church. Certainly Paul's letter to the Romans seems to have been formulated with a Jewish-Christian, rather than a Gentile-Christian, Church in mind.

Even so, a Gentile-Christian Church rapidly emerged. The letter written AD 96 which is known as 1 Clement is sometimes thought to have been written by Jewish Christians, but this thesis is impossible to prove – which in itself demonstrates the strength of the non-Jewish tradition by the end of the century. The letter was addressed to the Church in Corinth, and those who carried it there all have Gentile names, and are said to have been Christians from their youth. Even the shadowy figure of Clement himself is a witness to the non-Jewish element in Roman Christianity. It is often suggested that he was a freedman of the house of Titus Flavius Clemens, and obviously neither Titus nor his wife Domitilla were of Jewish origin.

174

If it is accepted that there were differing Christian traditions in Rome, one springing from the Jewish, the other from the non-Jewish community, then a passage in Clement's letter becomes somewhat easier to understand. He wrote:

> It was due to jealousy and envy that the greatest and most righteous pillars [of the Church, see also Gal 2:9] were persecuted and contended unto the death. Let us set before our eyes the good apostles. There was Peter, who because of unrighteous jealousy endured not just one or two but many hardships, and having thus borne his witness, went to the place of glory he deserved. Because of jealousy and strife, Paul showed how to win the prize of patient endurance . . . and when he had borne his witness before the rulers, he departed from the world an outstanding example of patient endurance. (1 Clem 5)

Professor Raymond Brown has very reasonably suggested that this description of the deaths of the two apostles, which are attributed to 'jealousy and envy', hints that they were brought about by strife among the Christians of the community, some of whom reported others to the Roman authorities.

There is no evidence at this date of a bishop governing all parties in the Roman Church. One may presume that Peter played a leading role, given his status among the apostles, but nothing directly suggests that this was the case. And nothing suggests that he was bishop of Rome. Ignatius of Antioch remains the earliest identifiable monarchical bishop, and geographically the origins of this office seem to lie in Asia Minor. Rome was not the first place, nor one of the earliest places, to have a single, ruling bishop.

The letter of Clement used to be quoted to demonstrate the early appearance of the office in Rome. Here, it was alleged, was the first example of a bishop of Rome writing to another Church in order to call the Christian community back into line. Not only was a bishop acting, he was exercising authority – primacy – over another group of Christians. But unfortunately for such an interpretation, Clement does not call himself a bishop. He does not write in his own name, but in that of the Christians of Rome. And not long afterwards, when Ignatius himself wrote to Rome, he did not address their bishop, though he never failed to mention an episcopal colleague wherever else one existed. Then the *Shepherd* of Hermas, a mystical text consisting of visions and revelations thought to have been written between about 120 and 140 in Rome (though Hermas actually claims to be a contemporary of Clement), speaks of a local Church which is headed by presbyters and not by a single bishop.

What evidence there is about the episcopal office in first- and early second-century Rome is negative: no such office existed. Not that there is a shortage of lists of bishops of Rome showing a line of descent from Peter (and including Clement). Eusebius quotes lists from Irenaeus and from Hegesippus, a Church historian who lived in Rome for a time during the second century. But these lists were constructed at a time when monepiscopacy had become the accepted norm. They are arguments produced with hindsight, and no proof in themselves that the situation was as they described it.

It was noted earlier that the first bishop of Rome whose date of death can be determined with any certainty is Zephyrinus, who died in 217. Clearly, however, he was not the first bishop. There is little reason to doubt that Polycarp visited Rome and met Anicetus, as a colleague bishop, *c.* AD 155. So that leaves a period between the earliest date for the *Shepherd*, 120, and the visit of Polycarp perhaps thirty-five years later, for the emergence of monepiscopacy in Rome. From then on succession can be taken as reasonably continuous, though not all Roman bishops were powerful, well-known figures, and information about them has been lost. In the middle of the third century, on the other hand, a number of them played leading roles in the Church at large, but towards the end of the third century the Roman bishops fade from centre-stage. More is known of Bishop Dionysius of Alexandria than of his Roman contemporaries.

CHURCH ORDER

The tone of the letter known as 1 Clement, written to the Church at Corinth, is far removed from Paul's letter to the same Church. It is not clear what had happened at Corinth to occasion the letter. The main fault of the Corinthians appears to have been an attempt to remove some presbyters from their liturgical functions. Clement responds to the crisis with a good deal of talk about the divinely assigned order of the Jerusalem liturgy, drawing parallels between the Jewish cult and its Christian equivalent. He goes on to assert quite clearly that deacons and bishops were appointed to their tasks by the apostles themselves. Clement follows this with a quotation from Isaiah, adapted to suggest that there were bishops even in Old Testament times. Such bishops, says Clement, are to be obeyed:

> Hence you who are instigators of the revolt [in Corinth] must submit to the elders and accept discipline in repentance, bending the knees of your hearts. Learn obedience, laying aside the arrogance and proud wilfulness of your tone. For it is better for you to find a small but creditable place in the flock of Christ than to appear eminent but be excluded from his hope. (1 Clem 57)

Contrast this with St Paul's words to the same Church, only forty odd years earlier:

> Now you together are Christ's body: but each of you is a different part of it. In the Church, God has given the first place to the apostles, the second to prophets, the third to teachers; after them miracles, and after them the gift of healing; helpers, good leaders, those with many languages. Are all of them apostles, or all of them prophets, or all of them teachers? Do they all have the gift of miracles, or all have the

176

The opening of the letter from Clement to the Corinthians in the codex Alexandrinus.

gift of healing? Do all speak strange languages, and all interpret them?
(1 Cor 12:27–30)

Paul describes a Church filled with the Spirit and guided by charismatic leaders. In 1 Clement, and even before the institution, at least in Rome, of the monarchical episcopate, there is described a Church constitution which is based upon an individual's office rather than upon spiritual gifts. The dichotomy between the New Testament Church and that of 1 Clement should not be over-emphasized. The notion of an office-based constitution has New Testament warrant – in Luke and Acts, for example, and in other texts which, perhaps significantly, are associated with Peter. But one New Testament model of the Church has, of necessity, triumphed over another.

Had Christianity remained a Church headed by charismatic leaders who claimed the authority of the Spirit for their guidance, it would have run grave risk of remaining a private cult, appealing only to an exclusive élite, and a prey to Gnosticism. But Christians constantly harped on authority, civil as well as religious. This had two effects: it gave witness to the world about them that Christians were capable of being good citizens, and it provided the Church with a tight-knit organization able to exercise discipline over its members and to withstand the onslaught of persecution when it came. The offices which emerged in the Church at the very end of the first century or at the beginning of the second may not have had scriptural warrant in the New Testament, but they were essential if Christianity was both to create and sustain a community, and face up to the imperial authorities.

177

CHRONOLOGY OF THE POPES

48–69	Peter (Galilean)	230–235	Pontianus (Roman)
69–78	Linus (Italian)	235–236	Anterus (Greek)
78–90	Cletus (Roman)	236–250	Fabian (Roman)
90–99	Clement I (Roman)	251–253	Cornelius (Roman)
99–105	Evaristus (Greek)	251–258	*Novatian**
105–115	Alexander I (Roman)	253–254	Lucius I (Roman)
115–125	Sixtus I (Roman)	254–257	Stephen I (Roman)
125–136	Telesphorus (Greek)	257–258	Sixtus II (Greek)
136–140	Hyginus (Greek)	259–268	Dionysius (Greek)
140–155	Pius I (Italian)	269–274	Felix I (Roman)
155–166	Anicetus (Syrian)	275–283	Eutychianus (Italian)
166–175	Soter (Italian)	283–296	Caius (Dalmatian)
175–189	Eleutherus (Greek)	296–304	Marcellinus (Roman)
189–199	Victor I (African)	308–309	Marcellus I (Roman)
199–217	Zephyrinus (Roman)	309	Eusebius (Greek)
217–222	Callistus I (Roman)	311–314	Miltiades (African)
217–235	*Hippolytus**	314–335	Sylvester I (Roman)
222–230	Urban I (Roman)		
* anti-pope	All dates before 175 are conjectural.		

But perhaps the dichotomy between the two models of Church government should not be taken as absolute. Choice of bishop may have lain with the people – though neighbouring bishops then ordained him to office – but the Spirit sometimes took a hand. According to Eusebius, Fabian was elected bishop of Rome 'by a miracle of divine and heavenly grace'.

Whatever the mechanics of the election, the choice of Fabian was inspired. During his period of office (236–250), the Church of Rome seems to have been at peace. He used his time well. He divided the city into seven ecclesiastical regions, with a deacon in charge of each. Cornelius, Fabian's successor, in a letter to Bishop Fabius of Antioch, described the staff of the Roman Church as Fabian must have left it. In addition to the one bishop:

> there are forty-six presbyters, seven deacons, seven sub-deacons, forty-two acolytes, fifty-two exorcists, readers and door-keepers, and more than fifteen hundred widows and distressed persons. (*History of the Church*, 6:43)

It has been calculated on the basis of these figures that, in the middle of the third century, the Christians in Rome numbered some forty thousand. The material needs of this community, and particularly the needs of the widows (who constituted a definite class in the Church everywhere, sometimes distinct from, at other times united to, the group of virgins), were met by the community through the ministrations of deacons, assisted by sub-deacons. These were not liturgical offices but administrative ones, and

178

because of their charitable work around the city the holders of these appointments were well known and influential in the community. Fabian himself appears to have been a layman at his election, but it was from the ranks of the deacons rather than from among the presbyters that bishops were commonly chosen.

In accounts of the early Church in Rome, women are mentioned only as recipients of charity. Thus the leading role which women had played in the primitive Church had been entirely lost in the West. In the East it had survived, and continued to survive, but was confined to ministry to women in a culture which was hostile to the idea of men associating with women who were not close relatives. Since in the Roman Church deacons were such powerful individuals that they frequently came to rule the Church, it is perhaps not surprising that women were not admitted to the same, or to a similar, rank.

If Fabian is credited with the organization of the Church's staff, Dionysius, bishop from 259 to 268, is credited with the division of Rome into parishes, each with its clergy. On the basis that there would have been two priests to each 'church', in the mid-century there were perhaps some two dozen, and by the Peace of the Church in 313 the number may have risen to forty or so. Outside the city proper a number of other churches, many of them governed by bishops, came under the general supervision of the bishop of Rome: sixty bishops attended a council in 251.

Imperfect though they be, these figures reveal a Roman Church which was expanding rapidly. They also, perhaps, reveal a Church of some wealth: it had already begun to acquire estates beyond the boundaries of the city. It was well organized, and seemingly close-knit. But its members were not theologically gifted, and in that differed from many of the Churches of the East – most notably Alexandria. They therefore had a particularly difficult time when they had to cope with the many unorthodox thinkers who flocked to the imperial capital.

HANDLING HERESY

What came to be thought of as 'normative' Christianity or 'orthodoxy' (the word means 'right thinking') emerged slowly. Even within the New Testament there were competing interpretations of Jesus' message; outside the New Testament the differences became even more evident.

Marcion was a typical case. He abandoned all the Old Testament and rejected most of the New apart from the writings of St Paul. In order to propagate his views he came to Rome, where he donated 200,000 sesterces to the Church (a considerable sum, though only a fifth of a proconsul's annual salary). But then, in about AD 144, the eccentric nature of his views proved too much. The money was returned and Marcion was expelled, to return to Asia Minor. Rome had toyed with Marcionism, but had finally rejected it. That was a pattern frequently to be repeated.

In about the year 200, for example, the doctrines of Noetus arrived in Rome. Noetus had been expelled from his own Church of Smyrna for teaching that God and Jesus were so closely identified as Father and Son that, when Jesus suffered, God the Father suffered with him. The doctrines, known as 'Patripassionism' to later generations, seemed at first to win some support among Roman Christians, though it was a variation on this teaching on the Trinity which made most headway. Called Sabellianism, from Sabellius, a Libyan who came to Rome during the time of Bishop Zephyrinus, it claimed that God's unity was such that Father, Son and Holy Spirit could only be three aspects, or modes, of the same God. Both Zephyrinus and his successor Callistus were claimed as supporters for this 'modalism'.

Meanwhile a different group of Asian immigrants to the Empire's capital was arguing that Jesus was simply a man upon whom a divine power had descended, and who had by this means been 'adopted' into the Godhead. Belief in the Trinity, of the presence in the Godhead of Father, Son and Holy Spirit, was one of the great hallmarks of Christianity. Both Sabellianism and adoptionism ran the risk of turning Christianity back into Judaism by denying the reality of the Trinity and insisting too strictly on the oneness of God.

All these divergences from 'normative' Christianity eventually foundered in Rome, but not because the bishop of the city led an attack upon them. Quite the contrary. Callistus, indeed, seems to have been a personal friend of Sabellius. Hippolytus, a Roman presbyter who died in about the year 236 and who may have had designs upon the bishopric himself, was scathing about Zephyrinus' intelligence. That the views of Noetus, Sabellius and the adoptionists did not make more headway in Rome and elsewhere was thanks to the opposition of the theologians such as Tertullian in Carthage or Hippolytus in Rome rather than to any action on the part of the Roman bishops – though it is true that it was Callistus who eventually expelled Sabellius.

On that occasion theologians in Rome and in Carthage ranged themselves together, but on another issue, which involved Church discipline as much as Church doctrine, the two Churches went their separate ways. Many apostasies had resulted from the persecution of Decius in 250–251, and when the danger was passed those who had apostatized wished to be received back into the Church. But what was their punishment to be? In Carthage Cyprian had already come to his conclusion: the *lapsi* might be reconciled to the Church only after a long and severe penance, or if they were in danger of death. In keeping with the usual practice, Cyprian told Rome what he had decided. His letter was answered by a certain Novatian who, following the martyrdom of Bishop Fabian and in the absence of a properly elected successor, seems to have taken charge. He heartily approved of Cyprian's decision, but added that

180

It is thought that the three figures on the left depict the Christian doctrine of the Trinity.

formal endorsement would have to wait upon the election of the new bishop. Maybe Novatian hoped to be elected himself, but if so he was disappointed. The choice was Cornelius.

Novatian had himself consecrated as a rival to Cornelius, and immediately insisted on much stricter terms for the reception back into the Church of the *lapsi*. Relations between Cornelius and Cyprian went fairly well, as they did at first under Cornelius' successor Stephen. When Cyprian learnt that the bishop of Arles was refusing to reconcile the *lapsi* even on the point of death, he wrote to Stephen asking him to bring pressure to bear upon the bishop.

The cause of the quarrel between Stephen and Cyprian was the rebaptism of those who had been baptized by heretics, but who now wished to be received into the Church. It was the Carthaginian view that rebaptism was essential, as has been seen, but Stephen insisted that Roman practice was to receive such converts into the Church by a ceremony of laying-on hands.

In such theological controversies the Church of Rome played a fairly minor role, even though its opinion was constantly sought. Its attitude was more pragmatic than theological. To impose limits upon admission to the

Church, to require that every candidate for baptism should feel him or herself to be divinely inspired, to insist on the most rigorous moral code for Christians: such attitudes would have made the Church sectarian. Had these views become the common inheritance of Christianity, the Church would have been side-tracked into the byways of history. Roman pragmatism was one of the factors which prevented that happening: Christianity remained open to all.

CHRISTIANITY WEST OF ROME

The history of Christianity in the rest of Europe is particularly difficult to untangle. According to French legend it was Mary Magdalen who brought Christianity to southern France. In Spain, on the other hand, missionary work was said to have been undertaken by St James the Greater, the brother of John and one of the sons of Zebedee. While in England tradition has it that Joseph of Arimathea, he who requested Jesus' body from Pilate and laid it in his own tomb, brought to Glastonbury the Holy Grail, the chalice Jesus had used at the Last Supper.

The stories are vivid, but they are no more than legends. The oldest of them concerns Spain. St James (the 'Sant Iago' of Santiago de Compostela) begins to feature in accounts of the conversion of the country from the sixth century. The Mary Magdalen story in France dates from the eleventh or twelfth century. It is not until the thirteenth century that stories can be

Possibly the oldest surviving Christian sarcophagus, which was found not in Rome but at Gayolle in France. It dates from the third century and is Greek in style. The Christian symbols, including those of the Good Shepherd and a figure with hands raised in prayer, are clearly visible.

found of Joseph of Arimathea's visit to Britain. The legends sprang up to fill the gaps, for very little is known of the early history of Christianity in any of these countries.

The first evidence of Christianity in France comes in a letter written by Irenaeus. In or about the year 177 some forty Christians were put to death in the amphitheatre at Lyons. The bishop of the city died in the persecution, as did Attalus who came from Pergamon, and Alexander of Phrygia. Their names are a witness to the mixture of races: about half appear to have been Romano-Gallic, though many had Greek names and Irenaeus himself, who probably succeeded the martyred leader of the community as bishop of Lyons, was a native of Smyrna. The persecution seems to have had the effect of dispersing the Christian community, driving its members into other Gallic towns – to Autun in particular which, along with Lyons, was one of the great trading centres of Gaul. So the persecution was a spur to further evangelism, but after that little is known about what happened to the Christian community which survived until the Peace of the Church of 313.

Even less is recorded of Christianity in Britain during the period. Aaron and Julius are known to have been martyred in the middle of the third century, but the tradition has been to date Alban's death much earlier, possibly to the very first years of the third century. Evidence for this earlier date is slender. It turns upon the use of the word 'Caesar' to describe the

183

rank of the individual under whom Alban met his death. It is hardly enough evidence to warrant putting half a century between the two persecutions.

Tertullian and Origen, it is true, make passing reference to Britain in their writings. According to the former 'parts of the inaccessible to Rome have been subjected to Christ', while the latter alleges that 'Christianity was a unifying force among the Britons'. Not too much faith should be put in such phrases. Apart from the obvious question of how they knew when so little, apparently, was recorded about Britain, the words occur in oratorical flourishes. Irenaeus makes a similar sort of remark about the Iberian peninsula.

Nevertheless the fact that evidence about Christianity in Britain is so sparse should not be taken to imply that the faith was weak or non-existent there. At the Council of Arles held in August 314 thirty-three bishops were present. Of these, three were British: Eborius, bishop of York, Restitutus, bishop of London, and Adelfius, whose see is uncertain but may have been Lincoln. Attending them were a priest and a deacon. Their presence attests a fairly strong, reasonably well-organized Christian community in Britain in the first decades of the fourth century. It is also clear that the Church, structurally, was town-based along the lines of the Roman model, and not clan-based as it was to become in Ireland after the Celtic form of Christianity had taken hold.

More is known about primitive Christianity in Spain. The first important evidence, however, comes not from Spain itself but from Carthage. In 254, or in the opening months of 255, Cyprian sent a letter to Spain in which he reflected upon a case which had been brought before him and over thirty of his brother bishops. It appears that two Spanish bishops had apostatized. When the Decian persecution was over they wanted to return to their former status, but in the meantime others had been consecrated in their place. One of them, Basilides, had taken himself to Rome to win redress and had been supported by Bishop Stephen. His opponents were appealing to the wisdom of Cyprian in Carthage against Stephen's decision.

Much has been made of these two visits: the recognition of papal primacy by Basilides, and the rejection of it by Cyprian. The appeal to Carthage has also been used, along with evidence from the text of the Bible and other sources, to support the theory that Christianity first came to Spain from Africa. There is no proof one way or the other, and it is most likely that Christianity first reached Spain as it had reached Gaul, brought by troops, travellers and traders.

Nonetheless, the story does reveal something about the Church in Spain, even if it says nothing about its origins. By the middle of the third century there were a number of Christian communities in the peninsula. It is clear, for instance, that there were more bishops than the four (two deposed and two elected in their stead) who are named, for they had taken

184

part in the ordination of Sabinus who had replaced Martial as bishop. It is also clear that apostasy was not the only charge against Martial, for his conduct had not been all that the early Church might have expected. It transpired that, upon his conversion to Christianity, he had not broken off all contact with his former pagan friends. On the contrary, he had remained a member of a burial society, and had interred his own children in the cemetery belonging to that society. From this we may assume that Christians in Spain already had their own burial grounds.

Not all the clergy were so ill-behaved. Shortly after this, Bishop Fructuosus, together with his deacons Augurius and Eulogius, died a martyr's death in Tarragona. Fructuosus' death was a noble one, and he showed himself to be everything a Christian apologist could have wished for, being on friendly terms with, and much respected by, the pagans around him.

Then came the astonishing Council of Elvira. The date of its meeting is uncertain, but its location is not. The council took place in what is now a suburb of Granada, either between the years 300 and 302 or in 309. It was attended by nineteen bishops and twenty-four presbyters, most of whom came from towns in southern Spain. Taken together, the forty-three clergy looked after some three dozen Christian communities, which would appear to suggest that, at least in Spain, a Church governed by a bishop was not the invariable rule even at the beginning of the fourth century. The result of the deliberations at the Council was a rather incoherent sequence of 81 canons, or rules for the Church. There has been some claim that not all the canons can be ascribed to the same occasion because some of them seem to reflect a rather later position taken by the Church. The problems that arise from dividing up the canons, however, are greater than those involved in accepting the traditional view that they were all drawn up at the Council of Elvira.

A great deal can be learned from the results of the meeting at Elvira. Those who were gathered there self-consciously modelled their proceedings upon the practices of Roman local legislative assemblies, as earlier synods, especially those in Africa, had also done. But this juridical concept of the role of Christian leaders was a world removed from the part played by the charismatic prophets and preachers who had first provided leadership in the Church in Asia Minor, two and a half centuries before. The canons of Elvira throw some light on the reasons why the Church had changed so much.

Amid all the turmoil and tension of the late Roman Empire, with the conflicting claims of the imperial cult, of the mystery religions and of Judaism, the Christian Church felt confident enough to emphasize its own distinctive identity. Canon 17, for example, declares that 'If any should perchance join their daughters in marriage to priests of the idols, they shall not be given communion, even at the end.' The phrase 'even at the end' is

The Visigoths entered Spain at the beginning of the fifth century. They were Christians of a sort, as the Chi-Ro symbol on this Visigothic sarcophagus demonstrates.

chilling. In common with the mystery religions, Christianity had offered to its adherents the hope of life after death and, unlike the mystery religions, had offered it widely. But what had once been an attractive promise was now turned into a deadly threat: the offer of everlasting life had become a means of social control. It could be used by the bishops and priests to prevent members of their communities associating with competing religious groups.

One method of marking out Christians from others, emphasized by members of the Council, was sexual behaviour. Another was the treatment of priests of the imperial cult, which rather suggests that these *flamines* were converting to Christianity in considerable numbers. Sexual conduct, however, was the major topic, even in those canons which did not dwell upon it explicitly, such as the prohibition against women receiving letters or consorting with long-haired men and hairdressers. Sexual misbehaviour was to be punished more severely than other failings. A woman who had beaten her slave-girl to death escaped more lightly than one who had had an abortion.

Canon 33 contains the first formal statement of the necessity for clerical continence:

Bishops, presbyters and deacons and all other clerics having a position in the ministry are ordered to abstain completely from their wives and not to have children. Whoever, in fact, does this, shall be expelled from the clerical state.

The canon is oddly phrased. It does not forbid clerics to marry. They might do so, but had 'to abstain completely from their wives' so as not to have children. It is the act of sexual intercourse which is forbidden. Subsequent councils were to refine the prohibition, but Elvira made it the distinguishing mark of the clerical caste, cutting its members off from the laity by their lifestyle and the ascetical demands laid upon them. These were not decisions imposed from above, but freely chosen by those whom they affected. The clergy, and especially the bishops, were defining themselves against the laity.

The Council of Elvira occurred at a time when there was growing autocracy in the Roman Empire at large. The clerics, who saw themselves as leaders in the Christian community, may already have been measuring themselves against the leaders of civil society. Their comparative leniency with Christians who killed slaves may have been an act of solidarity with the slave-owning classes, with whom the Christian leaders identified themselves. The priests of the imperial cult, the *flamines*, were men of the equestrian class, ranking only just below the senatorial order, and were the civil as well as the religious leaders in the provinces. Their conversion to Christianity in large numbers may reflect a loss of confidence in the imperial system, but apostasies among their ranks were also a problem. The clerics at Elvira were particularly harsh on *flamines* who reverted to their old ways, which suggests that there were power struggles in the Spanish cities between pagan and Christian priests.

It is unreasonable to imagine that the canons of Elvira marked a sudden shift in the life of the Spanish Church. The minds which formulated and approved them must have been moulded in a tradition created over several generations of Christian leadership. But they imply a vastly different form of Christianity from that which took root in first-century Palestine. This change is commonly attributed to the period after Constantine, and to the uneasy marriage of Church and State which occurred in the fourth century. Whatever the date of Elvira, it took place before the Edict of Milan brought toleration for Christianity, and must in any case represent a tradition of thought which was far older. The changes which had come about were occasioned by pressures internal to the Church as it became an increasingly powerful institution in a society whose certainties were in decline.

187

9
RITUAL AND WORSHIP

At the time Christianity was born and established itself, people lived in a threatening universe. Alongside the real world was another, parallel but unseen world of spirits, good and bad. The bad spirits predominated, and from them one needed protection. The security of a religious belief which proved itself by its ability to lay hold of the God's favour was enormously attractive. Those who came to the defence of Christianity against pagans such as Origen had no embarrassment in claiming that the Christian's magic was much greater than that of non-Christians. Irenaeus believed – and preached – that Christian leaders had even raised people from the dead by calling upon the name of Jesus.

But miracles of healing and raising people from the dead were not the common way of reaching out to the divine. Prayer, sacrifice, and elaborate ceremonial – these were all part and parcel of almost any form of religion – were more usual, and Christianity was certainly no exception. It was exceptional, however, in the form which these took.

THE PRAYER OF THE EARLY CHRISTIANS
In the first instance, the model for prayer was Jewish. Jesus was a Jew and he observed Jewish practices until his death. He attended the synagogue services with his disciples. St Luke's Gospel makes it clear this was his habit: 'he went into the synagogue on the sabbath day as he usually did' (Lk 4:16), and there are indications that he attended the synagogue on other days as well. Jesus took an active part in the worship. Not only did he read the Scriptures but he also preached, and it seems clear that he fulfilled all the liturgical observances required by Jewish Law.

For a long time Jesus' followers kept up the Jewish practices. The apostles, together with Mary and the other women, continued to pray in the synagogues. Peter and John are recorded as going up to the Temple at the ninth hour to pray. Paul invariably called at the local synagogue when visiting a city. It is reasonable to presume that the distancing of the new faith from the old was a gradual process which arose from a dawning awareness among Christians that they were not simply yet another Jewish sect, on a par with the Pharisees or the Essenes. But the first generation of Christians had grown up with the synagogue service, and continued to use its structures in their own form of worship, at least until AD 70. These roots were forgotten by those who came later.

The *Didache*, compiled in about AD 100 to instruct the faithful in forms

188

A fragment of the second-century Didache.

of worship among other things, tells them to recite the Lord's Prayer three times a day, and this may reflect the synagogue tradition of three services each day. It also insists upon a Wednesday and a Friday fast: Jews too fasted twice a week, but on Tuesdays and Thursdays. Hippolytus, writing his *Apostolic Tradition* in third-century Rome, recommended prayer specifically at nine o'clock in the morning, at midday and at three in the afternoon, at midnight and at cockcrow, as well as morning and evening prayers. This appears to be a heavy schedule, but it is intended for private devotions; the only public service he mentions is a morning one of instruction and of prayer to be attended by the clergy and by such of the laity who were able to be present.

The form of prayer said in common at the morning service was again closely modelled on that of Judaism. It was the equivalent of the *berakah*, prayers of praise and remembrance in which God is named, his past actions are recalled, and trust is expressed for the future because of God's faithfulness to his promises in the past. In its Jewish form, this prayer ended with another expression of praise to God, the 'doxology'. In Christian circles this soon seems to have become an expression of praise to the Trinity, to God the Father, God the Son and God the Holy Spirit. Prayers in the Jewish morning service were said standing, the leader speaking the words aloud and the congregation listening and answering 'Amen' at the end. Again the Christians copied this custom.

Even the singing of hymns, usually the psalms, was taken over from

Judaism – but with a difference, for the Psalms were interpreted as referring to Christ. Very soon, however, the Christians began to compose their own hymns, some of which may be traced in the text of the New Testament. Many of these, too, were modelled upon Jewish forms of prayer, and were often constructed out of interwoven passages from the Old Testament. An example of this is the Magnificat, the prayer put into the mouth of Mary when she goes to visit her cousin Elizabeth, as recounted at the beginning of the Gospel of Luke.

The early Christians did not have to rely solely upon the Psalms and upon the New Testament hymns, however. Though few other types survive, they do exist. There is extant a Greek evening hymn which quite possibly dates back to the second century. The earliest known hymn of the Western Church is some five hundred years later. It is an early version of 'Glory to God in the highest', still sung in Western liturgies.

THE SACRED MYSTERIES

In addition to daily attendance at the Temple for prayer, the Acts of the Apostles records other forms of worship practised by the first Christians: 'They went as a body to the Temple every day but met in their houses for the breaking of bread; they shared their food gladly and generously; they praised God and were looked up to by everyone.' (Acts 2:46–7)

This brief account seems to imply two sorts of meetings. There were those 'for the breaking of bread', and those at which 'they shared their food gladly', the one a Eucharist, the other a social gathering. The Eucharist was the central act of the Christian's life, for it did two things. First it recalled the action of Jesus at the Last Supper which was, at least according to the Synoptic Gospels, a celebration of the Jewish Passover:

For this is what I received from the Lord, and in turn passed on to you: that on the same night that he was betrayed, the Lord Jesus took some bread, and thanked God for it and broke it, and he said 'This is my body which is for you; do it as a memorial of me.' (1 Cor 11:23–4)

Secondly, it gave a promise of what was to come. It had the eschatological overtones of the resurrection: 'This is the bread come down from heaven; not like the bread our ancestors ate; they are dead, but anyone who eats this bread will live for ever' (Jn 6:58). The Eucharist, then, was a powerful medicine, the 'medicine of immortality', as Ignatius of Antioch called it in his letter to the Ephesians, echoing the sort of language the mystery cults might have used. The powers of the Eucharist lay very close to magic.

Although there are earlier hints, the first extended description of what happened during a Eucharistic service is to be found in Justin, who was writing in the middle of the second century. (It is worth remarking the fact that Justin does supply a description. At this date there was no obvious attempt to be secretive about what happened in the Christian assemblies. Later on the 'mystery' surrounding the Eucharist may have been one of the

190

several elements which helped to bind the Christian community together.) According to Justin, there were readings from the Old and the New Testaments followed by a sermon given by whoever was presiding over the occasion. All then stood, and intercessory prayers were offered. This was followed by the kiss of peace – and in the early Church a kiss meant a kiss, not some symbolic gesture of friendship. Bread and wine were then brought in, and over them the president of the assembly said a prayer of thanksgiving ('Eucharist' means 'thanksgiving'). Finally the deacon distributed the bread and wine to those attending, and some was carried to those absent through sickness. Members of the community took the consecrated elements home with them so they might receive the Eucharist during the week.

The outline to be found in Justin is not unlike modern Eucharistic liturgies. There was even a collection, the proceeds of which were handed over to the president so that he might 'help orphans and widows, and those who through sickness and any other cause are in need, and those in prison and strangers sojourning among us; in a word, he takes care of all those who are in need.' Christianity was a very supportive club.

But it had its critics. There were stories of sexual irregularities, even of cannibalism and infanticide. The charge of sexual misconduct was a common one against the mystery religions, but there is some evidence in Christianity of gross sexual perversion being raised to the level of an act of worship by at least one sect, the Carpocratians, who were active in Alexandria. And if Epiphanius is to be believed, another Christian group, the Phibionites, not only engaged in promiscuous sexual activity but held that if a child were conceived because of it, the embryo was to be aborted and eaten by the initiates.

There is some evidence that sects such as these existed, but none to suggest that they existed in any number. Of much greater concern to Christian writers was the danger that the kiss which was part of the liturgy might give rise to lewdness. It was, after all, a kiss on the lips, and Athenagoras, who was writing at about the same time as Tertullian, was worried lest one kiss might lead to another:

We felt it a matter of great importance that those, who we thus think of as brother and sister and so on, should keep their bodies undefiled and uncorrupted. For the Scripture says, 'If one kisses a second time, because he found it enjoyable . . .' thus the kiss, or rather the religious salutation, should be very carefully guarded. If it is defiled by the slightest evil thought it excludes us from eternal life.

It is not known what was the 'Scripture' Athenagoras was recalling, and the final words of the quotation are missing.

But what is particularly interesting about the quotation from Athenagoras is the indication it gives of the narrow pathway that Christians had to walk. Most early Christian writers are clear that the power of the

191

Eucharist was the power of the risen Christ. It strengthened whoever received it against the machinations of the devil and of the evil spirits which surrounded every individual. Yet to receive it unworthily was in itself a mortal danger. This was acknowledged early on by St Paul: 'Everyone is to recollect himself before eating this bread and drinking this cup; because a person who eats and drinks without recognizing the Body is eating and drinking his own condemnation' (1 Cor 11:28–9). Even Paul appears to attribute to the reception of the consecrated bread and wine a magical significance.

So those who partook of the Eucharist had to live worthy lives. By the late second century those who did not, or were publicly known not to do so, were denied the Eucharist. By the beginning of the third century Churches would advise one another of who was, and who was not, 'in communion' with the bishops of the local Church. Christians who moved about from one city to another could carry a letter of recommendation, which gave them access to a warm welcome – and even to financial support should they need it, according to Justin's remarks about the treatment of 'strangers and sojourners among us'.

Certainly by the middle of the third century the Eucharist had come to be regarded as a sacrifice. As a form of sacrifice it had distinct advantages. It was symbolic, but it was also real. It might be received by everyone, of whatever class or nationality, who had been initiated into the sacred mysteries. It was a sign of unity in the Church, and a passport for those who travelled. The Eucharist did not merely commemorate local gods but recalled a God who had proved his efficacy by raising others and then himself from the dead. Its power was magical, and it was reserved for Christians. It formed a discipline, but it also formed a point of attraction. Those whom the Eucharist attracted took their first definitive step towards the eternal life it promised when they underwent the awesome rites of initiation.

THE AWE-INSPIRING RITES

St John Chrysostom described baptism as 'the awesome mysteries about which it is forbidden to speak'. The words occur in a sermon delivered in about 390 in which the saint was berating those newly converted who, shortly after taking part in the ceremony of initiation into Christianity, had been distracted by chariot races and theatres, and were to Chrysostom's mind paying far too little attention to their religious duties. By the late fourth century the element of mystery in the rite of Christian initiation seems to have become one of its central elements. Christians kept some of the teachings and practices of their faith secret from non-believers. This included the words of the Creed and of the Lord's Prayer, the meaning of the Eucharist, and the ceremonies associated with the reception of converts.

192

Above, a Christian feast – possibly a Eucharist – on a third-century sarcophagus and, below, a painting from the catacomb of Callistus recalling the miracles of the loaves and the fishes which Christians would have interpreted as referring to the Eucharist.

It had not always been so. In the second century, for example, Justin Martyr had written freely about the Eucharist in a book intended for pagans, but by the early third century Tertullian was advising his wife not to marry again should he die, because her next, presumably pagan, husband would not understand when she gave herself the Eucharist. This growing emphasis on secrecy, at a time when the need for it might have been expected to recede, marks the influence upon Christianity of the mystery religions. It has been argued that signs of this influence can be found as early as the letters of Paul, and especially in those passages in which the apostle talks about baptism. But closer examination suggests that the 'mystery' words found in Paul's writing are for the most part those in fairly common usage at the time. He does not use the exact phrases of the mystery religions: he speaks about resurrection, for example, and not about rebirth. In any case, the details of the religions which, it is alleged, influenced Paul's thinking are known only from a period long after his death. It is probably sufficient explanation that both the mystery cults and Christianity attemped to meet the same basic needs of humankind, and so both fell into using the same sort of language.

To find the origins of baptism, therefore, it is not necessary to turn to the oriental cults. The Old Testament laid down a large number of ceremonial washings, or 'lustrations', by which ritual purity might be achieved. In New Testament times the Qumran community had frequent washings of this sort: baths may have been taken as often as three times a week. None of these, however, exactly constitutes baptism in the Christian sense. Not only were lustrations frequently repeated, they were self-administered. A much closer parallel to the Christian sacrament was the baptism of Jewish proselytes.

This baptism was undoubtedly a form of initiation. It was administered once only. It was preceded by a type of catechetical instruction which certainly influenced Christian practice. But once again there are problems about chronology. The earliest evidence for proselyte baptism is later than references to baptism by St Paul, though the context in which it arises suggests that it was being practised by the Jews at about the time Paul was composing his first letters. The most that can be said about the connection between proselyte and Christian baptism is that they may have arisen at around the same time.

Then there was the baptism of John. As recounted by the Gospels, John seems to have preached in the region associated with the Qumran sect. It is possible that he was in some way linked to the sect, though his message was both more radical and more urgent than theirs. His baptism was once and for all. It marked a change not, as in proselyte baptism, from Gentile to worshipping Jew, but from a life of sin to one of righteousness. It was a baptism of repentance.

No single one of these antecedents can wholly explain the origins of Christian baptism, but no doubt they all in some way contributed to its theory and practice in the early Church. Christ enjoined baptism. Baptism was the response of the apostles when, after Peter's sermon at Pentecost, three thousand were converted. The story is told in the Acts of the Apostles, and baptism recurs frequently in that book, as it does in the letters of St Paul. Paul may even drop some hints about the rite as it was practised in his own day when he talks about the newly baptized Christians putting off the old life and putting on the new: this may be a reference to dressing in new clothes after the ceremony.

Apart from this briefest of clues, the New Testament does not describe the rite. One can only suppose that, in its simplest form, it consisted of a confession of faith and an immersion in water. The *Didache*, which is roughly contemporary with the last New Testament writings, insists that baptism is necessary before the reception of the Eucharist, and briefly describes what happens. Baptism is to take place in cold running water (though warm is reluctantly allowed), and both baptizer and the one to be baptized should have fasted for two days before the ceremony.

A rather more detailed account of how the service was performed at Rome in the early years of the third century is preserved in the *Apostolic Tradition*. Hippolytus describes how candidates for baptism are to be treated during the three-year period of preparation. He gives in greater detail the immediate run-up to the ceremony: the exorcisms, the Thursday bath, more exorcisms and the Saturday night vigil of Scripture readings and final instruction. And then the baptism:

And at the hour when the cock crows they shall first pray over the water. When they come to the water, let the water be pure and flowing. And they shall put off their clothes. And they shall baptize the little children first. And if they can answer for themselves, let them answer. But if they cannot, let their parents answer or someone from their family. And next they shall baptize the grown men; and last the women, who shall have loosed their hair and laid aside their gold ornaments. Let no one go down into the water having any alien object with them.

There follow more anointings to drive away the devil. 'After these anointings let him go over to the presbyter who stands at the water. And let them stand in the water naked. And let the deacon likewise go down into the water with him.' Three times the candidate for baptism is pressed down into the water as, three times, his or her faith is questioned. There is further anointing, and then the candidate dresses.

There follows the solemn Eucharist. At communion, between the reception of the bread and the cup, the new member of the community is given a mixture of milk and honey, a symbol, perhaps, of the neophyte's arrival in the promised land.

This liturgy of baptism, confirmation and Eucharist no doubt had its moments of high drama, but was it really 'awe-inspiring' – an expression which one scholar has suggested might just as well be 'hair-tingling' or 'spine-chilling'?

This painting of the baptism of Jesus comes from the catacomb of Peter and Marcellinus and shows him standing in the River Jordan. In the fifth-century baptistery, right, found in what is now Turkey, the neophytes stood in a baptismal pool.

196

To understand the impact of baptism it is important to remember the length of the preparation and the atmosphere of the occasion. It had been preceded by at least three years of instruction, with the promise of more secrets to come at the moment of baptism. There was therefore a heightened sense of anticipation. Immediately before the ceremony came a fast, a long period of prayer, an all-night vigil in a darkened building. Then, in the dim light of wavering torches, the devil was solemnly abjured to flee in a series of exorcisms. The candidate entered the baptistery. First he or she turned towards the west to renounce Satan, then towards the east to confess Christ. There were repeated anointings with oil, the symbol of strength. Once at least the naked candidate was anointed from head to toe. Then, oiled as if for bathing, the candidate entered the font, climbing in, perhaps, as must have happened at Dura Europos, or stepping down until knee-deep while a deacon poured water over the head, or pressed the candidate's head down into the pool. There was another anointing perhaps – rituals differed – before the candidate dressed in new clothes. All this took place in the half-light, to the sound of hymns, in a state of high exaltation. Then came confirmation – another anointing – and the new Christian moved out of the torchlight into the dawn of a brightly lit church to receive his or her first Eucharist.

Accounts vary slightly according to local custom: in one place, for example, the neophyte's feet were washed, while in the Syriac tradition

197

there is no evidence for the final anointing now called confirmation. But the description above is a basic form of the ceremony as it had come to be practised by the third century. It is very far removed from the simple ritual hinted at in the New Testament.

THE PROBLEMS OF PRIESTHOOD

Discussion of the Eucharist and of baptism inevitably gives rise to the question of Christian ministers. So far we have discussed the role of bishops, deacons and deaconesses, and of presbyters, but not of priests. The role of priest in Jewish tradition was hereditary. There was only one place where sacrifice might be offered, the Jerusalem Temple, and those who offered it were the priests. Presbyters, on the other hand, were simply the senior members of the synagogue, no more than a council of elders. It has already been shown how the bishop emerged out of the Christian equivalent as the leading figure who presided over the Eucharist. In the early days of Christianity the Eucharist was not seen as a sacrifice, except as a commemoration of Christ's own sacrifice. So the word 'priest' in the New Testament is reserved for Christ and, figuratively, for the Church. It is not used of the presbyters. It is not even used of the bishops.

In the New Testament, prophesying emerges as the most important of all the Church ministries which are listed. Paul thinks both men and women will be inspired. Even while he is instructing women to wear a veil over their heads during services, he still presumes that a woman may prophesy or pray. Nothing at all is said about either men or women presiding at a Eucharist. But if anyone did preside at a Eucharist in first-century Palestine – and one must presume this was the case – according to Jewish practice the most likely person to do so would have been the head of a household, whether man or woman.

In his letters Paul never mentions presbyters at all, and there is no hint that there was any sort of division of the faithful into clergy and laity. It is true that the Acts of the Apostles depicts him appointing presbyters, but since he never talks of this himself it may be that the author of Acts is reading back into Paul's own lifetime a slightly later development. By the time Clement of Rome came to write to the Christians of Corinth, a distinction between clergy (if 'presbyters' can be described as clergy) and laity had come about, but Clement does not make the laity subordinate to the clergy. He tells the laity they ought not to act irresponsibly in deposing presbyters from office; he does not tell them that they cannot do so.

Although it is possible to find hints of a 'sacrificial' priesthood in the New Testament when applied to the Church as well as to Christ, especially in the Epistle to the Hebrews, the concept was slow to develop. In his *Apostolic Tradition* Hippolytus uses language which recalls the idea of a sacrificial priesthood, but he does not refer to it. The bishop 'offers' the gifts of the Church, but that is as far as it goes. Hippolytus is much more concerned with Church government, and with the forgiveness of sins.

This was not the first time 'sacrificial' or 'sacerdotal' language had been used about presbyters and bishops. Tertullian had used it, and without apology, as if the practice was already well established. He enumerated the functions for which a person needed to be ordained in order to indicate what it was improper for women to undertake – which may suggest that women were still acting in priestly roles in orthodox Christianity as they were in some of the less orthodox movements, Montanism in particular. Yet although Tertullian and Hippolytus were using sacerdotal terms, and although Tertullian made a link between priests and the altar – implying sacrifice – neither was explicitly sacrificial in the understanding of the Eucharist or of the priesthood.

On the other hand there were a number of factors which encouraged them to view the Christian 'clergy' in a new light. In the early days of the Church it was important to Christians that they mark their distinctiveness. The Jews had a sacrificing priesthood: for the Christians there was only one priest, Christ. And even Christ was not descended from Judaism's priestly caste. With Christ there had been a break with the past. But a century and a half later it was no longer quite so necessary to mark the distinction. By now that was well established, and similar institutions might be mentioned without fear of confusion.

It was not only Judaism that had priests, of course. Pagan cults had them too, and in the cities they played a significant part in civic life. In his study of Christian priesthood the theologian R.P.C. Hanson imagines the following conversation between a pagan and a Christian. The pagan might say, 'What is this leader of your cult called?' To this the Christian could only reply lamely, 'Ours is called an inspector'. The enhancement in the status of the Church's officials goes hand in hand with its growing self-confidence, so that by Cyprian's time the Christian bishop was clearly a man of distinction in the Roman city. It is no accident that Cyprian was the one who most distinctly associates priesthood with the celebration of the Eucharist, and identifies the apostles as the first bishops. That was something which had not occurred to earlier writers such as Irenaeus, despite the latter's strong belief in the apostolic succession. According to Cyprian, when a bishop offered the gifts (to use Hippolytus' language) he was doing precisely what Christ had done: he was offering the sacrifice of Christ's own body and blood.

The role of Christian presbyter was no longer one which might change according to the gifts of the Spirit. It had become a status in the Church, one to which governance, 'sacrifice' of the Eucharist and forgiveness of sin were inextricably attached.

REPENTANCE

At first sight it is odd that the problem of the reconciliation of Christians

Two Christians venerating a martyr standing in the attitude of prayer are shown in this picture from the confessio under the basilica of SS John and Paul. A Christian woman, right, stands in the same pose, between two shepherds, in a painting in the catacomb called Coemeterium Maius.

who had fallen away should have become a matter of such debate in the early Church. A great deal of Jesus' preaching was about repentance. There was no sin so bad that it could not be forgiven and its perpetrator reconciled both with God and with the community. There were of course those who rejected reconciliation. There is a passage in the letter to Titus, towards the end of the New Testament period, which shows this: 'If a man disputes what you teach, then after a first and second warning, have no more to do with him: you will know that any man of that sort has already lapsed and condemned himself as a sinner' (Titus 3:10–11).

Repentance, a change of heart, already had a community dimension, and this is re-echoed in the *Didache*. 'But on the Lord's Day come together', it says, 'break bread and give thanks, after you have first confessed your sins.' The homily known as the Second Letter of Clement is rather more practical: 'Almsgiving is good as a penance for sin; fasting is better than prayer, and almsgiving better than both.'

The serious sinner, then, is invited to repentance, but if the invitation is rejected the sinner is either cut off from the Church or he excommunicates himself. Forgiveness is symbolized by the acceptance back into the community after some form of suitable penance has been completed.

But then, some time in the middle of the second century, along came Hermas. He believed, and wrote, that all sins might be forgiven. Nothing, however serious, was so wicked that it might cut a person off from God for ever. The possibility of forgiveness, though, was on offer once and once only: the sinner who repeated the fault clearly could not have had, in Hermas' view, the true spirit of repentance.

As before, forgiveness was symbolized by the reconciliation of the sinner with the Church: Hermas seems to go a step further when he hints that this acceptance of the sinner back into the fold was the responsibility of the clergy.

Tertullian did not think they had any right to do so. He took particular exception to an 'edict' of an unnamed 'Pontifex Maximus', possibly Bishop Callistus of Rome, which claimed that sins of adultery and fornication could be forgiven. This severe attitude Tertullian displayed when he was in his Montanist period, and he admits that in his earlier life he had been a supporter of forgiveness: the rigorism inherent in Montanism may have owed something to the seeming laxity of the Catholic Church.

From Tertullian's writings, both in his Catholic and in his Montanist periods, it is possible to build up a fairly clear picture of what was involved in an act of reconciliation. The first thing needed was, of course, a change of heart, but this had to be demonstrated to the community by acts of mortification, by wearing sackcloth and ashes, by fasting and by prayer on bended knees (the usual posture for prayer was standing). There was also the act of confessing the sin. This was to be done publicly, and twice, the first time outside the church, the second inside the door. The actual reconciliation was left to the bishop to carry out. The same restriction remained that is to be found in Hermas: the ceremony can only be gone through once.

In Rome the practice seems to have been somewhat less rigorous – hence, perhaps, the conflict between Tertullian and the bishop of Rome. Certainly there was a disagreement between Cyprian of Carthage and the bishop of Rome over those who had lapsed into paganism during the persecution of Decius. In the course of this dispute Cyprian provides a clear description of penance in his day. It is under the supervision of the priests. They determine the time the penance is to take, ensure that it is performed, and decide when enough has been done. There does not seem to have been a formal, public confession of sin as part of the liturgical rite, but that may have gone before, perhaps privately. There was, however, a public act of formal penance performed before the bishop, priests and lay people, which concluded with the bishop laying his hands on the penitent.

What has just been described was the practice of the Western Church. In Alexandria they ordered matters slightly differently, but the chief difference was one of mentality. There they believed that sinners weaned themselves away from sinful attitudes by a slow process. The long-term result was that while the Western Church came to think of penance in legal terms, in the Eastern Church it became closely associated with the guidance of an individual's spiritual life. In that guidance a holy person could play as great a part, simply by reason of his or her holiness, as could a priest through his status.

The theory of penance developed in the fourth and subsequent

A woman in prayer, from Vigna Massimo. The extended arms of the 'orant' (person praying) indicate piety.

centuries, but its main lines were already visible in the third, and they determined what sort of community the Christian Church was going to be. If the possibility of penance was denied, or if it were on offer only once in a person's lifetime, Christianity was destined to be a Church only for the holy. It might be a beacon to others, an ideal to which to aspire, but as a strict discipline it would be suitable only for a handful. If, on the other hand, penance were to be offered readily, as was Rome's view, the body of the Church would be open to all. Christians might lose something of their power to move by example, the Church might lose some of its power to coerce its members and some of its renown for moral stature – recognized, as has been seen, by its opponents as well as by its friends – but at the same time it could, in its more welcoming guise, be a Church for the masses.

10

CHRISTIAN ATTITUDES

Christian attitudes changed as the Church came to terms with the world in which it had to operate. This is demonstrated by the attitude displayed at various times towards wealth.

THE FATE OF ANANIAS AND SAPPHIRA

One of the most radical positions adopted by the earliest Christians is described in a particularly vivid story to be found in the Acts of the Apostles:

> There was a Levite of Cypriot origins called Joseph whom the apostles surnamed Barnabas (which means 'son of encouragement'). He owned a piece of land and he sold it and brought the money and presented it to the apostles.

The fate of Ananias (whose body is being borne away) and Sapphira (standing in front of St Peter) is portrayed on this reliquary. Below, the Emperor Trajan distributes the alimenta, or bounty, to poor children which was intended, it is thought, to increase the birth rate among poor families, and thus boost recruitment into the army.

There was another man, however, called Ananias. He and his wife Sapphira agreed to sell a property; but with his wife's connivance he kept back part of the proceeds and brought the rest and presented it to the apostles. 'Ananias,' Peter said, 'how can Satan have so possessed you that you should lie to the Holy Spirit and keep back part of the money from the land? While you still owned the land, wasn't it yours to keep, and after you had sold it wasn't the money yours to do with as you liked? What put this scheme into your mind? It is not to men that you have lied, but to God.' When he heard this Ananias fell down dead. This made a profound impression on everyone present. The younger men got up, wrapped the body in a sheet, carried it out and buried it.

About three hours later his wife came in, not knowing what had taken place. Peter challenged her, 'Tell me, was this the price you sold the land for?' 'Yes,' she said, 'that was the price.' Peter then said, 'So you and your husband have agreed to put the Spirit of the Lord to the test! What made you do it? You hear those footsteps? They have just been to bury your husband; they will carry you out too.' Instantly she dropped dead at his feet. When the young men came in they found she was dead, and they carried her out and buried her by the side of her husband. This made a profound impression on the whole Church and on all who heard it. (Acts 4:36–5:11)

That it made a profound impression is hardly surprising. But the message is not wholly clear. At first sight it seems that Ananias and Sapphira died because they retained money for their own use, but more careful reading indicates that their real fault was lying rather than covetousness. It is clear enough that, at least at this early stage, there was a form of communism practised by the Jerusalem community ruled over by Peter. But it was what has been called 'love communism'. It was a free association. Ananias and Sapphira could have been Christians without being members of a community which shared its possessions.

It is significant that the passage refers to the Church in the last sentence quoted. 'Church' in this early usage meant the messianic community, a community looking forward to the imminent coming of a new age. And one of the signs that the new age had arrived was the sharing of goods – as also practised among the Essenes.

This sharing does not seem to have been obligatory even upon those who belonged to the community, and there is no record of it happening elsewhere during the first century. Quite the contrary. The Jerusalem community does not appear to have been a success. Paul had to take collections for them, and there is no evidence that the community of goods survived the fall of Jerusalem in AD 70. But the really wealthy, Sadducean, class also disappeared after AD 70, so the rhetoric of poverty, the tradition which presented the poor as especially beloved of God simply because they were poor and therefore oppressed, lost a good deal of its point. A breakaway group called the Ebionites managed to preserve the tradition, but possibly because they really were poor. Much later on, in the middle of the third century, Cyprian is recorded as having given up his considerable wealth on becoming a Christian, but it is also clear that he, or his Church, continued to be rich and able to make large donations to needier Christians.

It was the question of what money was for, rather than the rights and wrongs of having it, which gave rise to debate among Christians. After all, as the Church grew it needed increasing amounts of money in order to run its affairs. In Rome the catacombs were provided by wealthy Christians, who also set aside part of their houses for meetings for worship and, most important of all, were a source of alms.

Christian generosity towards members of its own community was one of its more attractive features. Churches gave financial support to widows, orphans, the destitute. The Roman *collegia* did likewise, it is true, but scarcely on such a grand scale. In comparison with the Church they were very small institutions, and tended to be at the whim of their patrons. Christian Churches, besides being larger bodies, had more 'patrons', though because of their numbers individual rich people had less say in how their money was spent. And it was not spent to advance their own interests. As early as the date of the *Didache* it is clear that Christians were supposed to pass their offerings to the priest, who decided which way they were to be distributed. Thus the rich were deprived of the power their money might bring them, and this power was transferred to the clergy.

The Church, then, did not reject riches. Irenaeus believed that people could become wealthy only through fraud and deceit, but he never hinted that money acquired in this way should be given up. Clement had a good many rich students in his catechetical school at Alexandria, and he was one of the few early Christians directly to address the question of money. But he did not tell his students that if they did not give up their wealth they were in danger of losing their souls – which was Jesus' message. Rather he taught that riches were not evil in themselves and could be used for good purposes, especially alms. Clement proposed a simple solution to the tension between the poverty proclaimed by the Gospel and the wealth enjoyed by his pupils. Money was not to be hoarded or spent on oneself, but used for the benefit of others. The obligation of the rich was to be detached from their money, to lead a simple life – Christian apologists were always insisting on the virtue of frugality – and not to go in search of yet greater wealth.

Tertullian pointed out that the danger lay not so much in wealth itself as in the consequences of being wealthy. Roman society was strictly stratified, but a person's position was determined more by birth than by wealth. There could be poor members of the equestrian order just as there could be, and often were, rich people among the freedmen. There were even rich slaves. But in practice the upper classes were also frequently the wealthy, and they were obliged to serve in public offices which, as will be seen, constantly involved compromise with paganism. That was incompatible with life as a Christian.

In general, however, the 'love communism' of Acts and the attempt to interpret literally Jesus' teaching on riches were soon abandoned as impracticable. Christianity was increasingly attracting the wealthy. A compromise had to be reached if the Church was to retain their allegiance and the considerable advantages which that entailed for the community as a whole. Clement's teaching, that the solution was detachment from wealth rather than abandonment of it, has remained the common doctrine to the present day.

CHRISTIANS AND THE STATE

Though there were ambiguities in Christian attitudes to wealth, there ought perhaps to have been fewer in the Church's relationship to the state. Paul made the position clear at the end of his letter to the Romans:

> You must all obey the governing authorities. Since all government comes from God, the civil authorities were appointed by God, and so anyone who resists authority is rebelling against God's decision and such an act is bound to be punished. (Rom 13: 1–6)

Nothing could be clearer. Paul has provided a Christian rationale for the state, and not for any state but, quite specifically, for the Roman Empire.

This was no passing aberration. Even after a persecution had occurred, the author of 1 Peter could still write:

> For the sake of the Lord, accept the authority of every social institution: the emperor as the supreme authority, and the governors as commissioned by him to punish criminals and praise good citizenship. God wants you to be good citizens, so as to silence what fools are saying in their ignorance. (1 Pt 2:13–17)

Yet, at about the time that 1 Peter was being written, the seer of Patmos was portraying the evils, and foretelling the final fall, of the Roman Empire. This confusion runs through the writings of the early authors.

Attempts have been made to reconcile the differences, and to produce a coherent theory. One solution to the apparent contradictions is to draw attention to the two dimensions in which Christians existed. They lived in a society which, for all its incidental variations from place to place, brought under one government, and one manner of life, a very large proportion of the then known world. Its inhabitants, including Christians, tended to think of it as universal in space and eternal in time. They could not think themselves outside it. That the Empire was divinely ordained, no one doubted. Such a vision neatly coincided with the Empire's own ideology, according to which the emperor was the defender of peace and of liberty. The Empire had, in its own eyes, a providential mission to bring all peoples

A third-century relief showing the payment of taxes.

together to enjoy the benefits of order and of civilization. The Empire had its own theology, and it was a theology with which Christians might to some extent concur.

But then there was the other dimension to a Christian's life, the expectation of Christ's return and the establishment of his kingdom. In that context the Empire did not fare at all well. Hippolytus identified it with Antichrist, and before him Hermas had insisted:

> You slaves of God live in a foreign country, for your city is far from this city. So if you know your city in which you are going to live, why do you prepare lands and expensive establishments and buildings and useless rooms here? (Si 1:1f.)

The two approaches were not necessarily exclusive. It was quite possible to believe that the Empire was providentially willed by God, but that nonetheless as a forerunner of the kingdom it was the realm of Antichrist. Christians did not attempt to speed up the coming of the kingdom. There is no evidence that they wished the Empire ill, even in times of persecution. Quite the contrary. In his Apology Justin went so far as to claim that Christians were defenders of public morality and their aims and those of the Empire went hand-in-hand. Consequently, he argued, the Empire should join them in their campaigns against prostitution, magic and the practice of abandoning infants. Christians were not rebellious, agreed Tertullian, and what is more they always paid their taxes.

209

But if Christians were such good citizens, why did they not play an active part in affairs of state? In Christianity's early years this is not hard to explain. For the most part the very first Christians were drawn from the lower classes and would not have expected to play a public role. But in the second century, and increasingly in the third, the position changed. The Church attracted converts from a wider cross-section of society.

One of Celsus' complaints about Christians was that they avoided public office. Origen's reply hints at the eschatalogical dimension of the Church:

> And we call upon those who are competent to take office, who are sound in doctrine and in life, to rule over the Churches... If Christians do avoid responsibilities, it is not with the motive of shirking the public services of life. But they keep themselves for a more divine and necessary service in the Church of God for the salvation of man. (*Contra Celsum*, VIII 75)

It was obviously Origen's view that the Church had first call upon the managerial skills of its members.

As time went on it seems likely that a number of ambitious Christians were quite prepared to undertake the burdens of public office. But the burdens were real. The obligation upon office-holders of a certain rank to provide games and other services for citizens became extremely expensive. Pagans such as Celsus may have resented Christians playing little or no part in the government of the municipalities, for some pagans were probably just as eager to avoid their civic duties as were the Christians.

From the beginning of the third century the problem was compounded. In the conspiracies of the reign of the Emperor Commodus and in the civil wars which followed his assassination many of the traditional ruling class lost their lives. There was a new mobility in society, and ambitious Christians may have felt they could improve their standing by accepting elevation to public office.

The chief Christian objection to holding these offices was their association with the pagan cults. Local civil leaders had the responsibility of ensuring that appropriate feasts were held in honour of both the local deities and the gods of Rome, and they had to find funds for the cult of the emperor. Whatever compromises Christians were prepared to make, flirting with idolatry was not one of them. It seems quite possible that, except in times of persecution, the Roman state itself was prepared to compromise during the third century, and to make it possible for Christians to accept magistracies while steering clear of the pagan ceremonial attached to them.

Persecution remained a problem, however, even for those who were prepared as time went by to countenance some compromise with the state. It was a theoretical problem as much as a practical one. As has just been indicated, some theologians looked upon the Empire as Antichrist, but a much more common view was that it played a providential role, and that its political authority was necessary for the preservation of order and the

This relief shows Roman legionaries. Armed service posed moral problems to Christians.

restraint of violence. Origen addressed himself directly to the issue of persecution. God conferred political power so that it might be put to beneficial use. In origin and purpose it was good, and those who turned it to an evil end would be punished by God. Melito, the bishop of Sardis who died c. 190, linked the Church's fortunes with those of the Empire: both had begun, and both had extended their frontiers, at about the same time, and the Empire's prosperity required the prayers of Christians. Melito even hinted that the success of Marcus Aurelius' attempt to have his son Commodus follow him to the throne was linked to how well the state treated the Church.

As bishops, Melito and Irenaeus had responsibility for the pastoral care of all in their Churches, the weak and the waverers as well as those determined in their faith. It may be that which made them rather more sympathetic towards the state and its needs – the pagan cult apart. Tertullian, on the other hand, was a layman, and something of a fanatic. He doubted the opinion that it was possible to hold office and yet avoid being tainted by paganism, and he drew attention to some of the moral dangers attached to the office of magistrate. A magistrate would have to send people to be tortured, or even condemn them to death. That raised the vexed question of the taking of life and, in particular, the problem of service in the imperial forces.

THE MORALITY OF WARFARE

Just as Celsus had complained about Christians failing to fulfil their civic duties, he criticized them for avoiding military ones as well. Origen replied:

We who by our prayers destroy all demons which stir up wars, violate oaths and disturb the peace, are of more help to emperors than those who seem to be doing the fighting... And though we do not become fellow-soldiers with him, even if he presses for this, yet we are fighting for him and composing a special army of piety through our intercessions to God. (*Contra Celsum*, VIII 73)

It is a neat argument, but it does not alter the facts: Christians would not serve in the army.

Though Hippolytus' *Apostolic Tradition* is basically a liturgical treatise, it contains the following prescription:

The soldier who is of inferior rank shall not kill anyone if ordered to, he shall not carry out the order, nor shall he take the oath. If he does not accept this, let him be dismissed [from the Church]. Anyone who has the power of the sword or the magistrate of a city who wears the purple, let him give it up or be dismissed. The catechumen or believer who shall wish to become a soldier shall be dismissed, because they have despised God.

Nothing could be clearer, yet about a century later, bishops at the Council of Arles determined that Christians had to remain in the army in peacetime. Anyone who rejected military service was to be put out of the Church. That was in 314. A year earlier, however, Emperor Constantine had exempted Christian clergy from fulfilling official state duties. It would appear that the bishops felt obliged to reciprocate.

The powerful profile of Diocletian, emperor from AD 284–305, on a Roman gold coin.

The recruitment of Christians into the army was not a problem in the very early Church, when military service was a voluntary occupation. Not everyone was eligible for service: slaves were not, nor were freedmen. Legions were recruited from among Roman citizens at first in Italy and only later, as the government gradually became militarized, from elsewhere in the Empire. Like other occupations it became hereditary during the crisis years of the third century.

There was no doubt about the basic Christian attitude. The Ten Commandments of the Old Testament forbade killing and idolatry, yet both of these were an inevitable part of a Roman soldier's life. On the parade ground at Carthage a trooper refused to commit an act of idolatry. He was expected to acknowledge the pagan gods before receiving a donation from the emperor, but instead of doing so he threw down his arms. It was this act which occasioned the first formal Christian treatise on military service, Tertullian's *De Corona*, 'On the Crown'.

For Tertullian the danger of idolatry was the chief argument against Christians joining the army, though he acknowledged others. He summed up his views succinctly in his book 'On Idolatry': 'When the Lord disarmed Peter he also disarmed all the soldiers to come' (*De Idolatria* 19:3). The fundamental objection was against the shedding of blood. The universalism of Christianity, which treated men and women as equals, improved the standing of the individual as such. Christianity was opposed to killing, and even more so to the casual brutality in which armies were wont to indulge.

In accounts of the death of martyrs there are instances of Christians being defended by soldiers, and this action was followed not infrequently by the soldiers' conversion. More commonly, however, the troops were remarkable for their cruelty to Christians. Christians were therefore forbidden to join the army. Those who became Christians when doing military service were expected to resign – no easy task because the Roman state, even though it exempted the Jews from bearing arms, did not recognize conscientious objection. The only way to withdraw was to arrange an ignominious discharge – a very unattractive proposition for anyone approaching retirement and the benefits available to veterans who had completed their twenty-five-year term of duty.

Perhaps a few followed that path, but in the third century it is clear that Christians were being recruited into the army, and staying there. In their desperate need for more troops the military authorities may have turned a blind eye to the Christians' stand against idolatry. Diocletian made a point of restoring the religious observances of the legionaries, which suggests that these had fallen into disuse. He did, moreover, discover that large numbers of his soldiers were Christians, and he dismissed them.

None of the Christian authors of the first three centuries seemed to find it strange to talk of *militia Christi*, 'soldiering for Christ', and to use the language of spiritual warfare or battle with the devil while condemning the

A Roman marriage ceremony with the matron of honour joining the couple's right hands.

real thing. Christians were, they insisted, a peaceful people, and the coming of Christ had brought an era of peace. Christian tradition was staunchly opposed to military service in the pay of the emperor. Until, that is, the interests of emperor and Church came to coincide, after Constantine granted toleration.

MARRIAGE AND VIRGINITY

Nothing presented quite such a problem to the early Church as sexuality. The first believers emphasized continence, purity, self-control, no doubt in opposition to the moral climate of the times. But they overdid it. The extreme views of the Marcionites, Montanists and others have already been mentioned, and the practice of rejecting marriage entirely can be traced back to the very first century.

Hostility to marriage was particularly strong in the apocryphal litera-

214

ture. The Acts of Thomas, for example, pointed out the problems which children caused their parents. In the view of the writer of these stories, parents who cared for their children became uncaring of others, and were frequently covetous and mean. The only true liberty was to be found in renouncing marriage.

Clement of Alexandria seems to have been a little more balanced, but even he argued that the advantages of marriage stem from the patience a husband learns as he copes with the problems that children, a wife, slaves and general material responsibilities bring in their train. One of the benefits of the married state, Clement remarked, is the attentiveness of a wife to her husband. She will relieve him of household chores, and look after him in sickness and old age. Virginity, on the other hand, would free those who embraced it for the service of God.

In eastern Syria there were communities which imposed the obligation of continence at the moment of baptism. Purity was a requirement of a full Christian life. It was however widely acknowledged in the Church that virginity, a higher choice than marriage, needed safeguarding by prayer and fasting. And, according to Origen, it needed strengthening by works of mercy. Spiritual works, that is. The temporal ones were to be undertaken by penitents. It was also widely acknowledged that virginity in itself did not guarantee holiness.

Christian marriage was, of course, tolerated. Early writers usually agreed that it had been ordained by God, but only as a concession to men's concupiscence. Once married, the partners had to stay faithful. That, too, was a departure from the pagan customs of the age. On the other hand the Church put the begetting of children as the first aim of marriage – a doctrine which came straight from Roman Law.

The Law did not give everyone equally the right to marry. Under the Law marriage was *obligatory* for all free citizens (in the Church it was not), but only within one's rank. The only possibility for those of differing social status was concubinage. Pope Callistus was criticized because he appeared to tolerate this consequence of the Law. A slave who was herself a concubine, he maintained, might be received as a catechumen provided she remained faithful to one man. If marriage was possible, however (which, technically, it was not for slaves), it had to be undertaken.

Divorce was not tolerated for Christians, and in this, too, they departed from the practice of their time. The early writers believed that it was quite acceptable for a man to divorce an adulterous wife, but not for a wife to divorce an adulterous husband. Men's failings were tolerated, those of women were not. Yet fidelity was required of both partners and, again in contrast to pagan marriage, husbands and wives were regarded as equals. By the beginning of the fourth century, adultery had come to be looked upon a little more leniently. In 314 the Council of Ancyra (Ankara) punished it with a temporary excommunication of seven years.

A Roman gold glass depicting a happily married couple.

As for the marriage ceremony, very little is known about it. Among Jewish Christian communities the earliest Christians probably retained the domestic ritual of a Jewish marriage. The parents would improvise prayers, the nuptial blessing being recited during the wedding feast; a member of the clergy might be expected to draw up a marriage contract, and possibly offer a prayer for the bride and groom.

Ignatius of Antioch proposed that Christians should marry only with the consent of the local bishop. There is no evidence that this suggestion constituted an obligation, and it was not necessary for the validity of the marriage. Ignatius' proposal may have been an attempt to encourage marriage between Christians, for inevitably marriages between Christians and pagans were common, especially in the early years. The Church did not at first discourage this practice, which had its advantages: it might bring others into the fold. But as time went on and the number of Christians increased, the Church looked upon marriages across religious boundaries with less and less favour. Such marriages were definitely forbidden by the Council of Elvira, though it is clear that they still occurred.

And in contrast to the picture on the opposite page, the archetypal philosopher, from a first-century BC wall painting. Philosophers lived lives of self-denial, and were constantly on the move, as the staff he is holding suggests.

Though in many ways the Church drew closer to the rest of society during the first three hundred years, the opposite was the case in terms of marriage and virginity. Christian and pagan practice grew increasingly apart. The Church's stance on sexuality, severe in contrast with that of other social groups, was one of the ways in which it identified itself. There were whole groups who embraced virginity in the belief that this was the more perfect form of Christian life.

SONS AND DAUGHTERS OF THE COVENANT

We have already seen that virginity was highly prized by the early Christian community. Later it became a vow – something promised to God – along with poverty and obedience. It became institutionalized and formal, defining the boundaries of what is called 'the religious life'.

The origins of this form of life are obscure. There are some hints, the most important of all being the baptismal liturgy of eastern Syria. Fragments remain which describe the last stage of the rite before the act of baptism itself. Those presenting themselves were asked to search their hearts to

217

decide whether they had strength enough to abandon their possessions, to renounce marriage, and to accept an ascetic way of life. If they were not ready, they were asked whether they ought not to postpone baptism until they were. Baptism was not simply initiation into a community of believers, but into a community of practitioners, people who were called to a holy war.

So strong was this strand in Syriac Christianity that no literature survives, even from later periods, which is directly concerned with the life of ordinary lay people. All writings were directed at those who had adopted this ascetic way of life. The two great Syriac authors, Aphraat and Ephraem, have only two styles of life to commend. Christians either live a life of virginity and holiness, or they live a 'consecrated' life, married but abstaining from all sexual activity. There must have been some lay people who did not fit into these categories, but about them such sources as exist are silent. As one scholar has put it recently, to think that only members of the 'covenant' (as this manner of life was called) existed is tantamount to believing that all Manichees were members of the 'elect'. Nevertheless, from the baptismal liturgy of the region it would seem that the option to be 'sons and daughters of the convenant', as this consecrated lifestyle was called, was put before everyone.

This is an extreme example, but Christians as a whole were different, and known to be so. Indeed they were admired for it. Galen, born in Pergamum in about AD 130, a philosopher though better known for his medical writings, was one of the Church's earliest and most perceptive critics. But even he was moved by the dedication shown by Christians:

> Their contempt of death is patent to us every day, and likewise their restraint in cohabitation. For they include not only men but also women who refrain from cohabiting all their lives; and they also number individuals who, in self-discipline and self-control in matters of food and drink, and in their keen pursuit of justice, have attained a pitch not inferior to that of genuine philosophers. (Quoted by Chadwick, *Alexandrian Christianity*, p. 36)

The comparison implied between Christian asceticism and the life of a Cynic philosopher is illuminating. 'Cynicism' in the first two centuries or so after Christ had few of the pejorative overtones it has since come to earn. The Cynics advocated self-sufficiency and the renunciation of all earthly possessions. Not only did they reject self-indulgence, they went about preaching its opposite, dressing simply but distinctively: their freedom of movement was a result of their renunciation of property. Their disciples were put through a rigorous training in this life of renunciation so that they might kill worldly ambition, free themselves of desire, learn to endure pain and make light of death. For this form of training the Greek word is 'asceticism'. It was so close to the Christian ideal that as Christian religious life spread, Cynicism declined.

218

Cynic philosopher, again with his staff, but also equipped with wallet and flask for his journey. Cynics dressed simply, and renounced all earthly possessions.

Christians seem quite consciously to have presented themselves as being in the same mould as the Cynics. Justin certainly did so, and he was teaching in Rome at the time Galen was there. Justin's pupils were, often enough, the children of Christian parents. They had been sent to the capital for their education, and had no sense that this, for them, was home. Justin stressed a rational philosophy that they all shared, no matter who or where they were. It was a universal appeal well suited to a society in which the old loyalties were crumbling. It was offered to all, regardless of status, thus establishing new bonds of commitment much less oppressive than the traditional patron-client dependency of Roman society.

Although not all Christians chose to adopt it, asceticism was one of the factors which distinguished the Christian from other members of society. As Galen's reflections quoted above indicate, the impressive lives of the few brought prestige to the many who would not, or could not, live similarly. And what made it more acceptable was that Christian asceticism fell into a pattern which was readily understood.

Where was Christian asceticism heading? When, towards the end of the second century, Clement of Alexandria takes up the theory, it becomes a much more demanding spiritual journey. The Christian may begin by suppressing his or her natural desires, but that is only the beginning. The aim of an ascetic life, Clement suggests, is union with God:

> ... leaving behind all the distractions of matter, he cleaves the heavens by his wisdom, and having passed through the spiritual entities and every rule and authority, he lays hold of the throne on high, speeding to that alone, which alone he knows. (Quoted by Chadwick, *Alexandrian Christianity*, p. 39)

It is not immediately easy to understand why a life of poverty and of chastity should be admired. The answer may lie in the nature of primitive Christianity. Christ had preached the coming of the kingdom, and the first Christians had kept that ideal before them. But as it became clear that the kingdom was not going to arrive in the immediate future, Christians reinterpreted this belief so that it became a religion of salvation, in which the goal was happiness in the after-life rather than in this world. Redemption became the focal point of the believer's commitment, rather than the goodness of creation. Deliverance from the world was the aim, and obviously both chastity and poverty freed the Christian from worldly ties. It is not surprising, therefore, that Christianity spawned so many sects which rejected worldly matters. What is more surprising, however, is that it was not entirely engulfed by them, and that it became as popular as it did.

The roots of such sects went deep. Some of the evidence that survives for early Christianity in Palestine suggests that to some people the possession of property was to be equated with sin – a much more rigorous view than that of the Jerusalem community. In the same group there circulated a letter, purporting to be from James, the 'bishop' of Jerusalem, recommending virginity. Jewish-Christian attitudes reflected the beliefs and practices of the Essene community to a surprising degree. In these Churches people fasted, and stayed awake at night to read the Scriptures; they took little care of their appearance, and viewed marriage with hostility even though there were married people among them.

The similarities between the community of the Dead Sea and Syriac asceticism are enough for some scholars to postulate a direct connection, possibly even the conversion of the Dead Sea community to Christianity. The Syriac sons and daughters of the covenant, unlike the Essenes, did not create specific communities but, like some at least of the Essenes, they lived at home, or just possibly in small groups attached to a church. Monasteries were still a thing of the future.

When they came, it was not first in Syria but in Egypt. They sprang from the life and work of a man called Anthony, most of whose achievements lie outside the scope of this book but whose beginnings lie very much within it.

THE COMING OF ANTHONY

No history of this period of Christianity would be complete without a note on Anthony. To him is attributed the inspiration for monastic life which

The great St Anthony of Egypt, shown here on a Cretan icon. If not the first, he was certainly among the earliest of the Christians to retreat into the desert, which he did in about AD 285. There he attracted a vast number of followers so that, in later centuries, he came to be regarded as the father of monasticism.

rapidly became a distinctive feature of the Catholic Church both east and west. That development took place in the fourth century and later, but it had its origins in the conversion of Anthony to a form of religious life similar to those described above.

Anthony was born sometime in the middle of the third century. When he was about twenty, and an orphan, he heard in church one Sunday the gospel message, 'Sell all you own and distribute the money to the poor'. It struck home. He sold his possessions and gave the proceeds away, keeping a small amount in reserve to maintain his sister. Then, and again in church, he heard the words, 'Take no thought for the morrow', so he disposed of what little money he had left, put his sister into a community of virgins, and went to live in a shed at the bottom of the garden of the house which had once been his home.

This was not such a surprising thing to do. There were already other men leading similar lives – Anthony consulted one of them regularly about his spiritual progress. The reasons for their adopting this type of existence may not, in every case, have been of so spiritual an order as Anthony's had been – at least as it is related by Bishop Athanasius of Alexandria.

In Egypt in the third century it was possible to build up substantial holdings of land and thus to become quite wealthy. Anthony's father seems to have done so. Yet at the same time the burden of taxation was rapidly increasing. Taxes were levied in villages as a whole, which put a strain upon village life, so the burden was psychological as well as fiscal. Setting up as a self-sufficient individual in the manner of a Cynic, therefore, was one way to cope with those pressures. The hermits, the people who followed Anthony's example, were certainly breaking out from social pressures, including the most demanding one of marriage. Not that Anthony himself managed to avoid some of these pressures. His spiritual progress is marked by retreat further and further into the desert, as his fame brought new demands upon him from which he wanted to escape.

Anthony was about thirty-five years old when he decided to go into the desert. By that time he had already had his struggles with the devil, so beloved of painters. These took place in one of the tombs outside his home village and were of such ferocity, or so it is recounted, that they left him unconscious. A friend finding him in this state and believing him dead carried him up to the village church, but there he recovered and asked to be taken back to do battle with the demons that beset him. Having survived this he crossed the Nile to the edge of the desert, where he shut himself inside an abandoned fort. Bread was brought to him only twice a year.

When next Anthony emerged, twenty years later, he was described as being 'perfect' in every way. He was physically fit and alert, despite his long sojourn in isolation. He was so close to God that he could perform miracles and cast out demons. In the last years of his life, after travelling with nomads into the interior of the desert, he grew his own food at an oasis. His crops flourished, and he could talk to animals: he was in touch with nature as well as with God. His latter years are presented as a return to Eden, to the state of innocence before the Fall. This is put forward as a model for monastic life.

In its original Greek meaning the word 'monastery' implies little more than a lodging. There is no reason to think that the first monasteries held more than one monk. Those whom Anthony had persuaded to follow his example were probably more like hermits than monks. Though they may have owed spiritual allegiance to Anthony as 'the father' or abbot, and though they may even have worn some common form of clothing, they did not come together for meals or for worship. They did, however, live in poverty and chastity, and acknowledged a form of spiritual obedience to their leading monk or spiritual guide. The letters of Anthony understand this form of life as a 'covenant'. It is possible that there is a direct connection between the Syriac sons and daughters of the covenant and Anthony's chosen way of life, though the link may be less straightforward. Philo of Alexandria speaks of a group called the Therapeutae, and though little or nothing is known of them beyond their name, they seem to have been linked with the Dead Sea community which, in its turn, may have been the inspiration for the Syriac form of religious life. It is also possible that the tradition of going into the desert to live an ascetic life was present in Egypt long before Anthony, though it is only with him that it takes on a distinctly Christian guise.

What certainly seems to have happened in the case of Anthony is that the followers of some forms of Christian practice who previously might have gone down unorthodox byways and become sectarian groups excommunicated from the Catholic Church, now found a way in which they could remain within the Church. Fervour and enthusiasm had been not so much tamed as channelled. There is no doubt that this life appealed to a quite extraordinary number of Christians. 'The desert was made a city by monks', commented Athanasius upon Anthony's success in persuading others to adopt his way of life.

That it should have proved so popular is often attributed to the end of persecution. Christians no longer lived on the edge of survival. The ascetic life was an alternative to martyrdom. This may be so, but it may also be that the popularity of this lifestyle owed much to the fact that Christian life had become so conventional. The life of the monks of the Egyptian desert was a reminder of the radical challenge presented by the first Christians.

11
THE FINAL CHALLENGE

I t is difficult for us today to visualize a thought-world which contained a heaven populated with dozens, perhaps even hundreds, of gods. Yet during the period encompassed by this book most of those who lived in the Roman world, apart from Jews and Christians, lived with the conviction that there was a variety of gods, quite distinct from one another, and all requiring some form of worship. All had their own temples, their priesthoods, their followers. Each had a particular role to perform. Some people, it is true, argued that there could be only one single god, but their influence was slight.

Three types of gods had their place in the Roman Pantheon. There were the gods of civic religion, such as Janus, Jupiter and Mars, inherited from

Opposite, a fresco from Herculaneum depicting the Egyptian cult of Isis. Sphinxes sit on either side of the goddess's shrine. A priest, flanked by two lesser priests, one a woman, the other a negro, holds up a vase to be venerated by worshippers. Roman civic religion was rather more restrained. The statue of Augustus, left, shows him with his toga drawn over his head: he is represented as the pontifex maximus, *or high priest, of the State cult.*

Italy's ancient inhabitants. There were the newly created gods, the emperors deified after their deaths – and sometimes even beforehand. And there were the gods of the mystery religions, Cybele, Isis, Mithras and others, oriental cults brought to Rome by travellers, soldiers and imported slaves. The God of the Jews and the God of the Christians were quite separate, but otherwise the various cults, civic, imperial and oriental, dwelt more or less happily together.

The role of the civic cults was to reinforce the cohesion of the state. Archaic forms of religion, already in decline and less favoured than the mystery religions, were revived by the Emperor Augustus to assure the people of Rome that the period of confusion and bloodshed following the assassination of Julius Caesar was over, and that Rome had regained its former stability. There were many of these cults. The Roman matrons had

their own, as did the aristocratic families in general. There were cults for tradesmen and cults for soldiers. Each had its own meeting-place, and their festivals brought people together socially and strengthened the bonds between them. Then there were the state cults involving acts of worship by the whole people, served by colleges of priests at the head of which, from 13 BC, was Augustus himself. As chief priest he was known as *Pontifex Maximus*, a title held by successive emperors until towards the end of the fourth century. In the fifth century it was appropriated by the Pope, who has used it ever since.

From the Hellenistic world the Romans had conquered they inherited the practice of ruler worship. From Augustus onwards most of the emperors were deified. Again there were the temples and the companies of priests; usually these were non-professionals, for to serve the imperial cult in the office of priest might be, for a young patrician, a stepping-stone to higher office in the state, or, alternatively, it might be a way of rewarding the devotion of a loyal servant out in the provinces. The importance of such cults was as much dynastic as anything else. Adhesion to the imperial cult signified support for a family which the godly emperor had founded, or from which he had come. The cult was, therefore, an amalgam of loyalty and of

226

patronage. It spread throughout the Empire. In addition to demanding the offering of incense before a bust, a statue, or some other image of the emperor, it provided games in honour of the imperial house, the carnival atmosphere of a splendid sacrifice, and competitions in music and poetry.

None of this had much to do with personal religion. Perhaps for the majority of people the external acts associated with the civic or imperial cults were enough to satisfy whatever need they felt for religious observance. But there were those for whom it was not enough. They felt the need for assurance of personal salvation in a world increasingly filled with demons and other unseen powers able to impair their enjoyment of a blissful eternity. For persons such as these, the mystery cults provided an answer.

These cults had in common the fact that they were built around some classical or oriental myth, typically one of death and rebirth. They were also secret. Even today little is known about them, and what is known may have been coloured by the views of Christians. There were elaborate

In the relief opposite, the Emperor Marcus Aurelius is shown offering sacrifice before the temple on the Capitoline Hill dedicated to the Roman gods Jupiter, Juno and Minerva. By the end of the second century the cult of the Greek god Zeus, who is represented above on a silver medallion, had become almost monotheistic.

initiation ceremonies; there were purifications; there were ritual meals. Those who had been initiated were assured some form of communion with the divinity they worshipped, a communion which in turn guaranteed them salvation. What made them especially attractive was that, in contrast to the civic cults, they cut across boundaries of class and race.

They had, in that, much in common with early Christianity, even though there is little if any sign of the influence of the mystery religions upon the early formulations of Christian belief. And even when such an influence can be detected, it is not all one way. Rather than looking for direct influence of one upon the other, it is simpler to see both Christianity and the oriental cults as two ways of responding to the same basic human needs.

There were a number of reasons why the Roman state looked askance upon the oriental cults. Some were thought to foster promiscuity, to pose a threat to the stability of the family, while the ceremonies of others might cloak subversive meetings, and were therefore a threat to the stability of the

The cult of the fertility goddess Cybele began in Phrygia, and it had arrived in Rome as early as 205 BC – though worship of her was at first severely restricted by the Roman authorities. Helios the sun god, shown opposite in the chariot which he drove daily across the sky, grew in importance in Greece and later in Rome, where, from the time of the Emperor Aurelian onwards, he became principal god of the Empire, subsuming under himself most, if not all, the other gods.

state. But despite such inauspicious beginnings, the cults eventually gained respectability.

The Jewish religion enjoyed an unusual position under the Romans. The Jews were, of course, unwilling to tolerate polytheism. Yet Roman nobles, including Augustus himself, sent offerings to the Temple in Jerusalem, and the Temple was placed under Rome's special protection. Apart from Caligula, Augustus and his immediate successors did not attempt to force the imperial cult upon the Jews. The emperors were happy enough to know that there were twice-daily sacrifices to the Jewish God for the well-being of the pagan Roman state and the imperial family. In deference to the beliefs of the Jews, portraits of the emperor on coins were avoided in Palestine as far as was possible, and so were statues. Even military standards, which bore the imperial image, were laid aside as the legions entered Jerusalem, and the Sabbath rest was respected.

Roman tolerance for a wide variety of deities extended as far as the exclusive deity of the Jews. For as long as they could be identified with the Jews, Christians appear to have enjoyed a similar privileged position. But this was a situation that was not long to last.

PERSECUTION BY THE EMPERORS
Why persecution of the Christians broke out at all is not clear. In the first

229

century, as already mentioned, there was undoubtedly persecution. Milder persecution also took place under Domitian, but it would be wrong to infer from these incidents that Christians were being punished by death or by exile throughout the territories ruled over by these two emperors. Such evidence as there is suggests the opposite. In about the year 113 Pliny wrote to the Emperor Trajan because, in the province of Bithynia and Pontus of which Pliny was governor, some people had been accused of being Christians. Pliny did not know what to do, so he punished them not so much for the crime with which they had been charged, but for their obstinacy in continuing to profess Christianity even under duress. Then as usually happens, Pliny goes on, there had been a rash of further accusations made by informers. He describes to Trajan in detail what he did:

> Whoever denied that they were or had been Christians, when they called upon the gods – repeating the words after me – and when they worshipped with incense and with wine your image, which I ordered to be introduced for this purpose with the deities' statues, and when especially they have cursed Christ...those persons I have thought ought to be dismissed.

In all this there is no mention of a precise offence, beyond the fact that the accused were said to be Christians.

No general rule could be established for their treatment Trajan replied to his governor, but Pliny had behaved perfectly correctly. If a Christian, having been punished, is prepared to pray to the Roman gods, he shall be pardoned.

Less than a decade later the Emperor Hadrian was writing in a similar vein to the proconsul of Asia, in a letter which Eusebius has preserved in his history of the Church. There had, it seems, been accusations against Christians, and once again a government representative had asked for advice. The emperor replied:

> If then the provincials can so clearly establish their case against the Christians that they can sustain it in a court of law, let them resort to this procedure only and not rely on petitions or mere clamour. So if someone prosecutes them and proves them guilty of any illegality, you must pronounce sentence according to the seriousness of the offence. But if anyone starts such proceedings in the hope of financial reward, then for goodness' sake arrest him for his shabby trick, and see that he gets his rewards. (*History of the Church*, 4:9)

A good deal of scholarly debate has centred around the authenticity of this imperial instruction, but if it is indeed genuine it is a remarkable example of the attitude of the Roman state in the earlier part of the second century. Clearly Christians were not the objects of systematic persecution by the imperial authorities. Indeed, the evidence of both Trajan and Hadrian points to the opposite: neither emperor wanted the peace disturbed by pointless accusations.

This fresco from Pompeii shows a Roman trial of the kind that Christians must have faced. The magistrate on the dais sits between two assessors with the accused kneeling below.

For a long time a remark of Tertullian's caused confusion. He refers to an *Institutum Neronianum* in such a way as to suggest that Nero had issued some general instruction on the persecution of Christians. But nothing of the sort is known, nor is anything similar mentioned in any accounts of the trials and deaths of Christians which have survived. One can only guess that some of the common criticisms of Christians may have been made the basis for accusations against them. That certainly seems to have occurred at Lyons, where informers falsely accused the Christians of incest and cannibalism.

Another possible charge against Christians may have been that they established new *collegia* without permission. It was suggested earlier that in the various cities of the Empire in which they flourished Christian communities seem to have acted as if they were *collegia*, though *collegia* with a difference. In the early years of Christianity, however, new *collegia* were viewed with suspicion by the civic authorities: they might be used as cover for groups conspiring against the security of the state.

Christians were not of course conspiring against the state, but there was

sufficient evidence in the form of their unwillingness to take part in local politics, their opposition to the army and so on, to encourage anyone with hostile leanings that they might be doing so. And while they were suspected of forming illegal associations or *collegia* they were in danger of being prosecuted.

For them to be prosecuted someone would have to bring a charge against them, locally and individually. This does indeed seem to have been what happened. Eusebius accuses Nero and Domitian of persecuting Christians, but he does not lay that charge against any other emperor – apart from the very doubtful instance of Septimius Severus (193–211) – until the middle of the third century. In the meantime, of course, martyrdoms occurred. As has been seen, there were deaths at Smyrna and at Lyons, and these took place during the reign of one of the most distinguished Roman emperors, Marcus Aurelius.

Marcus Aurelius' involvement in persecuting Christians has been so unacceptable to some historians of the Late Empire that they have argued it was the better emperors who persecuted, because these were the ones who were most concerned for the unity and thereby safety of the Empire. As will

The bust of Septimius Severus, opposite, comes from what is now Algeria. Left, a libellus, or certificate, to prove that Aurelia Demos had offered the sacrifice ordered by Decius. Aurelius Irenaeus wrote it out for her, because, says the libellus, she was illiterate.

be seen, there may be something in this argument in the case of the third century, but it could hardly have been true of the first two hundred years of Christianity. The number of adherents to the new sect was too small for them to be regarded as a significant threat.

It is much more likely that though the persecutions at Smyrna and at Lyons took place during the reign of Marcus Aurelius, they did not occur as a result of any action on his part. Quite clearly in both these cities it was the mob which took the initiative.

Christians lived under constant threat of persecution, but outbreaks were sporadic and local until the middle of the third century. They occurred because Christians constituted a distinctly different group in Roman society and therefore aroused the hostility of other, more conformist, groups. As *collegia*, and therefore technically illegal, they were at risk once charges had been laid against them. Such charges were brought in individual cities at different times and for different reasons. Persecution did not happen throughout the length and breadth of the Empire at the same time. Each Christian community was quite separate, so the known incidence of suffering in one city should not lead us to suppose the same of another.

233

At the beginning of the third century the tempo of persecution changed. The major cities of the Empire, Alexandria, Carthage, even Rome itself, were all affected. So were Corinth and Antioch. Even the remote province of Cappadocia was touched.

It is not clear whether the Emperor Septimius Severus had anything to do with this concerted campaign against the Christians. Certainly the tradition which the emperor himself inherited was one of toleration, especially where the Eastern mystery religions were concerned. And there is extant no edict ordering persecution. There is, however, evidence of an imperial instruction or rescript which forbade conversion to Judaism – a fairly traditional prohibition – and to Christianity. This last was certainly not traditional, and if the rescript can be regarded as genuine it definitely marks a shift in attitude towards Christianity, for which there is ample evidence in the degree of persecution during the first decade of the third century.

The shift may have been gradual. The account of the martyrdom of Perpetua and her companions in Carthage indicates that there was still a good deal of mob hostility, though it may be that the mob was rather more aware than before of imperial support. But if so, why the change of policy from one which appears to have been neutral to one of veiled hostility? The answer may be the growing strength of Christianity. By the end of the second century it had definitively emerged from the shadow of Judaism. Judaism was itself not a popular religion, but it was a particularly privileged one. By distancing itself from Judaism, Christianity had implicitly renounced the privileges accorded to the Jews, while still laying claim to the exemptions from civic duties and military service which the Jews enjoyed.

What is more, Christianity seems to have had great success making converts fast. It was not simply a question of numbers: there was also the development within the Church of a more powerful voice, with spokesmen such as Clement of Alexandria, Tertullian and Origen. The Church, therefore, was both more visible and more of an active threat to the traditional – and by the third century, rather frail – structure upon which Roman society depended.

Just how frail was soon to be demonstrated. In 235 the Emperor Alexander Severus was assassinated. There began half a century of anarchy, during which the selection and disposal of emperors was determined by the army. This was at a time when the Empire could least afford the chaos brought by the coming and going of rulers: it was threatened from without by barbarian attacks on its frontiers, and from within by galloping inflation. Naturally at such a time a premium was put on loyalty to the state. This loyalty was to be demonstrated by devotion to the emperor and, under Aurelian (270–275), to the cult of the Unconquered Sun, *Sol Invictus*, in whom, it seemed, everyone, whatever their belief, might recognize something of his or her own particular deity.

Eusebius claims that persecution broke out immediately after Alexander's assassination because of the hostility of his successor, the Emperor Maximian, to everything the Severan dynasty had stood for – and that had included tolerating Christianity even in those close to the imperial family. Again according to Eusebius, the persecution took on a new and more dangerous form. It was aimed solely at the destruction of Christian leaders. But Maximian's reign was brief (235–238). It was followed by a period of peace for the Church until the equally brief reign of the Emperor Decius.

Though once again no edict is extant, it seems both from Eusebius' account and from the letters of Cyprian that this time at least the proscription of Christians by Decius was universal. It was not left to local antipathy to the new religion, or to the apathy of magistrates. Commissioners were appointed, before whom all were to be summoned and made to sacrifice, to sprinkle incense on a brazier, or to pour a libation. Those who did so were given a certificate to prove it, a *libellus*. Those who did not were imprisoned, exiled or executed.

Similar penalties were attached to the rescripts of Valerian (253–260), which again are known largely by way of the letters of Bishop Cyprian. Among the penalties was included the confiscation of property belonging to Christians. Gallienus, however, son of and co-emperor with Valerian, who survived as sole emperor for a further eight years after his father's ignominious capture by the Persians, restored the churches which had been seized, and then the cemeteries. It may be that, in this unexpected act, Gallienus was attempting to win the political support of Christians. If so, there must already have been a strong Christian lobby among the powerful in the Empire's major cities – a supposition which the events of Diocletian's reign make credible.

Lack of devotion to the Roman gods did not make Christians into martyrs. The authorities may have needed to have tighter control of the population, to find scapegoats for a collapsing economy and for the constant frontier wars. But Christians were persecuted because they were different and distinctive. The motives were not directly religious, at least until the reign of Diocletian.

THE CHRISTIANS WHO DIED

This brief account of the emperors who persecuted Christians suggests not only that the pogroms were sporadic and localized but that relatively few Christians actually died. Whether the number was great or small in relation to the size of the Christian community we do not know. By the time the community had grown in size persecutions tended to concentrate only on its leaders (at least until the persecution of Diocletian, as will be seen later), so deaths may have been fairly rare, if well publicized.

Actual numbers are impossible to calculate. Eusebius names less than

150, though he does speak of 'immense numbers' in Egypt and the Upper Nile under Diocletian. Indeed he makes several references of the same sort – 'an alarming number', 'countless martyrs' – and even refers to the destruction of a whole village.

Presumably there were few examples of this kind, otherwise Eusebius would not have picked out one incident for special mention. Apart from this, the largest single number of people put to death seems to have been the 48 at Lyons in 177. There is no reason to believe, of course, that Eusebius knew of every case. Nonetheless, over the almost three hundred years from the death of Christ to the edict which brought toleration in 313,

This painting from the extensive Cemetery of Commodillo is thought to represent Christ flanked by two martyrs.

the number of executions does not seem to have been enormously high.

There were, of course, other sufferings. Many Christians were condemned to the mines or marble quarries. Many more were imprisoned, and Roman imprisonment was particularly brutal. Prisoners were often kept in underground cells without light or sanitation; they were frequently chained to the wall or to the floor. One young man who fled from Rome to Cyprian's hiding place near Carthage told the bishop that he had been chained to the floor with his legs held wide apart, so that he could not move at all.

In apparent contrast to this brutal treatment, however, was the readiness of the local authorities to allow visitors into the prisons. Priests

237

came in to offer the Eucharist, and were permitted to enter and leave without hindrance. The guards must have known them to be Christians, but all was well as long as those visiting the prisons had not themselves been denounced. And as has already been seen, Christians were so generous with gifts of food that life inside the gaol was often tolerable.

For many, of course, prison was only a stage on the way to execution. It has entered the mythology of martyrdom that Christians were regularly thrown to the lions or to other wild beasts. That may have been to some extent true of Rome, but by far the more common method of execution was beheading. The Colosseum in Rome has sometimes been presented as a regular venue for battles between Christians and wild animals, but there is no evidence of this having occurred, and even, before the seventeenth century, no claim that it ever happened.

Whatever the manner of the death, those Christians who were executed seem to have gone willingly to meet their Lord. There is evidence that some of them may even have courted death: Origen, when a youth, wanted to follow his father to martydom, and rather later, Anthony made his way to the court house to put himself in danger. But this kind of behaviour was exceptional and indeed frowned upon by the Church authorities. Ignatius of Antioch's attitude seems to have been more typical. Once he was condemned to death he was anxious that no one should interfere with the final outcome.

A good deal is known about the final hours of martyrs. The 'acts' were often faithfully recorded, and have been preserved. Accounts of their trials have sometimes been based, or so it appears, upon court records. Occasionally the 'acts' are either the work of eye-witnesses, or depend upon earlier eye-witness texts. A number of these accounts are plainly legendary, but others demonstrate quite unexpected traits which tend to give credence to their authenticity. Roman officials, for example, are sometimes shown as sympathetic and interested in the doctrines of Christianity.

The care which was taken to preserve these accounts of the trials and deaths of the martyrs is an indication of the high regard in which they were held. By a rather curious extension of the Church's penitential discipline those in prison awaiting death (even if, finally, martyrdom was denied them) were thought capable of granting forgiveness to those who had lapsed from the faith during persecution, so that they might be allowed back into the Church. The status of martyr was a privileged one.

THE IDEA OF MARTYRDOM

The basic paradox of early Christianity was that to live, one first had to die. And to die twice: first came rebirth at baptism, and then there was the second rebirth, into eternal life at death. The two notions were linked, for martyrdom was a form of baptism, a baptism of blood. The first Christians stood the terminology of death on its head.

The traditional language for a Christian's dying was that he or she had 'fallen asleep'. At that point the dead person entered a place of rest and of refreshment, and was at peace. Tertullian, however, invented a whole new image. He spoke of the day of a martyr's death as his or her 'birthday'. This new idea eventually took over, and the day was celebrated as such. Tertullian talks of annual offerings, which, in this context, must have meant the offering of the Eucharist on the anniversary of a martyr's death to commemorate the victory that had been won.

Cyprian objected to Christians holding banquets on such occasions, as the pagans did, on the grounds that there was too great a risk that such feasts might lead to immorality. He was in favour of prayers being offered for the deceased during the Eucharist, but there is no evidence to suggest that at this time the prayers for those who had died for the faith were any different from those offered for other Christians who had died of natural causes.

They were not, however, entirely forgotten. Cyprian might have been opposed to funeral banquets and even to grief (Christians had not so much died as gone before, so there was little point in grieving), but he was in favour of maintaining a calendar which recorded the martyrs' deaths. These dates were marked by a celebration of the Eucharist – in Rome this often took place in the catacombs, the tomb itself serving as an altar.

It was determined quite early on, and certainly by Tertullian's day, that those who had died a violent death for their faith, as witnesses (the word 'martyr' means witness) to fidelity to Christ, gained immediate entry into Paradise, and there awaited reunion with their bodies at the resurrection of the dead. They were therefore not in the same need of their fellow Christians' prayers in order to achieve salvation. Indeed, as has been seen, they were in a position before their deaths to offer others less constant than themselves the hope of reconciliation. It was not long before Christians were seeking to be buried in proximity to those who had died for their faith. The cult of the saints had yet to reach fruition – but by the end of the third century it was in evidence.

Such reverence was, however, still limited to those who had died or been imprisoned for their faith. With the exception of groups such as the followers of Montanus, Christians by this time did not believe in the imminent arrival of the kingdom of God and the return of Jesus. But there were still remnants of that once strong eschatological tradition, according to which the Second Coming would happen only after a period of suffering. Christians expected persecution as a sign of the dawning of the messianic age: this was part of their inheritance from Judaism.

Jewish and Christian ideas on martyrdom were close. The dispute which arose between Tertullian and Bishop Callistus in Rome over the sins which could not be forgiven, for example, paralleled the views earlier expressed by the Rabbi Akiba that Jews should go to their death rather than commit the

239

Christian martyrs met their deaths in a variety of ways, such as being torn to pieces by wild beasts in the arena, but the most prominent practice was beheading, as shown in the picture above from the basilica of SS John and Paul, which depicts three Christians being executed.

240

sins of murder, apostasy and idolatry. They had, of course, already done so. During the Maccabean revolt the orthodox followers of Judaism were forced to eat unclean food, or to die. The scribe Eleazar, whose story is told in the Second Book of Maccabees, chose to die rather than commit what he regarded as a form of apostasy. Indeed, he refused even to pretend to eat the pork that was put in front of him. And when the idolatrous eagle was erected by Herod over the gateway to the Temple, those who pulled it down did so in order to be martyred. It has even been claimed that the account of the martyrs of Lyons of 177 is consciously modelled upon the story of the Maccabees.

THE LAST GREAT CHALLENGE
The story of Diocletian is told by Lactantius, a pagan convert who later became tutor to Constantine's son, in his book *On the Deaths of the Persecutors*:

> Diocletian's anxious disposition made him an investigator of future events; and while he was busy in the regions of the East, he was once sacrificing cattle and looking in their entrails for what was going to happen, when certain of his attendants who knew the Lord and were present at the sacrifice, placed the immortal sign [the sign of the cross] on their foreheads; at this the demons were put to flight and the rites thrown into confusion. The *haruspices* [the pagan priests] began to get agitated at not seeing the usual marks on the entrails, and as if they had not made the offering, they repeated the sacrifice several times. But the slaughter of victim after victim still revealed nothing; and finally their Tagis, the chief of the *haruspices*, whether through suspicion or through the evidence of his own eyes, said that the reason why the sacrifices were not yielding an answer was that profane persons were present at the sacred ceremonies. Diocletian then flew into a rage; he ordered that not only those who were attending the rites but all who were in the palace should offer sacrifice, and that any who declined should be punished by whipping; he also sent letters to commanders ordering that soldiers should be compelled to perform the abominable sacrifices, and that any who disobeyed should be discharged from military service. This far his rage and anger went; he did nothing further against the law and religion of God. (*De mortibus persecutorum*, chapter 10)

Diocletian's persecution, along with that of Marcus Aurelius, has tended to lend credence to the belief that it was the 'best' emperors who persecuted. But from Lactantius' account it would seem that before the incident described Diocletian was not a major persecutor of Christians. Until then they had been tolerated in his retinue and were serving in the army.

In order to understand the next step in the development of the Christian Church, it is necessary to look at the rather complicated political background against which it was set. Lactantius claims that Diocletian increased the size of the Roman army four hundred per cent. That is certainly an exaggeration, but a two hundred per cent increase is probable. The civil service expanded likewise, both in Rome and in the provinces. There were, indeed, more provinces created, which were in turn grouped together into dioceses. This made for tighter control, and more efficient taxation to raise the money needed to keep the army going. Diocletian's reforms paid dividends: they slowed down, and eventually stopped, the spiralling inflation which had plagued the Empire during the third century, and his better organised army gained the upper hand in the border territories invaded by barbarians.

Diocletian also reorganized the Empire's central government. He was himself proclaimed emperor in 284, and two years later he made another army officer, Maximian, a co-emperor with responsibility for the western part of the Empire. To Maximian he gave the title of 'caesar', while Diocletian was called 'augustus'. Then, in 293, two more officers were made co-emperors, thus forming the 'tetrarchy' or 'rule of four'. Maximian was promoted to the title of augustus along with Diocletian, and both took an assistant with the title of caesar: Galerius was caesar to Diocletian, and Constantius to Maximian. Then, in 305, Diocletian and Maximian retired, to be replaced by Galerius and Constantius as augusti, with Maximinus Daia and Severus as their respective caesars.

It was the view of early Christian writers that the emperor mainly responsible for the persecution which bears Diocletian's name was actually Galerius, and that he was motivated by straightforward hatred of Christianity. When the first edict of persecution was issued in February 303 it was believed that Diocletian had exacted a promise from Galerius that there would be no bloodshed. Certainly there was nothing in the edict which should itself have led to martyrdom: churches were to be destroyed, and Christians who enjoyed civil rights in the Empire were to be deprived of them. In the west, under Constantius, some churches do indeed seem to have been pulled down, but that was the extent of the persecution. Things were rather different in the east, where the edict was fully enforced. This led to rioting, and when the palace in Nicomedia caught fire Christians were blamed. A second edict was issued, ordering the arrest of all the clergy: 'priests and deacons were arrested and condemned without any proof or confession and then led off with all their dependants,' says Lactantius, and he adds that the prisons were full.

An amnesty was offered. A third edict promised that all clergy who sacrificed to the gods would be released. If they refused they were tortured, or made to go through the motions of sacrificing. Then a fourth edict, in 304, ordered everyone, not just the Church leaders, to offer sacrifice to the pagan gods.

Little of this appears to have been implemented in the west. Most of the suffering was in the eastern part of the Empire under Galerius and his caesar Maximinus Daia, who was an enthusiastic pagan. Daia took steps to revive pagan ceremonial, and on at least two occasions tried to make all citizens participate. But for the most part, and despite comparatively large numbers of deaths and imprisonments, the Christians stood firm. Indeed there is evidence that the exiling of people for their faith to remoter parts of the Empire simply helped to spread knowledge of Christianity outside the urban centres.

It has been suggested that the failure of the Great Persecution under Diocletian and Galerius can be attributed, at least in part, to a significant shift in the balance between paganism and Christianity in the second half of the third century. In that period, it is argued, the countryside of

The last of the great persecutions was instituted by the Emperor Diocletian, who built this plain and functional Senate House in Rome.

This porphyry statue, on a corner of St Mark's basilica in Venice, represents the 'tetrarchy', or rule of the four emperors. Right, a view of the Christian quarter of Hippo Regius. The town, which predated the Romans, became the seat of a bishop. From AD 395–430 that bishop was St Augustine, and the columns in the picture mark the ruins of his basilica.

244

Anatolia, Egypt and North Africa was evangelized. The Christian community could no longer be easily identified and isolated. Moreover, it was now even dangerous to do so. The Empire depended heavily for its grain supplies upon Egypt and Africa: it was unwise to alienate their inhabitants.

Galerius eventually came to believe that the persecutions had gone far enough. Lactantius attributes Galerius' change of heart to the disease which afflicted him, and which indeed killed him a few days after the 311 edict of toleration. But the text of the edict, as it is preserved in *On the Deaths of the Persecutors*, reveals both Galerius' concern for the old ways which he wished to restore for the good of the Empire, and his admiration for the constancy with which the Christians had endured their sufferings. If they were to be

245

Christian though he may have been, the Emperor Constantine was thought of by many in a classical pagan context. This cameo shows him with his family being borne heavenward.

permitted to worship their own god, however, they must also pray for the safety and well-being of the state.

Except in those parts of the Empire ruled over by Maximinus Daia – Egypt and eastwards – this edict effectually brought persecution to an end, and permitted Christians to restore their churches. And eventually, even Daia was forced into line.

THE COMING OF CONSTANTINE

Constantine was the son of Constantius; his mother, Helena, may have been married to Constantius or may have been his concubine. When Constantius was promoted to the rank of caesar, under Maximian in 293, Helena was no longer considered a suitable consort and was sent off with Constantine to the East. In 305, Constantius became an augustus, and Constantine was allowed by Galerius to rejoin his father in the West.

In 306, Constantius died while at York. Constantine, who was with him, was proclaimed augustus, though the only title he claimed from Galerius was that of caesar. He went back to France, where he won the support for a time of the retired Emperor Maximian. He married Maximian's daughter Fausta, but then marched against Maximian's son Maxentius, who held Rome. At the entrance to Rome Constantine fought successfully for control of the Milvian Bridge. That was on 28 October 312: the victory proclaimed Constantine master of the western half of the Empire.

The control of the eastern part was still shared between Licinius, who had succeeded Galerius, and Maximinus Daia. Licinius and Constantine met in Milan. They made a political arrangement between themselves in which they agreed to allow Christians freedom of worship and to restore to them all the property which had been confiscated. The edict, which came to be known as the Edict of Milan, was of the greatest importance for Christianity, and set it on the way to becoming the established religion of the Empire. That was a remarkable about-turn for what had until shortly before been a proscribed sect.

Why did Constantine take this step? Perhaps no other single religion, apart from the cult of the emperor himself, commanded such wide respect, but Christianity was hardly strong enough to have commended itself to the emperor as a political tool. The reason must be that, to some extent, Constantine believed in Christianity. To what extent it is difficult to say. It is not just that the emperor delayed formal reception into the Church until his death-bed, in 337. In a period when the penitential discipline was still very strict, there were many who did likewise. But Constantine appears to have learnt about Christianity gradually, under the tutelage of a number of religious advisers, chief of whom was Bishop Hosius of Cordoba.

The Chi-Ro symbol with which Constantine embellished the shields of his soldiers before the battle of the Milvian Bridge is said to derive from the first two letters of the name 'Christ' in Greek. Some scholars believe, however, that the symbol was a common one, and was no more than a form of good-luck charm.

247

Constantine's own account of his conquest of the Empire has two major references to Christianity. First of all, when he was in Gaul (what is now France and part of Germany) Constantine saw in a dream the form of the cross with the words *In hoc signo vincis*: 'In this sign you will conquer'. Then, just before the battle at the Milvian Bridge he had another vision which encouraged him to put the Chi-Ro symbol – an emblem for Jesus, a monogram constructed from the first two Greek letters of the word 'Christ' – upon the shield of his troops. He did conquer, as the dreams had suggested, and he won under the banner of Christ. What he himself made of this we do not know, but for the future of Christianity it was of enormous significance.

Constantine's victory brought more than toleration for the Church. Catholicism, as distinct from other brands of sectarianism which were to emerge remarkably promptly, received privileged treatment from then on. A measure of toleration to Christianity had of course been conceded by Galerius. But in 313 the tone of the so-called Edict of Milan (it was not strictly an edict, but apparently a letter of a governor; and it was not issued in Milan, though, it is perfectly true, Milan was the city where Licinius and Constantine struck a bargain for the future governance of the Empire) was much more generous, and much more favourable to Christianity:

> We grant both to Christians and to all men freedom to follow whatever religion each one wishes, in order that whatever divinity there is in the seat of heaven may be appeased and made propitious towards us and towards all who have been set under our power...We have resolved that all the conditions which were contained in letters previously sent ... are to be ... completely set aside ...
>
> And since these same Christians are known to have possessed not only the places in which they had the habit of assembling but other property too which belongs by right to their body... you will order all this property, in accordance with the law we have explained above, to be given back without any equivocation or dispute to all those same Christians ... In this way it will come about ... that the divine favour towards us, which we have experienced in such important matters, will continue for all time to prosper our achievements along with the public well-being.

This might have been a pagan emperor writing about the future of the cults. But it was not. It was a Christian emperor (Constantine), or at least one with Christian sympathies, writing about the future of Christianity. The faith, once a persecuted sect springing from a remote part of the Empire, had achieved repectability – though one may doubt whether respectability was what all Christians wanted. After the upheavals of the previous three hundred years, it is little wonder that, in the century which followed the Edict of Milan, many chose to seek a new sort of martyrdom, that of the religious life.

A silver coin struck at Pavia in AD 315 is the first such object to show Constantine associated with the supposedly Christian Chi-Ro monogram, here attached to his helmet.

In their thousands Christians followed the example of Anthony and went into the Egyptian desert, there to live lives of radical poverty, of chastity, and of obedience to charismatic leaders. It was a return to the way of life of some at least of the first-century Christians, the practices of whom had been preserved more by heretical sects such as the Montanists and Marcionites than by the main-stream Church. The lives of the monks who took their lead from Anthony were a vivid reminder of how much Christianity had changed in less than three centuries. Which raises the question of whether the Christianity that had survived to the Edict of Milan was the same as the one to be found in the New Testament.

How much an institution can change and still remain the same is not an historical problem at all but a philosophical one. The question can, however, be put another way. Despite all the changes in its structures and all the developments in its theology, did the Christian community to which Constantine granted toleration in 313 believe itself identical with the Church Jesus had founded?

The answer is clear. Of course it did.

BIBLIOGRAPHY

The main books and articles consulted are listed below.
To keep the list as short as possible, where articles appear in collections only the title of the collection and the name of its editor are given.

Ash, James L, 'The Decline of Ecstatic Prophecy in the Early Church', Theological Studies, vol. 37 (1976), 227–252.

Aune, D E, 'The Odes of Solomon and Early Christian Prophecy', New Testament Studies, vol. 28 (1982), 435–460.

Avila, Charles, Ownership: Early Christian Teaching, London, Sheed and Ward, 1983.

Bammel, Ernst and Moule, CFD (eds.), Jesus and the Politics of his Day, Cambridge, Cambridge University Press, 1984.

Barnes, T D, Constantine and Eusebius, Cambridge (Mass.) Harvard University Press, 1981.

Barnes, T D, Tertullian: A Historical and Literary Study, Oxford, Clarendon Press, 1971.

Bauer, Walter, Orthodoxy and Heresy in Earliest Christianity, Philadelphia, Fortress Press, 1971.

Baus, Karl, From the Apostolic Community to Constantine, London, Burns and Oates, 1980.

Baynes, Norman H, Constantine the Great and the Christian Church, London, Oxford University Press for the British Academy, 1972.

Benko, Stephen, Pagan Rome and the Early Christians, London, B.T. Batsford, 1985.

Bevenot, Maurice, 'Clement of Rome in Irenaeus' Succession List', Journal of Theological Studies, N.S. 17 (1966), 98–100.

Bevenot, Maurice, 'Cyprian and his Recognition of Cornelius', Journal of Theological Studies, N.S. vol. 28 (1977), 346–359.

Bevenot, Maurice, 'Cyprian's Platform in the Rebaptism Controversy', The Heythrop Journal, vol. 19 (1978), 123–142.

Brown, Peter, Society and the Holy in Late Antiquity, London, Faber and Faber, 1982.

Brown, Peter, The Cult of the Saints, London, SCM Press, 1981

Brown, Peter, The Making of Late Antiquity, Cambridge (MA), Harvard University Press, 1978.

Brown, Peter, The World of Late Antiquity, London, Thames and Hudson, 1971.

Brown, Raymond E and Meier, John, Antioch and Rome, New York, Paulist Press, 1983.

Brown, Raymond E [et al.] (eds.), The Jerome Bible Commentary, London, Geoffrey Chapman, 1969.

Chadwick, Henry, Alexandrian Christianity, Philadelphia, Westminster Press, 1954.

Chadwick, Henry, Origen: Contra Celsum, Cambridge, Cambridge University Press, 1953.

Chitty, Derwas, The Desert a City, Oxford, Basil Blackwell, 1966.

Coleman-Norton, P R, Roman State and Christian Church, London, SPCK, 1966.

Colgrave, B and Mynors, R B (eds.), Bede's Ecclesiastical History of the English People, Oxford, Clarendon Press, 1969.

Cornell, Tim and Matthews, John, Atlas of the Roman World, Oxford, Phaidon, 1982.

Countryman, L.W, The Rich Christian in the Church of the Early Empire, New York, Edwin Mellen Press, 1980.

Danielou, Jean and Marrou, Henri, The Christian Centuries, vol. I, London, Darton, Longman and Todd, 1964.

Davies, Stevan L, 'The Predicament of Ignatius of Antioch', Vigiliae Christianae, vol. 30 (1976), 175–180.

Davies, Stevan L, The Revolt of the Widows, Carbondale, Southern Illinois University Press, 1980.

Dunn, J D, Unity and Diversity in the New Testament, London, SCM Press, 1977.

Elliott, John H, Home for the Homeless London, SCM Press, 1982.

Empie, P C and Murphy, T A (eds.) Papal Primacy and the Universal Church, Minneapolis, Augsburg Publishing, 1974.

Eusebius, The History of the Church from Christ to Constantine Harmondsworth, Penguin Books, 1965.

Faivre, Alexandre, Naissance d'une Hierarchie, Paris, Beauchesne, 1977.

Frend, W H C, Martyrdom and Persecution

in the Early Church, Oxford, Basil
Blackwell, 1965.
Frend, W H C, Religion Popular and
Unpopular in the Early Christian Centuries,
London, Variorum, 1976.
Frend, W H C, The Early Church: From the
Beginnings to 461, London, SCM Press,
1982.
Frend, WHC, The Rise of Christianity,
London, Darton, Longman and Todd,
1984.
Frend, W H C, Town and Country in the
Early Christian Centuries, London,
Variorum, 1980.
Freyne, Sean, Galilee from Alexander the
Great to Hadrian, Notre Dame, University
of Notre Dame Press, 1980.
Fuellenbach, John, Ecclesiastical Office and
the Primacy of Rome, Washington,
Catholic University of American Press,
1980.

Gilmore, A (ed.), Christian Baptism,
London, Lutterworth, 1959.
Grant, Robert M and Tracy David, A Short
History of the Interpretation of the Bible,
London, SCM Press, 1984.
Grant, Robert M, Augustus to Constantine,
London, Collins, 1971.
Grant, Robert M, Early Christianity and
Society, London, Collins, 1978.
Grant, Robert M (ed.), The Apostolic
Fathers, Camden NJ, Thomas Nelson,
1964–1968.
Grant, Robert M, The Formation of the
New Testament, Hutchinson, 1965.

Hamman, Andre (ed.), Baptism: Ancient
Liturgies and Patristic Texts, Staten Island
(NY), Alba House, 1967.
Hanson, R P C, Christian Priesthood
Examined, London, Lutterworth, 1979.
Hengel, Martin, Acts and the History of
Earliest Christianity, London, SCM Press,
1979.
Hertling, L and Kirschbaum, E, The
Roman Catacombs, London, Darton,
Longman and Todd, 1960.
Hinson, E G, The Evangelization of the
Roman Empire, Macon, Mercer University
Press, 1981.
Hoffmann, R J, Marcion: On the Restitution
of Christianity, Chico, Scholars Press,
1981.
Hopkins, Clarke, The Discovery of Dura
Europos, New Haven, Yale University
Press, 1979.

Hornus, J-M, It is not Lawful for Me to
Fight, Scottdale, Herald Press, 1980.

Jones, Cheslyn [et al.] (eds.), The Study of
Liturgy, London, SPCK, 1978.

Katz, Steven T, 'Issues in the Separation of
Judaism and Christianity after 70 C E',
Journal of Biblical Literature, vol. 103
(1984), 43–76.
Kraeling, C H, The Excavations at Dura
Europos. Final Report. The Christian
Building. New Haven, Yale University
Press, 1967.
Kraeling, C H, The Excavations at Dura
Europos. Final Report. The Synagogue, New
Haven, Yale University Press, 1956.

Laeuchli, Samuel, Power and Sexuality,
Philadelphia, Temple University Press,
1972.

MacMullen, Ramsay, Christianizing the
Roman Empire, New Haven, Yale
University Press, 1984.
Male, Emile, La Fin du Paganisme en
Gaule, Paris, Flammarion, 1950.
Massyngberde, Ford J, Revelation, Garden
City (NY), Doubleday, 1975.
Meeks, Wayne A, The First Urban
Christians, New Haven, Yale University
Press, 1983.
Meier, John P, 'Presbyteros in the Pastoral
Epistles', The Catholic Biblical Quarterly,
vol. 35 (1973), 323–345.
Mullin, Redmond, The Wealth of
Christians, Exeter, The Paternoster Press,
1983.
Munier, Charles, Eglise et Cite, Paris,
Cujas, 1979.
Murray, Robert, Symbols of Church and
Kingdom: A Study in Early Syriac Tradition,
Cambridge, Cambridge University Press,
1975.
Mursurillo, Herbert, The Acts of the
Christian Martyrs, Oxford, Clarendon
Press, 1972.

Neusner, Jacob and Frericks E (eds.), 'To
See Ourselves as Others See Us', Chico,
Scholars Press, 1985.
Neusner, Jacob (ed.), Christianity, Judaism
and other Greco-Roman Cults, Leiden, E J
Brill, 1975.
Neusner, Jacob (ed.), Religions in
Antiquity, Leiden, E J Brill, 1968.
Norris, Frederick W, 'Ignatius, Polycarp
and I Clement: Walter Bauer

Reconsidered', Vigiliae Christianae, vol. 30 (1976), 23–44.

Osiek, Carolyn, *What are they saying about the Social Setting of the New Testament?* New York, Paulist Press, 1984.

Power, David, *Ministers of Christ and his Church*, London, Geoffrey Chapman, 1969.

Richardson, Cyril C, 'A New Solution to the Quartodeciman Riddle', Journal of Theological Studies, N.S. vol. 26 (1973), 74–84.

Roberts, Colin H, *Manuscript, Society and Belief in Early Christian Egypt*, Oxford, Oxford University Press for the British Academy, 1979.

Rowland, Christopher, *Christian Origins*, London, SPCK, 1985.

Rudolph, Kurt, *Gnosis*, Edinburgh, T & T Clark, 1983.

Sage, M, *Cyprian*, Cambridge (Mass.), Philadelphia Patristic Foundation, 1975.

Sanders, E P (ed.), *Jewish and Christian Self-Definition*, London, SCM Press, 1980–82.

Sandmel, S, *Philo of Alexandria*, Oxford, Oxford University Press, 1979.

Saulnier, Christiane, 'La Persecution des Chretiens et la Theologie du Pouvoir a Rome', Recherches de Science Religieuse, vol. 55 (1984), 251–279.

Saxer, Victor, *Morts, Martyrs, Reliques*, Paris, Beauchesne 1980.

Schillebeeckx, Edward, *Paul the Apostle*, London, SPCK, 1983.

Schillebeeckx, Edward, *The Church with a Human Face*, London, SCM Press, 1985.

Schurer, E, *The History of the Jewish People in the Age of Jesus Christ*, Edinburgh, T & T Clark 1973, 1979.

Schussler-Fiorenza, Elizabeth, *In Memory of Her*, London, SCM Press, 1983.

Scobie, Charles H H, 'The Origins and Development of Samaritan Christianity', New Testament Studies, vol. 19 (1973), 390–414.

Searle, Mark, *Christening: The Making of Christians*, Leigh-on-Sea, Kevin Mayhew, 1980.

Segal, J B, *Edessa, 'The Blessed City'*, Oxford, Clarendon Press, 1970

Smith, Terence V, *Petrine Controversies in Early Christianity*, Tubingen, J C B Mohr (Paul Siebeck), 1985.

Soggin, J Alberto, *A History of Israel from the Beginning to the Bar Kochba Revolt*, London, SCM, 1984

Sotomayor, Manuel, *Historia de la Iglesia en Espana*, I, Madrid, BAC, 1979.

Stanton, G N, 'Aspects of Early Christian-Jewish Polemic and Apologetic', New Testament Studies vol. 31 (1985), 377–392.

Stone, M E (ed.), *Jewish Writings of the Second Temple Period*, Philadelphia, Fortress, 1984.

Trevett, Christine, 'Prophecy and Anti-Episcopal Activity', Journal of Ecclesiastical History, vol. 34 (1983), 1–18.

Vermes, Geza, *Jesus the Jew*, London, Collins, 1973.

Vermes, Geza, *The Dead Sea Scrolls in Perspective*, London SCM Press, 1982.

Voobus, Arthur, *History of Asceticism in the Syrian Orient*, vol. 1 Louvain, CSCO, 1958.

Walsh, John Evangelist, *The Bones of St. Peter*, New York, Doubleday, 1982.

Wegman, Herman, *Christian Worship in East and West*, New York, Pueblo Publishing, 1985.

Whitaker, Edward Charles, *Documents of the Baptismal Liturgy*, London, SPCK, 1960

Wilken, Robert L, *The Christians as the Romans saw Them*, New Haven, Yale University Press, 1984.

Wink, W, *John the Baptist and the Gospel Tradition*, Cambridge, Cambridge University Press, 1968.

Yarnold, E J, *The Awe-Inspiring Rites of Initiation*, Slough, St Paul Publications, 1972.

The author wishes to thank Darton, Longman & Todd Ltd for their kind permission to reproduce quotations from *The Jerusalem Bible*.

PICTURE CREDITS

Illustrators: David Eaton, Aziz Khan